MENTAL CAPACITY ACT MANUAL

SECOND EDITION

by

RICHARD M. JONES M.A. (Kent and Brunel)
Solicitor, C.Q.S.W.
Consultant, Morgan Cole, Solicitors

LONDON
SWEET & MAXWELL
2007

First edition   (2005) Mental Capacity Act
                  Manual

Published in 2007 by
Sweet & Maxwell Limited of 100 Avenue Road,
http://www.sweetandmaxwell.co.uk
Typeset and printed in Great Britain by Hobbs, Totton, Hampshire

No natural forests were destroyed to make this product;
only farmed timber was used and re-planted.

British Library Cataloguing in Publication Data

A CIP catalogue record for this book
is available from the British Library

ISBN 978-1-84703-037-5

PREFACE

April 2007 saw the bringing into force in England of the provisions of this Act relating to the new independent mental capacity advocate (IMCA) service, some directly related elements of the Act to support it, the *Code of Practice* to provide guidance and the criminal offence of ill-treatment and wilful neglect (for England and Wales). All of the remaining provisions of the Act will be brought into force for both England and Wales in October of this year. Details of the current commencement provisions can be found in the notes to s.68.

Apart from reproducing regulations relating to the IMCA service and the conduct of research, this edition contains key extracts from the *Code of Practice* on the Act that has been approved by Parliament. The annotations have been revised and extended to take into account developments that have occurred since the publication of the first edition. Of the cases that have been considered, particular mention should be made of the decision in *Re SA (Vulnerable Adult with Capacity: Marriage)* where Munby J. held that in certain circumstances the inherent jurisdiction of the High Court can be exercised for the protection of vulnerable adults who do not lack the mental capacity to make the decision in question. The inherent jurisdiction of the High Court has therefore not been ousted by this Act; it will be possible for the jurisdiction to be exercised by the new Court of Protection to protect mentally capable vulnerable adults. *Re SA* is considered in the notes to s.15.

A list of the contact details of relevant organisations can be found at Annex A.

In preparing this edition I have taken into account judicial decisions and other material that was available to me on April 19, 2007.

Richard Jones
e-mail: richard.jones2@morgan-cole.com

PREFACE TO THE FIRST EDITION

The Mental Capacity Act 2005 is a measure which is likely to touch the lives of everyone because, at some point, all adults will probably be affected by a lack of capacity to make decisions relating to their everyday lives, either personally, or through contact with people who are unable to make decisions for themselves. As the Government has noted, a

> "wide range of conditions can result in incapacity to take decisions. In some cases, the capacity to take decisions is never attained (for example in the case of some people with a learning disability). In other cases, capacity is attained but is subsequently lost. This may occur for a number of reasons, including medical disorders or traumatic injury. The loss of capacity may be temporary for example during a toxic confusional state, which might result from an illness, or use of drugs. In some cases, capacity may fluctuate during periods when they are well, but may lose it during periods of illness. Finally, the loss of capacity may be permanent, as for example in some cases of dementia or the persistent vegetative state" (*Who Decides? Making Decisions on Behalf of Mentally Incapacitated Adults*, Cm. 3803, para.2.1).

The following factors can be said to have driven the process that cumulated in the passing of the Act: the legal context, demographic tends and improvements in healthcare, the community care policy, and the protection of human rights.

The legal context

As is pointed out in the "Introduction and General Note" to the Act, the legal context that confronted the Law Commission when it commenced its investigation into the adequacy of legal procedures for decision-making on behalf of mentally incapacitated adults was most unsatisfactory. It was described as "one of incoherence, inconsistency and historical accident" (Law Comm. No.231, para.2.45). The High Court had attempted to respond to this situation by using the doctrine of necessity and the declaratory jurisdiction to determine the legality of action proposed to be taken in respect of a mentally incapacitated person, but this approach, which is aimed at responding to individual problems, was ill-suited to developing a coherent legal framework It was clear that the law did not offer sufficient protection either for the mentally incapacitated, or for those who look after them.

Demographic trends and improvements in healthcare

The number of elderly people is rising steadily in the population. The mental faculties of the elderly often decline with age and the number of persons suffering from dementia, which leads to a progressive loss of mental capacity, is increasing markedly. More than 700,000 people in the United Kingdom are estimated to suffer from dementia and this is projected to rise to around 840,00 by 2010 (The Alzheimer's Society (January 2004)). Recommendation 1035 (1986) of the Parliamentary Assembly of the Council of Europe on ageing of populations in Europe noted that during the period from 1990 to 2020:

"increases of 20% and more are expected in the 45–60 age group and of 15–20% in the 65 and over and there will be a disproportionate growth in the number of very old people, aged 80 and over, which would be one-third of the size of this group".

In the United Kingdom context, the House of Lords Select Committee on Economic Affairs estimated that the proportion of the population aged 65 or over as a percentage of those aged 16–64 would be 24.4% in 2000, 32.8% in 2025, and 39.2% in 2050 (Session 2002–03, 4th Report, *Aspects of the Economics of an Ageing Population*, Vol.1, p.10).

Medical advances, in particular the development of antibiotics, have saved the lives of many people who would in earlier times have died from disease or trauma. Some of those who survive will do so with impaired mental capacity or even, exceptionally, lapse into a persistent vegetative state. In the case of Tony Bland, a young man who as a result of being crushed at the Hillsborough disaster was in a persistent vegetative state, Lord Browne-Wilkinson expressed his concern about the "scale of the problem that is presented by modern technological developments" and said that it seemed to him "imperative that the moral, social and legal issues raised by this case should be considered by Parliament" (*Airedale NHS Trust v Bland* [1993] 1 All E.R. 821 at 878, 879, HL). Also, as the Law Commission noted, the

"achievements of medical science have also created difficult dilemmas about the appropriate measure of medical care which should be given at the end of life, particularly where unconscious or incapacitated people have, in advance, indicated an unwillingness to be kept alive once their health has deteriorated" (Law Comm. No.231, para.2.38).

A further concern in the medical context was the recognition that certain procedures involving the mentally incapacitated were almost certainly unlawful. The most prevalent example was the practice of carrying out research on a person who was mentally incapable of consenting to participating in it, and where that person would receive no benefit from the results of the research.

The community care policy

The community care policy comprises two distinct threads. The first relates to the policy of discharging mentally disordered people from large, isolated long-stay hospitals into community based provision. This has lead to significant changes to the ways in which such people are cared for. The second thread concerns the manner in which social care needs of the population should be assessed and provided for. The White Paper *Caring for People: Community Care in the Next Decade and Beyond* (1989) Cm. 849, states at para.1.1:

"Community care means providing the services and support which people who are affected by problems of ageing, mental illness, mental handicap or physical or sensory disability need to be able to live as independently as possible in their own homes, or in 'homely' settings in the community. The Government is firmly committed to a policy of community care which enables such people to achieve their full potential."

Preface to the first edition

One of the consequences of this approach, which has been delivered through the legislative framework of the National Health Service and Community Care Act 1990, has been the emphasis on avoiding institutional care for elderly and disabled people unless their particular needs positively require such an outcome.

The combination of these two policy initiatives has lead to a decrease in reliance on institutional care for the mentally disabled. Institutional care tends to encourage a paternalistic approach to meeting patient/resident needs, while community based care increases the opportunities for mentally disabled individuals to make many of the decisions that occur in everyday life either by themselves or with support. Some of the decisions that may be required to be taken will raise the question of whether the person concerned possesses the required level of mental capacity to make the decision in question. If the answer is in the negative, disputes, in particular about the most appropriate living situation for the person, can sometimes arise between relatives, or between relatives and a public authority.

The protection of human rights

The Act is indicative of a growing shift in attitude toward those who, for whatever reason, lack the mental capacity to make key decisions for themselves. In particular, there has been a growing international recognition of the unacceptability of discrimination against the mentally disabled. In 1971, the United Nations proclaimed the Declaration of the Rights of Mentally Retarded Persons. Its seven paragraphs read:

"1. The mentally retarded person has, to the maximum degree of flexibility, the same rights as other human beings.

2. The mentally retarded person has a right to proper medical care and physical therapy and to such education, training, rehabilitation and guidance as will enable him to develop his ability and maximum potential.

3. The mentally retarded person has a right to economic security and to a decent standard of living. He has a right to perform productive work or to engage in any other meaningful occupation to the fullest possible extent of his capabilities.

4. Whenever possible, the mentally retarded persons should live with his own family or with foster parents and participate in different forms of community life. The family with which he lives should receive assistance.

5. The mentally retarded person has a right to a qualified guardian when this is required to protect his personal well-being and interests.

6. The mentally retarded person has a right to protection from exploitation, abuse and degrading treatment. If prosecuted for any offence, he shall have a right to due process of law with full recognition being given to his degree of mental responsibility.

7. Whenever mentally retarded persons are unable, because of the severity of their handicap, to exercise all their rights in a meaningful way or it should become necessary to restrict or deny some or all of these rights, the procedure used for that restriction or denial of rights must contain proper legal

safeguards against every form of abuse. This procedure must be based on an evaluation of the social capability of the mentally retarded person by qualified experts and must be subject to periodic review and to the right of appeal to higher authorities."

Although a Declaration of the United Nations is not legally binding, the Declaration on the Rights of Mentally Retarded Persons was supported by the UK Government when it was adopted by the General Assembly. The Declaration can therefore be categorised as identifying non-binding "soft law" principles which provide guidance to the UK Government when it legislates in this field. Despite is dated terminology, the Declaration represents an important milestone in that it established some important rights, in particular the person with a learning disability has "the same rights as other human beings" which cannot be restricted without due process that "must contain proper legal safeguards against every form of abuse". The Law Commission paid "careful regard" to aspects of the Declaration when it made its final report (Law Comm. No.231, para.2.27). The philosophy that lies behind the Declaration is one of minimum intervention in the lives of the learning disabled, consistent with providing proper care and protection and maximum help to enable them to realise their full potential and make best use of their abilities. Many countries have enacted legislation embodying its principles: see *Report on Incapable Adults,* Scottish Law Commission, Cm. 2962, para.1.5.

Subsequent to the 1971 Declaration, the General Assembly proclaimed the Declaration on the Rights of Disabled Persons in 1975, and adopted twenty-five "Principles for the protection of persons with mental illness and the improvement of mental health care" (Resolution 46/119 of December 17, 1991). Principle 23.1 requires States to "implement [the] Principles through appropriate legislative, judicial, administrative, educational and other measures, which they shall review periodically." In the European context, Recommendation No.(99)4 of the Committee of Ministers of the Council of Europe on Principles Concerning the Legal Protection of Incapable Adults, and the Convention on Human Rights and Biomedicine, together with its Additional Protocol, are reproduced as Annexes A to C[1].

The only international instrument against which UK law can be judicially tested is the European Convention on Human Rights. Although the Convention is not part of substantive domestic law, the Human Rights Act 1998 makes Convention rights enforceable in domestic courts. The Joint Committee on Human Rights said that the provisions of the Draft Mental Incapacity Bill:

"engage a wide range of [Convention] rights, including the right to respect for family life, the right to property, and the right to be free of degrading treatment. In our view, however, the safeguards built into the Draft Bill are sufficient to ensure that there is no significant risk of the implementation of the Draft Bill leading to an incompatibility with any of them" (Session 2002–03, 15th Report, *Scrutiny of Bills and Draft Bills: Further Progress Report* (HL 149/ HC 1005), para.4.7).

Further reports of the Joint Committee were more questioning of whether particular provisions of the Bill risked violating either Arts 2, 3, 5, or 8 of the

---

[1] Not reproduced in this edition.

Convention. Generally speaking, the Committee was satisfied with the responses that it received from the Government either in terms of amendments to the Bill, or from assurances the it received regarding the contents of the *Code of Practice* (Session 2004–05, 4th Report (HL 26/HC 224), Ch.4).

Another aspect of the rights based approach to the provision of services has been an increasing demand for the mentally incapacitated to enjoy the benefits of a lay advocate. In particular, it is considered that the support of an advocate would be beneficial in respect of an incapacitated person who did not enjoy the benefits of an involvement with caring relatives.

Running in tandem with the development of a rights agenda for the mentally incapacitated has been a gradual abandonment of the paternalistic approach to medical provision for the mentally capacitated, and a growing recognition of the principle of patient autonomy. The House of Lords Select Committee on Medical Ethics (1993–94) commented that the principle of patient autonomy "has become important in relation to medical treatment as the relationship between doctor and patient has changed to one of partnership" (HL 21–1, para.40). One manifestation of this trend has been the recognition at common law of the right of a capacitated patient to make a "living will". At the European level, the importance of patients being empowered to make informed choices in healthcare is reflected in the European Charter of Patients' Rights which proposes fourteen rights that all patients in Europe should be granted. The Charter, which was developed by the Italian patients' rights organisation Cittadinazattiva—Active Citizens Network, was launched in Rome in 2002.

Ten years elapsed between the publication of the Law Commission's Mental Incapacity Bill on February 28, 1995 and the Mental Capacity Act receiving its Royal Assent on April 7, 2005. This delay can be partly explained by the sensitivity of successive Governments to concerns that had been expressed by a number of bodies about the prospect of the provisions on advance decisions enabling euthanasia to be introduced "by the backdoor". This concern, which was a recurring issue throughout the parliamentary debates on the Bill, led to the enactment of s.62. The fact that the legislation had been the subject of detailed scrutiny over a number of years did not prevent the Bill being amended frequently during its passage through Parliament. Although the amendments improved the Bill, they did not ameliorate the following concerns:

- The fact that the Act provides for advance decisions to be made orally will inevitably result in many purported oral advance decisions being invalid because they will not be applicable to the treatment in question for one or more of the reasons set out in s.25(4).

- There is much to be said in favour of the opinion of House of Lord's Select Committee on Medical Ethics that advance decisions should be advisory only. A number of witnesses to the Joint Committee pointed out that healthy patients tend not to make the same choices as sick ones.

- Although the potential for the donee of a lasting power of attorney to act in a manner which is contrary to the best interests of the donor was recognised by the Government, the Act does not provide sufficient safeguards to protect the donor from such acts.

Apart from these concerns, there can be no doubt that the Mental Capacity Act represents a major advance in that it provides a comprehensive statutory framework for assisting those lacking capacity to make decisions for themselves wherever possible and for proper decisions to be made by others when that is not possible. However, the framework could prove to be an empty vessel if it is not "accompanied by changes in attitude which recognise the rights of those lacking capacity and the need to instil respect and good practice in dealing with them" (Joint Committee, para.30).

CONTENTS

Table of Cases

Table of Cases

Table of Cases

Table of Cases

PART 1

MENTAL CAPACITY ACT 2005

(2005 c.9)

ARRANGEMENT OF SECTIONS

SECTION

PART 3

MISCELLANEOUS AND GENERAL

Declaratory provision

Private international law

General

SCHEDULE 1

LASTING POWERS OF ATTORNEY: FORMALITIES

SCHEDULE 2

PROPERTY AND AFFAIRS: SUPPLEMENTARY PROVISIONS

Mental Capacity Act 2005

SCHEDULE 3

INTERNATIONAL PROTECTION OF ADULTS

SCHEDULE 4

PROVISIONS APPLYING TO EXISTING ENDURING POWERS OF ATTORNEY

SCHEDULE 5

TRANSITIONAL PROVISIONS AND SAVINGS

SCHEDULE 6

MINOR AND CONSEQUENTIAL AMENDMENTS

SCHEDULE 7

REPEALS

An Act to make new provision relating to persons who lack capacity; to establish a superior court of record called the Court of Protection in place of the office of the Supreme Court called by that name; to make provision in connection with the Convention on the International Protection of Adults signed at the Hague on 13th January 2000; and for connected purposes. [7th April 2005]

PROGRESS OF THE BILL

1–002 *Hansard*, HL Vol.667, col.1333 (1 R).

Hansard, HC Vol.422, col 928 (1 R); Vol.425 col.22 (2R), (Prog), (MR), (Carry-over Motion); Vol.428, cols 101 (1R), 1531 (Prog), (RS); Vol.432, cols 1362 (Prog), (Lords' Amendments), 1641 (Royal Assent); Vol.668 cols 11 and 42 (2R); Vol.669 cols 102,191, 734 (Comm),1101 (MfA); Vol. 670, cols 845 (MfA), 1275, 1441 and 1483 (Rep.); Vol.671, cols 412 (3R), 950 (Royal Assent).

INTRODUCTION AND GENERAL NOTE

1–003 The Law Commission's Fourth Programme of Law Reform (1989, Law Com. No. 185) proposed an investigation into the adequacy of legal and other procedures for decision-making on behalf of mentally incapacitated adults. There followed an extensive consultation exercise in the course of which the Commission published the following consultation papers.

- Mentally Incapacitated Adults and Decision-Making: An Overview (CP No.119)
- Mentally Incapacitated Adults and Decision-making: A New Jurisdiction (CP No.128)
- Mentally Incapacitated Adults and Decision-Making: Medical Treatment and Research (CP No.129)
- Mentally Incapacitated and Other Vulnerable Adults: Public law Protection (CP No.130)

The current state of the law was described by the Commission at para.1.1 of its Final Report "Mental Incapacity" (Law Com. No.231) which was published in March 1995:

"It is widely recognised that, in this area, the law as it now stands is unsympathetic and full of glaring gaps. It does not rest on clear or modern foundations of principle. It has also failed to keep up with developments in our understanding of the rights and needs of those with mental disability."

The Report sought to provide:

"A new set of coherent answers to a single question. The question, put simply, is 'who decides?' Although it may be asked in a variety of situations and for a variety of reasons, it arises whenever a person lacks the mental capacity to make a legally effective decision for himself or herself. There are various supplementary questions which must then be put. 'On what basis?' and 'with what formalities?' are examples of these. The types of decision which may be called for can be divided into three broad categories: 'personal welfare'decisions, 'health care'decisions and 'financial'decisions" (para.2.1).

A draft "Mental Incapacity Bill" was appended to the Report. This was intended to "provide a unified and comprehensive scheme within which people can make decisions for themselves" (para.3.1).

Lord Mackay, the Lord Chancellor, announced in January 1996 that the "Government has decided not to legislate on the basis of the Law Commission's proposals in their current form and has also concluded that it would be inappropriate to make any proposals to Parliament in the absence of full public consultation" (Lord Chancellor's Department, Press Notice, January 16,1996).

The incoming Labour Government issued a consultation paper *"Who Decides? Making Decisions on Behalf of Mentally Incapacitated Adults"*, Cm.3803 (1997) which was based on the Commission's proposals. It also took into account the report of the House of Lords Select Committee on Medical Ethics (HL Paper 21-1) which had considered the issue of advance statements about healthcare. The consultative paper sought views on a possible framework for providing protection for mentally incapacitated adults and those who look after them, and for providing an organised framework of law to manage the welfare and affairs of mentally incapacitated adults. The consultation resulted in over 4,000 responses being received.The Government's response to the consultation was published in October 1999 as *"Making Decisions: The Government's proposals for making decisions on behalf of mentally incapacitated adults"*, Cm.4465. The proposals were largely based on the Law Commission's recommendations. The Lord Chancellor, Lord Irvine, announced in November 1999 that the Government had decided to bring forward legislation "to empower mentally incapacitated adults, so far as can safely be allowed, to make provision for the care they want before they lose capacity, and to ensure that when decisions come to be made about their care and welfare, they contain adequate safeguards and protection, they are made consistently and in line with each individual's particular best interests" (speech to the Law Society's Conference on Mental Incapacity, November 10,1999).

Judicial support for legislation was expressed in a number of cases. In *F (Adult: Court's Jurisdiction), Re* [2000] 2 F.L.R.512, CA, Butler-Sloss P. said at 524:

"The assumption of jurisdiction by the High Court on a case-by-case basis does not, however, detract from the obvious need expressed by the Law Commission and by the Government for a well-structured and clearly defined framework of protection of vulnerable, mentally incapacitated adults, particularly since the whole essence of declarations under the inherent jurisdiction is to meet a recognised individual problem and not to provide general guidance for mentally incapacitated adults. Until Parliament puts in place that defined framework, the High Court will still be required to help out where there is no other practicable alternative."

A"Draft Mental Incapacity Bill" (Cm.5859-1) was presented to Parliament in June 2003. In July 2003 the House of Commons and House of Lords appointed a Joint Committee to scrutinise the Draft Bill. The Joint Committee's Report, which contained 99 recommendations and was mainly supportive of the principles underlying the draft Bill, was published in two volumes in November 2003 (HL Paper 189-1, 2; HC 1083-1, 2). The Government's response to the report was published in February 2004

(Cm.6121). The great majority of the Joint Committee's recommendations were accepted by the Government.

Several witnesses to the Joint Committee suggested that the title "Mental Incapacity Bill" was inappropriate and had negative connotations and preferred "Mental Capacity Bill" which they saw as a more accurate description of the Bill, as well as being more positive and reassuring. The Joint Committee considered that the Bill "should avoid the pejorative implications of incapacity and instil confidence in those it is intended to serve" and recommended "that consideration should be given to changing the Bill's title to 'Mental Capacity Bill'" (paras 362–364). The Government accepted this recommendation.

The objectives of the legislation, which has the general aim of seeking to strike a balance between respect for individual autonomy and the need to protect the vulnerable, were explained by the Secretary of State for Constitutional Affairs and Lord Chancellor, Lord Falconer, when he moved the second reading of the Bill:

"The Bill seeks to do six main things. First, it allows adults to take as many decisions as they can for themselves and, in any event, to put them at the centre of the decision-making process about themselves.

Secondly, when adults fear that they may not be able to take decisions about their medical treatment in the future, it allows them, if they wish, and subject to effective safeguards, to make decisions in advance of incapacity about whether treatment should be carried out or continued.

Thirdly, where adults cannot make decisions and have not made any decision in advance about their own personal welfare or other property or affairs, the Bill ensures that the decisions which are made for them are made in their best interests.

Fourthly, where an adult lacks capacity to make a decision for himself about serious medical treatment, accommodation in a hospital or care home, or other residential accommodation, and they have no friends or family to be consulted, the Bill will require the relevant NHS body or local authority to appoint an independent [mental capacity advocate] to support the person in these most difficult decisions.

Fifthly, the Bill will provide protection against subsequent legal liability for those carers who have honestly and reasonably sought to act in the best interests of the person for whom they have cared.

Finally, the Bill will provide clarity and safeguards around the carrying out of research in relation to people who lack capacity" (*Hansard*, HL Vol.668, col.12).

The view of the Joint Committee on Human Rights is that the legislation "should be broadly welcomed from a human rights perspective, because it enhances the ability of people who lack capacity to make their own decisions where they can and makes it more likely that sound decisions will be made on their behalf where they cannot make those decisions for themselves" (Fourth Report, HL 26/HC 224, para.4.5). In *B v Secretary of State for Work and Pensions* [2005] EWCA Civ 929, para.25, Sedley L.J. said: "Mental capacity, although not listed in Art.14 [of the European Convention on Human Rights], is arguably at least as sensitive a personal characteristic, in relation to discrimination, as race or sex".

Research into the operation of the Adults with Incapacity (Scotland) Act 2000 (asp 4) found that lack of publicity about the Act and how it might benefit adults and carers was perceived as one of the main barriers to access (The Adults with Incapacity (Scotland) Act 2000: Learning from Experience (2004), Scottish Executive). The Department of Health has been proactive in publicising the Mental Capacity Act by producing a leaflet and a number of information booklets on the Act which are tailored to meet the needs of different audiences. They can be downloaded at *www.dca.gov.uk/legal-policy/mental-*

capacity/publications.htm. Hard copies can be ordered by e-mail from makingdecisions@dca.gsi.gov.uk.

Territorial Extent

This Act only extends to England and Wales, apart from the two exceptions set out in **1–004** s.68(5).

Territorial Application: Wales

The Welsh Ministers may make regulations under ss.30 and 34 and issue guidance under **1–005** s.32(3). They may also make regulations under ss.35, 36, 37 and 41. Section 68(2) provides that ss.30–41 will come into force by order made by the Welsh Ministers. Section 43(1) provides that the Welsh Ministers must be consulted by the Lord Chancellor before a *Code of Practice* is prepared or revised.

Matters not covered by this Act

The most significant omission from the Act relates to the recommendations that the Law **1–006** Commission made in Pt IX of its Final Report for the protection of vulnerable people at risk. In particular, the Commission recommended that, where local authorities have reason to believe that a vulnerable person in their area is suffering or is likely to suffer significant harm or serious exploitation, they should be under a statutory duty to investigate and to provide or arrange community care services or to take other action to protect that person (Law Comm. No.231, para.9.16).

Appointees

If an incapacitated person has little capital and receives income only from state benefits, **1–007** the necessary financial arrangements can be made under reg.33 of the Social Security (Claims and Payment) Regulations 1987 (SI 1987/1968) which provides that the Secretary of State may appoint someone aged 18 or over (the "appointee") to act on behalf of the claimant. The appointee has no power to deal with the claimant's capital but can:

  (i) exercise any rights and duties that the claimant has under the social security legislation;
 (ii) receive any benefits payable to the claimant; and
(iii) deal with the money received on the claimant's behalf in the interests of the claimant or his or her dependants.

Concern has been expressed about the nature of the enquiries conducted before appointments are made, and about the absence of regular supervision or monitoring of the performance of appointees: see R. Lavery and L. Lundy "The Social Security Apointee System" (1994) *Journal of Social Welfare and Family Law* 313.

The Government resisted amendments to the Bill which would have brought the appointee system under the jurisdiction of the Court of Protection. However, Baroness Andrews, speaking during the committee stage in the House of Lords, said:

"The Bill has enabled us to take stock of the arrangements for appointees and to improve them in the light of the Bill's principles. Officials and Ministers from the Department for Constitutional Affairs and Department for Work and Pensions have been discussing how they can use the Bill to improve the appointeeship system ...

During the process a DWP official—a benefits official—will visit the person lacking capacity and the prospective appointee. The official needs to be sure that the person does in fact lack the capacity to look after their own benefits, and that the appointee will act in their best interests. That process will be enhanced by the Bill and the code of practice. For example, it will be useful for the officials carrying out those visits to have the benefit of the extra advice on assessing capacity. DWP and DCA officials will work together to ensure that DWP guidance reflects the principles of the Bill and places best interests at its heart.

In addition DWP acknowledges that the question of monitoring needs to be addressed, and it will look at options for introducing a monitoring system. With half a million appointees, that is not going to be easy; but it is clearly important, and there will be visits, paper reviews, targeted monitoring—all those sorts of things can be looked at in the light of the Bill. DWP will act quickly to revoke appointments where allegations of mismanagement are made" (*Hansard*, HL Vol.668, col.1463).

Guidance on how an appointee can open a bank account and manage money on behalf of the claimant is contained in "Banking for mentally incapacitated customers" which can be downloaded from the website of the British Bankers Association (see Annex A).

The appointee should carry out his or her functions in accordance with the provisions of this Act, in particular ss.1, 3 and 4.

COMMENCEMENT
1–008   See s.68.

ABBREVIATIONS
1–009   "ANH": artificial nutrition and hydration
"*Code of Practice*": the *Code of Practice* laid before Parliament in draft in February 2007, pursuant to ss.42 and 43 of the Act, and approved in April 2007
"EPA": Enduring Powers of Attorney
"Explanatory Notes":Explanatory notes on the Mental Capacity Bill prepared by the Department for Constitutional Affairs and the Department of Health
"IMCA": independent mental capacity advocate
"Joint Committee": House of Lords, House of Commons, Joint Committee on the Draft Mental Incapacity Bill, Session 2002–3
"LPA": lasting power of attorney
"Oral and written evidence": House of Lords, House of Commons, Joint Committee on the Draft Mental Incapacity Bill, Session 2002–3, Volume II: Oral and written evidence, HL Paper 189-II, HC 1083-II
"the Bill": the Mental Capacity Bill
"the court": the Court of Protection
"the 1983 Act": the Mental Health Act 1983 (c.20)
"the 1985 Act": Enduring Powers of Attorney Act 1985 (c.29)

Throughout the Act, the capital letter "P" is used to refer to a person who lacks capacity or is believed to lack capacity to make a decision about a particular matter, and the capital letter "D" is used to refer to a person exercising powers in relation to P.

PART 1

PERSONS WHO LACK CAPACITY

The principles

The principles
1–010   **1.**—(1) The following principles apply for the purposes of this Act.
(2) A person must be assumed to have capacity unless it is established that he lacks capacity.
(3) A person is not to be treated as unable to make a decision unless all practicable steps to help him to do so have been taken without success.
(4) A person is not to be treated as unable to make a decision merely because he makes an unwise decision.

(5) An act done, or decision made, under this Act for or on behalf of a person who lacks capacity must be done, or made, in his best interests.

(6) Before the act is done, or the decision is made, regard must be had to whether the purpose for which it is needed can be as effectively achieved in a way that is less restrictive of the person's rights and freedom of action.

GENERAL NOTE

The Joint Committee recommended that a statement of principles should appear on the **1–011** face of the Act. The Committee believed "that such a statement inserted as an initial point of reference could give valuable guidance to the courts, as well as helping non-lawyers to weigh up difficult decisions. Evidence given to us indicates that this be welcome to a wide range of those who have to deal with the problems of substitute decision-making in practice. We also believe that such a statement would be valuable in helping to frame the Codes of Practice based upon the [Act]" (para.43). The principles apply to all actions and decisions taken under this Act. The statement set out in s.2(3) can be added to the principles contained in this section.

The status of this section is that decisions and actions carried out under the Act should be tested against the principles which act as benchmarks for decision makers. Although there is no duty placed on persons or bodies to apply the principles, a failure to do so could be cited in legal proceedings as evidence of unlawful conduct.

Subsection (2)

This establishes the fundamental principle that persons over the age of 16 (s.2(5)) are **1–012** assumed to be mentally capable of making their own decisions. This assumption of personal autonomy can only be overridden if the person concerned is assessed as lacking the mental capacity to make a particular decision for him or herself at the relevant time. Thus, in the absence of a capacity assessment, any doubts have to be resolved in favour of capacity. The approach to be taken when making the assessment is set out in ss.2 and 3. In legal proceedings, the burden of proof will fall on the person who asserts that capacity is lacking.

Subsection (3)

This provision, which is aimed at maximising the decision making capacity of individ- **1–013** uals, is expanded upon in s.3(2).

The Explanatory Notes suggest that "all practicable steps" could include "making sure the person is in an environment in which he is comfortable or involving an expert in helping him his views" (para.20). The Joint Committee said that such steps "might include using specific communication strategies, providing information in [a] more accessible form, or treating an underlying mental disorder to enable a person to regain capacity" (para.70). Providing information over time may allow a person to assimilate information more completely, thereby maximising their actual understanding. Consideration could be given to postponing the decision if it is felt that the person might regain capacity over time. Chapter 3 of the *Code of Practice* considers the steps that can be taken to help people make their own decisions. Resource and time constraints are clearly relevant to the practicability of the assistance that might be required. It is important not to equate "practicable" with "possible" (*Owen v Crown House Engineering* [1973] 3 All E.R. 618, 622 NIRC). In *Dedman v British Building and Engineering Appliances Ltd* [1974] 1 W.L.R. 171, 179, CA, Scarman L.J. said:

"The word 'practicable' is an ordinary English word of great flexibility: it takes its meaning from its context. But, whenever used, it is a call for the exercise of common sense, a warning that sound judgment will be impossible without compromise. Sometimes the context contemplates a situation rarely to be achieved though much to be desired: the word then indicates one must be satisfied with less than perfection ... [S]ometimes ... what the context requires may have been possible, but may not for some reason have been 'practicable'. Whatever its context, the quality of the word is that there are circumstances in which we must be content with less than 100 per cent: and it calls for judgment to determine how much less."

During the second reading debate in the House of Lords, Lord Brennan cited a dramatic example of the impact that appropriate help can have on the ability of a disabled person to communicate:

"[A] client whom I represented had for 12 years, while being able to walk and grunt but not talk, been treated as a zombie, because his family did not believe that he was capable of any cognitive function. After obtaining a judgment on liability and getting an interim payment, at the second meeting with a speech therapist who knew about communication my client was able to converse with her. When challenged by me in conference, he readily spelt the word 'encyclopaedia'. Yet his family—his carers—were convinced for 12 years that his life was pretty well worthless" (*Hansard*, HL Vol.668, col.84).

In *AK (Adult Patient) (Medical Treatment: Consent), Re* [2001] 1 F.L.R. 129, a patient who had lost the use of virtually all his muscles, apart from those in one of his eyelids, through motor neurone disease was assisted to communicate by means of a device known as an "E transport" which involved the painstaking spelling out of words letter by letter by a process linked to the line of sight.

Although all practicable steps must be taken to help a person make a decision, those assisting the person must beware of subjecting the person to undue influence. In the context of consent to medical treatment, Lord Donaldson M.R. said in *T (Adult: Refusal of Treatment), Re* [1992] 4 All E.R. 649, 662 that while it is acceptable for the patient to receive advice or for the patient to have been subject to the strong persuasion of others in reaching a decision, such persuasion must not "overbear the independence of the patient's decision". His Lordship identified the real question in each case as being: "does the patient really mean what he says or is he merely saying it for a quiet life, to satisfy someone else or because the advice and persuasion to which he has been subjected is such that he can no longer think and decide for himself? In other words, is it a decision expressed in form only, not in reality?" His Lordship identified two aspects of the effect of outside influence that could be of "crucial importance": the strength of will of the patient and the relationship of the "persuader" to the patient. With regard to the former, a patient who is "very tired, in pain or depressed will be much less able to resist having his will over-borne than one who is rested, free from pain and cheerful". With regard to the relationship between the persuader and the patient, his Lordship spoke of the potential strength of the parental and marital relationship, especially with regard to arguments based on religious belief. Other outside influences that could vitiate a person's consent include fraud, misrepresentation and duress. For the effect of a person's vulnerability to exploitation on the assessment of their mental capacity, see *Lindsay v Wood* [2006] EWHC 2895 (QB) which is noted in the General Note to s.3. Undue influence in the context of financial transactions was considered by the House of Lords in *Royal Bank of Scotland v Etridge* [2001] UKHL 44; [2001] 4 All E.R. 449.

Research into the decision-making capabilities of persons with learning disabilities has shown that the presentation of information in a user-friendly manner makes it possible to move some people from being assessed as incapable to being assessed as capable (M.J. Gunn, J.G. Wong, I.C.H. Clare and A.J. Holland, "Decision-making capacity" (1999) 7(3) Med. L. Rev. 269). Confirmation that capacity is not static, even among patients who have engaged in self-harm, is contained in a study which found that the number of patients judged to have capacity increased significantly following the presentation of an information sheet about the specific treatment being proposed, together with a verbal explanation (R. Jacob, I.C.H. Clare, A.J. Holland, P.C. Watson, C. Maimaris and M.J. Gunn "Self-Harm, Capacity, and Refusal of Treatment: Implications for Emergency Medical Practice" (2005) 22 *Emergency Medical Journal* 799.

For a publication which offers practical help in assisting with communication, see N. Grove and B. McIntosh, "Communication for Person Centred Planning" (2006) *Foundation for People with Learning Disabilities*. Models available from psychology that might be helpful in identifying means to improve capacity are identified in "Assessment of Capacity in Adults: Interim Guidance for Psychologists" (2006) *British Psychological Society*, p.25.

Guidance on creating the right environment for assessing capacity is given in *Assessment of Mental Capacity: Guidance for Doctors and Lawyers*, (2004) BMA/Law Society, para.2.3.

Subsection (4)

This provision underpins the right to personal autonomy by preserving the right of a per- **1–014** son to make an irrational, unusual or eccentric decision which, viewed objectively, is not in that person's best interests without the person being treated as being mentally incapable by virtue of that decision alone. It does not prevent a capacity assessment being undertaken in respect of a person who makes an unwise decision, a series of unwise decisions, a decision that puts that person at risk, or who makes a decision which does not reflect that person's values, beliefs or approach to risk-taking. The making of such decisions might suggest that the person is susceptible to undue influence, or it could be an indication of inadequate understanding or a lack of information being provided to the person about the decision in question. The Joint Committee "considered carefully the dilemma created when a person with apparent capacity was making repeatedly unwise decisions that put him/her at risk or resulted in preventable suffering or disadvantage". While the Committee recognised that "the possibility of over-riding such decisions would be seen as unacceptable to many user groups", they suggested that "such a situation might trigger the need for a formal assessment of capacity" (Vol.1, para.78).

That the nature of the decision taken might be indicative of a lack of capacity on the part of the decision maker was emphasised by Kennedy L.J. in *Masterman-Lister v Brutton & Co* [2002] EWCA Civ 1889; [2003] 3 All E.R. 162, para.54, where his Lordship said that although the role of the court was the investigation of capacity not outcomes, outcomes "can often cast a flood of light on capacity".

In the context of consent to medical treatment, Lord Donaldson M.R. said:

"Prima facie every adult has the right and capacity to decide whether or not he will accept medical treatment, even if a refusal may risk permanent injury to his health or even lead to premature death. Furthermore, it matters not whether the reasons for the refusal were rational or irrational, unknown or even non-existent. This is so notwithstanding the very strong public interest in preserving the life and health of all citizens" (*T (Adult: Refusal of Treatment), Re* [1992] 4 All E.R. 649, CA, at 664).

Butler-Sloss P., in confirming that a mentally competent person is entitled to refuse treatment even if she does not give good reasons for doing so, said that "there is a point at which refusal and irrationality, as others might see it, tips the usually competent person over into a situation where the person, for however long or short a period, is actually unable to see through the consequences of the act, because that capacity to see through those consequences is inhibited by the panic situation in which the patient finds [her]self" (*Bolton Hospitals NHS Trust v O* [2003] 1 F.L.R. 824, para.15).

The approach taken in this provision is consistent with the finding of the European Court of Human Rights in *Winterwerp v Netherlands* (1979–80) 2 E.H.R.R. 387, para.37, that Art.5 of the European Convention on Human Rights does not permit the detention of a person "simply because his views or behaviour deviate from the norms prevailing in a particular society."

Subsection (5)

The best interest principle, which must guide all actions done for or decisions made on **1–015** behalf a person who lacks capacity, is expanded upon in s.4.

A clinician who follows a valid and applicable advance decision (see ss.24–26) is not acting "for or on behalf of a person who lacks capacity", he or she is acting on the instructions of a capacitated individual. It follows that the best interests principle does not apply to such decisions and healthcare professionals must comply with a valid and applicable advance decision, even though they do not consider that it would be in the patient's best interests to do so.

Subsection (6)

1–016 Someone making a decision or acting on behalf of a mentally incapacitated person must consider whether it is possible to decide or act in a way that would interfere less with the person's rights and freedom of action, or whether there is a need to act at all. Put another way, the intervention should be proportional to the particular circumstances of the case. As only "regard" must be had to this principle, an option which is not the least restrictive option can still be in the person's best interests.

The Parliamentary Under-Secretary of State for Constitutional Affairs gave the following example of an approach that would satisfy this principle: "A care assistant might be worried about residents with dementia wandering into the kitchen of the establishment unsupervised in case they come into contact with cleaning fluids. However, to steer them away from the kitchen would be unnecessary if staff ensured that all dangerous liquids were locked in a cupboard.That would not interfere with the freedom of action of the person suffering from dementia" (St.Comm.A, col.25).

Preliminary

People who lack capacity

1–017 **2.**—(1) For the purposes of this Act, a person lacks capacity in relation to a matter if at the material time he is unable to make a decision for himself in relation to the matter because of an impairment of, or a disturbance in the functioning of, the mind or brain.

(2) It does not matter whether the impairment or disturbance is permanent or temporary.

(3) A lack of capacity cannot be established merely by reference to—

(a) a person's age or appearance, or

(b) a condition of his, or an aspect of his behaviour, which might lead others to make unjustified assumptions about his capacity.

(4) In proceedings under this Act or any other enactment, any question whether a person lacks capacity within the meaning of this Act must be decided on the balance of probabilities.

(5) No power which a person ("D") may exercise under this Act—

(a) in relation to a person who lacks capacity, or

(b) where D reasonably thinks that a person lacks capacity, is exercisable in relation to a person under 16.

(6) Subsection (5) is subject to section 18(3).

DEFINITIONS

1–018 "enactment": s.64(1).

GENERAL NOTE

1–019 This section sets out the Act's definition of a person (i.e. a person over the age of 16 (subs.(5)) who lacks capacity, bearing in mind the assumption is that a person has capacity (s.1(2)). The definition applies for "the purposes of this Act" only. Schedule 6 makes consequential amendments to statutes to ensure that the definition contained in this Act is used in relation to other relevant proceedings. Common law definitions of capacity, such as the capacity to make a will (*Banks v Goodfellow* (1869-70) L.R. 5 Q.B. 549) and to marry (*Sheffield City Council v E* [2004] EWHC 2808 (Fam); [2005] Fam 326), are not affected.

If a person satisfies the "diagnostic test" set out in this section, that person's capacity to make the particular decision in question is assessed using the formula set out in s.3. Therefore, the fact that a person may be suffering, for example, from a mental illness does not of itself render that person mentally incapable of making a particular decision. A finding of incapacity can only be made if it is established under s.3 that the impact of the mental illness on the person is sufficient to render him or her incapable of making that decision. If the person fails to satisfy the diagnostic test, there can be no finding of incapacity for the purposes of this Act.

The Law Commission proposed a "diagnostic threshold" to ensure that the test of capacity "is stringent enough not to catch large numbers of people who make unusual or unwise decisions" (Law Com. No.231, para.3.8).

J. Beckett and R. Chaplin report that the capacity of patients with schizophrenia has been extensively studied and has shown a broad range from the significantly impaired to full capacity in both the acute and chronic stages of the illness, and that patients with depression have shown relatively unimpaired capacity. Their own study found that many patients hospitalised with mania have capacity to make an informed choice regarding treatment even when compulsorily detained ("Capacity to consent to treatment in patients with acute mania" (2006) 30 *Psychiatric Bulletin* 419).

Subsection (1)

Impairment of, or a disturbance in the functioning of, the brain or mind. A wide range of **1–020** conditions can result in incapacity to make decisions. In some cases, the capacity to take decisions is never attained (for example a person born with a severe leaning disability). In other cases, capacity is attained but is subsequently lost, either on a temporary or permanent basis. The Explanatory Notes state that the diagnostic test contained in this provision could "cover a range of problems, such as psychiatric illness, learning disability, dementia, brain damage or even a toxic confusional state, as long as it has the necessary effect on the functioning of the mind or brain, causing the person to be unable to make the decision" (para.22). It will "clearly also apply to patients with grave physical illnesses, which, by reason of vital organ failure and consequent biochemical disturbances, will cause either confusion or impairment of consciousness" (Dr Fiona Randall, Oral and written evidence, Ev 301). It could also cover people who are suffering from the effects of pain, shock or exhaustion or who are drunk or under the influence of drugs. A person who is rendered unconscious will clearly satisfy the test.

Although medical evidence supporting a conclusion that the test has been satisfied is not required, it would be advisable for the assessor to seek such evidence in difficult or controversial cases; see further, the General Note to s.3.

Subsection (2)

The temporary nature of P's incapacity matters for the purposes of decision making **1–021** because a decision should be delayed if the person's mental capacity might return and the delay would be consistent with the person's best interests (see s.4(3)). Temporary loss of capacity could be caused by the effect of excessive alcohol consumption, the misuse of drugs, the nature of a person's mental disorder, the effect of prescribed medication or an emotional crisis. Also see the note on s.24(1).

Subsection (3)

This provision is aimed at preventing unjustified assumptions being made about a per- **1–022** son's mental capacity. It "gives further emphasis to the Bill's principle that everyone should be assumed to have capacity until it is shown that they do not. For example, it is not acceptable to say, on the assumption that someone has a learning disability, that he cannot or will not want to make decisions about where to live", *per* Baroness Andrews (*Hansard*, HL Vol.670, col.1319). Also see the notes to s.4(1).

Subsection (4)

1–023   "The balance of probability standard means that a court is satisfied an event occurred if the court considers that, on the evidence, the occurrence of the event was more likely than not", *per* Lord Nicholls in *H (Minors) (Sexual Abuse: Standard of Proof)*, Re [1996] A.C. 563 at 586.

Subsections (5) and (6)

1–024   Although the powers under this Act only generally arise where the person lacking capacity is 16 or over, powers in relation to property might be exercised in relation to a younger person who has disabilities which will cause the incapacity to last into adulthood (see s.18(3)). Any overlap with the jurisdiction under the Children Act 1989 (c.41) can be dealt with by an order made under s.21. Further exceptions to the general rule that this Act applies to those who are 16 and over are:

1. A lasting power of attorney can only be made be a person who has reached 18 (s.9(2)(c)).
2. An advance decision can only be made by a person who reached 18 (s.24(1)).
3. The offence of ill-treatment or neglect of a mentally incapacitated person established by s.44 has no age limit.

This Act does not effect the legal right of a person with parental responsibility over a child to consent to the medical treatment of that child on the child's behalf.

Inability to make decisions

1–025   **3.**—(1) For the purposes of section 2, a person is unable to make a decision for himself if he is unable—

(a) to understand the information relevant to the decision,
(b) to retain that information,
(c) to use or weigh that information as part of the process of making the decision, or
(d) to communicate his decision (whether by talking, using sign language or any other means).

(2) A person is not to be regarded as unable to understand the information relevant to a decision if he is able to understand an explanation of it given to him in a way that is appropriate to his circumstances (using simple language, visual aids or any other means).

(3) The fact that a person is able to retain the information relevant to a decision for a short period only does not prevent him from being regarded as able to make the decision.

(4) The information relevant to a decision includes information about the reasonably foreseeable consequences of—

(a) deciding one way or another, or
(b) failing to make the decision.

DEFINITIONS

1–026   "emergency worker": s.2(3)

GENERAL NOTE

1–027   This section sets out the test for determining whether a person who has satisfied the diagnostic test (s.2) is "unable to make a [particular] decision" and therefore lacks capacity for the purposes of this Act (see s.2). The approach taken is a "functional" approach to capacity as the definition relates to the ability of the person to make a particular decision at a particular moment in time, not on the person's ability to make decisions generally. The assessment of a person's capacity must therefore relate to the decision to be made. The functional approach can be contrasted with the "outcome" approach which uses the consequence of the decision-making process as the criterion for determining capacity, and the "status" or "diagnostic" approach under which a person's capacity is determined by his or her membership of a specific population, such as those who have a particular psychiatric diagnosis. With regard to the status approach T. Grisso and P. Appelbaum have pointed out that a "patient may be psychotic, seriously depressed, or in a moderately advanced stage of dementia, yet still found competent to make some or all decisions" (*Assessing Competence to Consent to Treatment* (1998), p.18). The rejection of the outcome approach, which is confirmed in s.1(4), was emphasised in *Masterman-Lister v Jewell* [2002] EWHC 417 (QB); [2002] W.T.L.R. 563, at para.19 where Wright J. said that "in principle, legal capacity depends on understanding rather than wisdom; the quality of the decision is irrelevant as long as the person understands what he is deciding". The appropriateness of adopting the functional approach has been confirmed by research that has shown that people with mild intellectual disabilities may have the capacity to make some financial decisions but not others (W.M.I. Suto , I.C.H. Clare, A.J. Holland and P.C. Watson "Capacity to make financial decisions among people with mild intellectual disabilities", Journal of Intellectual Disability Research (2005) 49, 199–209).

The functional approach, which allows individuals to have the maximum decision-making powers possible, reflects the position that obtained under common law. In *Masterman-Lister v Brutton & Co* [2002] EWCA Civ 1889; [2003] 3 All E.R. 163, Chadwick L.J. said at paras 57–58:

> "English law requires that a person must have the necessary mental capacity if he is to do a legally effective act or to make a legally effective decision for himself The authorities are unanimous in support of two broad propositions. First, that the mental capacity required by the law is capacity in relation to the transaction which is to be effected. Second, that what is required is the capacity to understand the nature of that transaction when it is explained."

The functional approach allows for a temporary loss of capacity, for example, unconsciousness following a road traffic accident, and for persons to lack capacity in relation to one matter but not in relation to another (perhaps more complex) matter. A striking example of a situation where a person was found to be capable of making a decision in relation to one matter, but not in relation to another is the deceased who on the same day was found by Karminski J. to have had capacity to marry (*Park, In the Estate of* [1954] P. 89), and by Pearce J. and a jury not to have had capacity to make a will (*Park, Culross v Park* (1950) *The Times*, December 2, 1950) (cited by Munby J. in *Sheffield City Council v E* [2004] EWHC 2808 (Fam); [2005] Fam 326 at para.25).

Although, strictly speaking, this section requires a fresh capacity assessment to be undertaken in respect of every decision that the person might be required to make, with a person who is profoundly mentally incapacitated this could result in a large number of separate capacity assessments having to be made during the course of a single day. For routine decisions such as what clothes the person should wear, what food he or she should eat, or whether he or she should go for an accompanied walk, it is likely that the capacity assessment, if it happens at all, will be undertaken in a perfunctory manner. If there is a challenge as to whether the person had capacity, the decision-maker would need to show that he or she had reasonable grounds for believing that the person lacked the capacity to make the decision in question at that particular time: see s.5. It is suggested that formal capacity assessments should only be undertaken in respect of significant or controversial decisions, or where the mental capacity of the person is disputed.

If there is any doubt as to whether a person lacks capacity, this should be decided on a balance of probabilities (s.2(4)). Prior to reaching a conclusion that a person lacks the capacity to make a particular decision, all practicable steps must be taken to help him or her to make the decision (s.1(3)). A person who wishes to challenge a finding of capacity can, if the matter cannot be resolved by discussion, mediation or the provision of a second opinion, make an application to the Court of Protection for a declaration (s.15(1)(a)).

The person who is required to assess an individual's capacity will be the person who has the power to make the decision in respect of, or to act on behalf of the person in question. In the context of decision making by multi-disciplinary care teams, it is not sufficient for a decision to be categorised as a "team decision": the person who has professional account-ability for a decision relating to an individual who may lack capacity must be identified, and it is that person who must undertake the capacity assessment. The assessment of a per-son's capacity to make most day-to-day decisions will be made by the appropriate carer and will not require the involvement of a professional. Where consent to medical treatment is required, the doctor proposing the treatment is responsible for the capacity assessment. If a professional, such as a psychiatrist or a psychologist, is brought in to assist the potential decision-maker with an assessment of the person's capacity to make a complex or serious decision, the ultimate decision about capacity is that of the potential decision-maker and not the psychiatrist or psychologist whose role is that of an advisor. The *Code of Practice*, at para.4.53, suggests that:

"Professional involvement might be needed if:

- the decision that needs to be made is complicated or has serious consequences
- an assessor concludes a person lacks capacity, and the person challenges the finding
- family members, carers and/or professionals disagree about a person's capacity
- there is a conflict of interest between the assessor and the person being assessed
- the person being assessed is expressing different views to different people—they may be trying to please everyone or telling people what they think they want to hear
- somebody might challenge the person's capacity to make the decision—either at the time of the decision or later (for example, a family member might challenge a will after a person has died on the basis that the person lacked capacity when they made the will)
- somebody has been accused of abusing a vulnerable adult who may lack capacity to make decisions that protect them
- a person repeatedly makes decisions that put them at risk or could result in suffering or damage."

It is a striking fact that during the Parliamentary debates on the Bill no-one questioned the ability of professionals, let alone lay people, to assess mental capacity. The available evidence suggests that professional competence in this area is poor (see the studies cited below). In the context of medical practice, T. Grisso and P. Appelbaum suggest that doctors approach the issue of capacity assessments intuitively:

"Whether they recognise it or not, most clinicians assess their patients' decision-making abilities as part of every encounter. Ordinarily, this occurs unconsciously, as clinicians take notice of patients' dress, demeanour, communicative skills, intelligence, ability to attend to a conversation, apparent understanding, and ability to reach a decision. Since we all assume, appropriately, that people with whom we deal are competent to make decisions about their own lives—indeed the law makes a similar assumption—only when our unconscious monitoring detects something unexpected do we attend to it directly" (above, p.61).

The authors suggest that the following factors alert clinicians to the need for a capacity assessment: abrupt changes in patients' mental states, patients' refusal of recommended treatment, patients' consent to specially invasive or risky treatment, and the presence of one or more risk factors to impaired decision making, such as diagnosis or age (above, pp.62–76).

For a person to be assessed as being mentally incapable or making a decision he or she must: (1) be suffering from an impairment of, or disturbance in the functioning of, the mind or brain (s.2(1)); and (2) fail to satisfy any one of the requirements set out in paras (a)–(d) of subs.(1). Paragraphs (a), (b) and (c), which will cover the vast majority of cases, are taken from the decision of the Court of Appeal in *MB (Medical Treatment), Re* [1997] 2 F.L.R. 426 at 437, where Butler-Sloss L.J. identified the test of capacity in medical cases in the following terms:

> "A person lacks capacity if some impairment or disturbance of mental functioning renders the person unable to make a decision whether to consent to or refuse treatment. That inability to make a decision will occur when:
>
> (a) the patient is unable to comprehend and retain the information which is material to the decision, especially as to the likely consequences of having or not having the treatment in question;
> (b) the patient is unable to use the information and weigh it in the balance as part of the process of arriving at the decision."

As the approach adopted by this section is clearly based on the common law test of capacity, the Court of Protection will almost certainly use the existing caselaw on capacity as a guide to interpretation.

The finding of Lord Donaldson in *T (Adult: Refusal of Treatment), Re* [1992] 4 All E.R. 649 at 661 that the required capacity is the capacity which is commensurate with the gravity of the decision which the person is purporting to make is likely to be followed under this Act. Thus the more serious the decision, the greater the level of capacity required.

To be valid, a consent must be truly that of the mentally capable person, given freely and uncontaminated by the undue influence of others. The nature of undue influence is considered in the note on s.1(3). Paragraph 3.1 of the *Reference Guide to Consent for Examination or Treatment* (Department of Health, 2001) considers the validity of consent given in a prison or psychiatric hospital environment:

> "When patients are seen and treated in environments where involuntary detention may be an issue, such as prisons and mental hospitals, there is a potential for treatment offers to be perceived coercively, whether or not this is the case. Coercion invalidates consent and care must be taken to ensure that the patient makes a decision freely. Coercion should be distinguished from providing the patient with appropriate reassurance concerning their treatment, or pointing out the potential benefits of treatment for the patient's health. However, threats such as the withdrawal of any privileges or loss of remission of sentence for refusing consent, or using such measures to induce consent are not acceptable."

In *B (Consent to Treatment: Capacity), Re* [2002] EWHC 429 (Fam); [2002] 1 F.L.R. 1090, at para.100, Butler-Sloss P. stressed the importance of distinguishing between capacity and best interests in the context of consent to medical treatment:

> "If there are difficulties in deciding whether the patient has sufficient mental capacity, particularly if the refusal may have grave consequences for the patient, it is most important that those considering the issue should not confuse the question of mental capacity with the nature of the decision made by the patient, however grave the consequences. The view of the patient may reflect a difference in values rather than an absence of competence and the assessment of capacity should be approached with this firmly in mind. The doctors must not allow their emotional reaction to or strong disagreement with the decision of the patient to cloud their judgment in answering the primary question whether the patient has the mental capacity to make the decision."

A person's ambivalence about whether to receive medical treatment is only relevant to the issue of capacity "if, and only if, the ambivalence genuinely strikes at the root of the mental capacity of the patient", *per* Butler-Sloss P. in *B (Consent to Treatment: Capacity), Re* above, at para.35. In this case the President said at para.94: "Unless the gravity of the illness has affected the patient's capacity, a seriously disabled patient has the same rights as the fit person to respect for personal autonomy".

If there is concern or doubt about the mental capacity of a person to consent to medical treatment, that doubt should be resolved as soon as possible, by doctors within the hospital or NHS trust or by other normal medical procedures. In the meantime, while the question of capacity is being resolved, the person must be cared for in accordance with the judgment of the doctors as to the person's best interests. In the rare case where disagreement still exists about competence, it is of the utmost importance that the person is fully informed of the steps being taken, such as enlisting independent outside expertise, and made part of the process. Those in charge must not allow a situation of deadlock or drift to occur. If all appropriate steps to seek independent assistance from medical experts outside the hospital have failed, the hospital should not hesitate to make an application to the Court of Protection or seek the advice of the Official Solicitor (*NHS Trust v T (Adult Patient: Refusal of Medical Treatment)* [2004] EWHC 1279 (Fam) ; [2005] 1 All E.R. 387, para.42).

A judge is not required to accept the evidence of psychiatrists as to a person's mental capacity (*W (Adult: Refusal of Medical Treatment), Re* [2002] EWHC Fam 901). In *Masterman-Lister v Jewell*, above, Wright J. said at para.16:

"Although the opinions of skilled and experienced medical practitioners are a very important element in the evidence to be considered by the court, that element has to be considered in conjunction with any other evidence that there may be about the manner in which the subject of the enquiry actually has conducted his everyday life and affairs."

The evidence of the patient's wife was preferred to the medical evidence in *Lindsay v Wood* [2006] EWHC 2895 (QB), largely because of the "difference between 'real life', as it is described, and the artificial conditions of medical assessment" (para.49). Stanley Burnton J. said at para.18:

"When considering the question of capacity, psychiatrists and psychologists will normally wish to take into account all aspects of the personality and behaviour of the person in question, including vulnerability to exploitation. However, vulnerability to exploitation does not of itself lead to the conclusion that there is a lack of capacity. Many people who have full capacity are vulnerable to exploitation, or more so than most other people. Many people make rash and irresponsible decisions, but are of full capacity. The issue is ... whether the person concerned has the mental capacity to make a rational decision."

Although the test set out in this section is easily understandable and, perhaps, gives the impression that the assessment of a person's mental capacity is a relatively straightforward task, the reality is that the assessment can sometimes be extremely difficult. Baroness Finlay of Llandaff gave evidence to the Joint Committee on this point:

"If I can give you two specific and very common instances, one where patients have been anxious, which is understandable because they are facing dying, and where the benzodiazepine group of drugs such as Midazolam are used to remove the churning drive of anxiety without sedating the patients so they can still function but they are relived in part of this desperate feeling of anxiety, butterflies and churning inside. With some of these patients you can have a conversation and they appear to understand everything that is said and have recall. The following day they have no recall whatsoever of that conversation. It may have been a few hours later in some patients. Another situation which arises is where patients' calcium goes up and that occurs in about ten per cent of all cancer patients. They become confused. That is a gradual onset and the outset is difficult to diagnose. They may appear to be arguing rationally but when their calcium level has been brought down and is treated they then are behaving differently and they have no recall of that previous conversation or the direction that they were trying to give in expressing what they wanted. Also they may completely change their mind which is a terribly important situation for a clinician. The difficulty is in judging whether they have capacity or not because at any one point in time the conversation appears to be logical and consequential. There are lots of other situations which arise, particularly with patients on steroids where the steroids may have created a very mild steroid psychosis which can be difficult to diagnose and just presents as emotional immobility. Again, their thinking and perception is distorted" (Oral and Written Evidence, Ev 126).

This Act requires judgments to be made about a person's mental capacity by people without a clinical background who will probably have had no training or experience in making such assessments. There must be a very considerable doubt as to their ability to do this. Similar doubts can be expressed about the competence of some medical practitioners to undertake this task. In its evidence to the Joint Committee, the Alzeheimer's Society emphasised the need for a skilled capacity assessment. One of its members wrote of her experiences:

"As a former nurse, my mother was extremely good at covering up her problems and was extremely plausible. Her doctor reacted with shocked amazement at our suggestion that my mother had dementia.—'There's nothing wrong with your mother. I saw her only the other day and had a conversation with her. She's fine.' This was at a time when my mother was putting the electric kettle on the gas ring, entertaining phantom meetings of teachers in her front room, turning up at the hairdressers at 2a.m. and living on a diet of biscuits having forgotten how to cook" (Oral and Written Evidence, Ev 384).

It has been noted that competency is rarely questioned when the patient consents to treatment (B. Hoffman and J. Srinivasan "A study of competence to consent to treatment in a psychiatric hospital" (1992) 37 *Canadian Journal of Psychiatry* 179). Also see R. Cairns, C. Maddock, A. Buchanan, A.S. David, P. Hayward, G. Richardson, G. Szmukler and M. Hotopf., "Reliability of mental capacity assessments in psychiatric in-patients" (2005) 187 *British Journal Psychiatry* 372, where the researchers found a probable bias towards judging a patient as having capacity if they made the apparently "correct" decision of agreeing to treatment.

Research into the application of the functional approach to capacity has been undertaken: see M.J. Gunn, J.G. Wong, I.C.H. Clare and A.J. Holland, "Decision-making capacity" (1999) 7(3) Med. L. Rev. 269. The authors concluded that the approach "can work, albeit the interface between legal definition and clinical practice is not a simple one to bridge" (at 306). Suto and her colleagues found that the quality of capacity assessment made by medical practitioners under Part VII of the 1983 Act, including those undertaken by psychiatrists, was poor and that most assessors relied on the status approach. The authors found little evidence of the use of the functional approach (W.M.I. Suto, I.C.H. Clare and A.J. Holland, "Substitute financial decision-making in England and Wales: a study of the Court of Protection" (2002) 24(1) *Journal of Social Welfare and Family Law* 37). There is also evidence that psychiatrists can be inconsistent in their approach to the assessment of patients' capacity to consent to treatment (A. Shah and S. Mukherjee, "Ascertaining Capacity to Consent: A survey of approaches used by psychiatrists" (2003) 43 *Medicine, Science and the Law* 231). A study of the recognition of the mental incapacity of acutely ill medical hospital in-patients found that clinical teams rarely identified patients who did not have the required mental capacity (V. Raymont, W. Bingley, A Buchanan, S. David, P. Hayward, S. Wessely, and M. Hotopf, "Prevalence of mental incapacity in medical inpatients and associated risk factors: cross sectional study" (2004) 364 *Lancet* 1421). The Royal College of Psychiatrists summarised the available research evidence by stating that "at present few doctors understand and are knowledgeable about capacity assessments, and many would fail to recognise that a person lacked capacity" ("Assisted Dying for the Terminally Ill Bill—Statement form the Royal College of Psychiatrists on Physician Assisted Suicide", April, 2006).

For an extensive analysis of the assessment of capacity from a psychological perspective, see "Assessment of Capacity in Adults: Interim Guidance for Psychologists" (2006)

British Psychological Society. Also see, *Assessment of Mental Capacity: Guidance for Doctors and Lawyers* (2004) BMA/Law Society.

Subsection (1) para. (a)

1–028 The nature of understanding is considered by T. Grisso and P. Appelbaum, above, at p.38:

> "As basic as the concept of understanding may seem, the psychological process related to it are not easily defined. A person's accurate assimilation of information involves a complex series of events. First the information must be received as presented, a process that is influenced not only by sensory integrity, but also by perceptual functions such as attention and selective awareness. Whatever is received then undergoes cognitive processing and is encoded in a manner consistent with the person's existing fund of information and concepts, which in turn influences how, and how well, the message is recorded and stored in the memory."

The authors point out that many medical conditions, as well as chronic mental disorders and disabilities, can "have a substantial negative influence on these functions" (p.39).

In the context of an individual's capacity to execute an instrument, it has been held that the degree or extent of the understanding required is relative to the particular transaction which it is to effect (*Re Beaney (deceased)* [1978] 2 All E.R. 585).

The information provided must include the information specified in subs.(4). As the information must be "relevant to the decision", the person should not be burdened with peripheral information. The information, which should be devoid of unnecessary technical jargon, should be given in an appropriate manner in the person's first language (subs.(2)). It is suggested that the person must have the ability to understand that the information provided applies to him or herself. All practicable steps should be taken to assist the person to understand the information (s.1(3)), with account being taken of any cultural or religious factors relating to the person which might inhibit communication.

In the context of consent to medical treatment, an explanation in "broad terms" of the nature of the procedure which is intended and its likely effects would be sufficient for the person's consent to be "real" (*Chatterton v Gerson* [1981] 1 QB 432 at 442). In *R v Mental Health Act Commission Ex p. X* (1998) 9 B.M.L.R. 77 at 87, DC, Stuart-Smith L.J. said that he could not "accept that a patient must understand the precise physiological process involved before he can be said to be capable of understanding the nature and likely effects of the treatment or can consent to it". The finding in *Chatterton v Gerson* was followed by the House of Lords in *Sidaway v Board of Governors of the Bethlem Royal Hospital* [1985] 1 All E.R. 643, where it was held that the decision on what risks should be disclosed to a patient was primarily a matter of clinical judgment and in making that judgment a doctor was required to act in accordance with a practice accepted at the time as proper by a responsible body of medical opinion. It would not matter that there may be another body of responsible medical opinion which takes a different view, However, Lords Keith and Bridge, speaking with the majority, considered that the court might in certain circumstances come to the conclusion that disclosure of a particular risk was so obviously necessary to an informed choice on the part of the patient that no reasonably prudent doctor would fail to make it. This approach was confirmed by the House of Lords in *Bolitho (Deceased) v City and Hackney HA* [1997] 4 All E.R. 771, where it was held that in a rare case, if it could be demonstrated that the medical opinion was not capable of withstanding logical analysis, the judge would be entitled to hold that the body of opinion was not reasonable or responsible. *Sidaway* and *Bolitho* were considered by the Court of Appeal in *Pearce v United Bristol Healthcare NHS Trust* (1999) 48 B.M.L.R.118, para.23, where Lord Woolf held that:

> "[I]f there is a significant risk which would affect the judgment of a reasonable patient then in the normal course it is the responsibility of a doctor to inform the patient of that significant risk, if the information is needed so that the patient can determine for him or herself as to what course that he or she should adopt."

Whether a risk is "significant" cannot be determined simply in terms of percentages. The doctor will have to:

"take into account all the relevant considerations, which include the ability of the patient to comprehend what he has to say to him or her and the state of the patient at the particular time, both from the physical point of view and the emotional point of view" (para.24).

If a patient asks about a risk, it is the doctor's legal duty to give an honest answer (*per* Lord Woolf at para.5).

In *R (A Minor) (Wardship: Medical Treatment), Re* [1991] 4 All E.R.177, a case concerning the capacity of a child to consent to treatment, Lord Donaldson M.R. said at 187:

"[W]hat is involved is not merely an ability to understand the nature of the proposed treatment—in this case compulsory medication—but a full understanding and appreciation of the consequences both of the treatment in terms of intended and possible side effects and, equally important, the anticipated consequences of a failure to treat."

The treating doctor should therefore provide the patient with information about what would happen to the patient if the treatment is provided, the likely consequences to the patient if the treatment is not provided, and the risks and side effects of the treatment. In the studies examined by Diana Rose and her colleagues, approximately half of those who received electroconvulsive therapy felt that they had been given insufficient information about the procedure ("Information, consent and perceived coercion: patient's perspectives on electroconvulsive therapy" (2005) 186 *British Journal of Psychiatry* 54).

The General Medical Council's guidelines "Seeking Patients' Consent: The Ethical Considerations" state at para.10:

"You should not withhold information necessary for decision making unless you judge that disclosure of some relevant information would cause the patient serious harm."

A similar approach to the existence of a "therapeutic privilege" that allows for certain information to be withheld from patients is taken by the *Code of Practice* on the Mental Health Act at para.15.16. Given that the notion of professional paternalism has been effectively buried by the recommendations made by *Learning from Bristol: the report of the public inquiry into children's heart surgery at the Bristol Royal Infirmary 1984–1995* (Cm.5207), it is suggested that Andrew Hockton is correct when he states that doctors invoke therapeutic privilege "at their peril" (*The Law of Consent to Medical Treatment*, 2002, para.1–002).

Subsection (1) para. (b)

RETAIN. See subs.(3).   **1–029**

Subsection (1) para. (c)

Understanding the information is not sufficient: the person must also be able to use the **1–030** information as part of the process of arriving at a decision. In using the information, the person can be assisted by relevant professional advice (*Masterman-Lister v Brutton & Co* [2003] 3 All E.R.162, CA), and by support from the person's care network. The *Code of Practice*, at para.4.22, offers the following examples of persons who able to understand, but not "use or weigh" the information:

"For example, a person with the eating disorder anorexia nervosa may understand information about the consequences of not eating. But their compulsion not to eat might be too strong for them to ignore. Some people who have serious brain damage might make impulsive decisions regardless of information they may have been given or their understanding of it."

In order to "use or weigh" information, the person must not be prevented by mental disorder from believing the information. In *B v Croydon HA* (1994) 22 B.M.L.R. 13, 20, Thorpe J. said that in the context of consent to medical treatment there is a difference between outright disbelief (due to mental disorder) which meant being "impervious to reason, divorced from reality, or incapable of adjustment after reflection", and "the tendency which most people have when undergoing medical treatment to self assess and then puzzle over the divergence between medical and self assessment". In *R (on the application of B) v Dr. SS, Dr. AC and the Secretary of State for Health* [2005] EWHC 86 (Admin), paras 188, 190, Charles J. found that the patient was refusing treatment because he did not accept or believe that he is, or may be, mentally ill. It therefore followed that the patient lacked capacity because he "does not believe or accept a cornerstone of the factors to be taken into account in considering the information he has been given about his proposed treatment and therefore is not able to use and weigh in the balance the relevant information as to his proposed treatment in reaching a decision to agree to it or to refuse it".

In *Re MB*, above, the court said that if a compulsive disorder or phobia from which the patient suffers dominates her thinking, the decision may not be a true one. In this case the patient's phobia to needles induced such panic in her that "at that moment the needle or mask dominated her thinking and made her quite unable to consider anything else" (at 431). *Re MB* was applied in *Re H (Adult Patient)* [2006] EWHC 1230 (Fam) where Potter P. said, at para.22, that "a compulsive disorder or phobia may prevent the patient's decision from being a true one, particularly if conditioned by some obsessional belief or feeling which so distorts the judgment as to render the decision invalid". Similar considerations apply if the patient's thinking is dominated by fear or pain.

A person who is subject to the undue influence of another would be unable to give a valid consent: see the notes on s.1(3).

Subsection (1) para. (d)

1–031   The rationale for this provision is explained in the Explanatory Memorandum at para.27:

> "This is intended to be a residual category and will only affect a small group of persons, in particular some of those with the very rare condition of 'locked-in syndrome'. It seems likely that people suffering from this condition can in fact still understand, retain and use information and so would not be regarded as lacking capacity under subs.(1)(a)-(c). Some people who suffer from this condition can communicate by blinking an eye, but it seems that others cannot communicate at all. [This provision] treats those who are completely unable to communicate their decisions as unable to make a decision. Any residual ability to communicate (such as blinking an eye to indicate 'yes' or 'no' in answer to a question) would exclude a person from this category."

Although the blinking of an eye or the squeezing of a hand can be used to communicate a decision without undue difficulty, it would be less easy to use such methods to identify whether the person has understood and applied the information provided. In *AK (Adult Patient) (Medical Treatment: Consent), Re* [2001] 1 F.L.R. 129, a patient who could only communicate by blinking one eyelid was held to be mentally capable of making a decision to refuse life-sustaining treatment.

This provision is concerned with people who are "unable" to communicate their decision; it does not encompass people who are unwilling to communicate their decision. If a person falls into the latter category, he or she must be assumed to be mentally capable unless the decision-maker assesses that person as lacking the capacity to make the decision in question (s.1(2)). If the failure of the person to communicate is assessed as being the consequence of "an impairment of, or a disturbance in the functioning of, [that person's] mind or brain" (s.2(1)), the decision-maker must consider whether the identified impairment or disturbance results in a failure of the person to satisfy the requirements of paras (a),(b) or (c). If there is such a failure, the person will lack the capacity to make the decision.

Subsection (2)

1–032   This provision, which expands upon the principle set out in s.1(3), was added at the third reading of the Bill so that there "is no longer any doubt: no one should be labelled incapable merely because insufficient efforts have been made to help him understand and communicate", *per* the Parliamentary Under-Secretary of State (*Hansard*, HC Vol.428, col.1632).

AN EXPLANATION. The explanation must be sufficiently specific to enable the person to use or weigh the information as required by subs.(1)(c).

Subsection (3)

SHORT PERIOD. The person must be able to retain the information for the time that it takes **1–033** to make the decision. Most decisions will therefore require the information to be retained for a brief period only. Significant or difficult decisions might require the person to retain the information over a number of days before a decision is made.

In "Summing up—a Judge's Perspective", [2006] Crim. L.R. 817, H.H. Judge Nic Madge makes reference to Professor Robert H. Margolis's review of the literature that shows that patient's retain about 50 per cent of the information provided to them by health care professionals. Of the information recalled, about half is remembered incorrectly, i.e. patients remember correctly only about a quarter of what they are told. An equally disturbing finding is that patient's often forget their own medical diagnoses. Information presented in a simple, easy to understand format is remembered better than information presented in a more complex manner. The more information presented, the lower the proportion that is recalled by the patient. When verbal presentation is supplemented by written explanations, recall can be significantly enhanced: see "Boosting Memory with Informational Counselling" *The ASHA Leader* (August 3, 2004) pp.10–11, 28, available at *www.asha.org/about/publications/leader-online/archives/2004/040803*.

Best interests

4.—(1) In determining for the purposes of this Act what is in a person's best **1–034** interests, the person making the determination must not make it merely on the basis of—

(a) the person's age or appearance, or

(b) a condition of his, or an aspect of his behaviour, which might lead others to make unjustified assumptions about what might be in his best interests.

(2) The person making the determination must consider all the relevant circumstances and, in particular, take the following steps.

(3) He must consider—

(a) whether it is likely that the person will at some time have capacity in relation to the matter in question, and

(b) if it appears likely that he will, when that is likely to be.

(4) He must, so far as reasonably practicable, permit and encourage the person to participate, or to improve his ability to participate, as fully as possible in any act done for him and any decision affecting him.

(5) Where the determination relates to life-sustaining treatment he must not, in considering whether the treatment is in the best interests of the person concerned, be motivated by a desire to bring about his death.

(6) He must consider, so far as is reasonably ascertainable—

(a) the person's past and present wishes and feelings (and, in particular, any relevant written statement made by him when he had capacity),

(b) the beliefs and values that would be likely to influence his decision if he had capacity, and

(c) the other factors that he would be likely to consider if he were able to do so.

(7) He must take into account, if it is practicable and appropriate to consult them, the views of—

(a) anyone named by the person as someone to be consulted on the matter in question or on matters of that kind,

(b) anyone engaged in caring for the person or interested in his welfare,

(c) any donee of a lasting power of attorney granted by the person, and

(d) any deputy appointed for the person by the court, as to what would be in the person's best interests and, in particular, as to the matters mentioned in subsection (6).

(8) The duties imposed by subsections (1) to (7) also apply in relation to the exercise of any powers which—

(a) are exercisable under a lasting power of attorney, or

(b) are exercisable by a person under this Act where he reasonably believes that another person lacks capacity.

(9) In the case of an act done, or a decision made, by a person other than the court, there is sufficient compliance with this section if (having complied with the requirements of subsections (1) to (7)) he reasonably believes that what he does or decides is in the best interests of the person concerned.

(10) "Life-sustaining treatment" means treatment which in the view of a person providing health care for the person concerned is necessary to sustain life.

(11) "Relevant circumstances" are those—

(a) of which the person making the determination is aware, and

(b) which it would be reasonable to regard as relevant.

DEFINITIONS

1–035   "treatment": s.64(1)
"lasting power of attorney": s.64(1)
"deputy": s.64(1)
"the court": s.64(1)

GENERAL NOTE

1–036   Section 1(5) establishes the principle that "an act done, or decision made, under this Act for or on behalf of a person who lacks capacity must be done, or made, in his best interests". This section sets out a checklist of factors which must be considered before the decision is made, or the act is carried out. In effect, the checklist establishes the course of action that should be followed in order to reach a determination whether a decison is in the person's best interests, a term which is not defined in this Act: it deals with the process of acquiring evidence, rather than specifying the criteria of best interests. A considerable latitude is therefore granted to the decision-maker when reaching a reasonable belief as to where P's best interests lie. In its report on *Mental Incapacity*, the Law Commission acknowledged that "no statutory guidance could offer an exhastive account of what is in the persons best interests, the intention being that the individual person and his or her individual circumstances should always determine the result" (Law Com. No. 231, para.3.26). As well as being in the person's best interests, the decision should also aim to satisfy the least restrictive option principle set out in s.1(6).

Any person or body that intervenes on behalf of P must believe that their act or decision is in that person's best interests and that belief will have to be reasonable (subs.(9)). The test of best interests is therefore an objective one. It is the best interests of P that is at issue, not the best interests of another. The test applies to all decisions made or actions taken under this Act, ranging from a decision of the Court of Protection to a minor decision made by an informal carer. Only one course of action can be in the best interests of P.

It is noteworthy that while the law requires a "significant harm" test to be satisfied before a child can be removed from the family home against parental wishes (Children Act 1989, s.31(2)), the court can order the removal of a mentally incapable adult from the family home under this Act merely on the basis that removal would be in the adult's best interests.

Only one course of action can be in the best interests of P. The practical effect of subs.(6) is to attempt to ascertain what P's subjective preference would have been had he or she been mentally capable. However, the effect of this is not to require the decision maker to make a form of substituted judgment on behalf of P as the matters itemised in subs.(6) must merely be considered by the decision-maker who may come to a decision which P would not have wanted. For example, "if someone had a lifelong aversion to needles, a decision could still be taken to give them the necessary injection when they were unconscious after a car crash", *per* the Parliamentary Under-Secretary of State, St.Comm. A, col.73. The concept of substituted judgment has been developed by the American courts and rejected by the English courts; see, for example, the observations of Lord Goff and Lord Mustill in Airedale *NHS Trust v Bland* [1993] 1 All E.R.821 at 872–3, and 891–2 respectively.

The provisions of subss.(3)–(7) do not provide an exhaustive list of factors that need to be taken into account as the decision maker must consider "all the relevant circumstances" (subs.(2)). The assessment of a P's best interests is clearly going to be influenced by either the personal or professional relationship that the decision-maker has with P. If P's incapacity is likely to be temporary, it might be possible for the decision to be postponed until capacity is regained: see subs.(3).

If someone disagrees with the best interests determination that has been made, the Department of Constitutional Affairs Consultation Paper CP 10/06, at pp.10–11, identifies the following options that may be explored:

- involving an advocate, who is independent of all the parties, to work with the person who lacks capacity and help them understand the situation or act as an advocate of their best interests;
- getting a second opinion in cases where the decision relates to medical treatment;
- holding a formal or informal case conference if the decision relates to medical treatment or social care;
- using the informal or formal complaints processes if the decision in question is to be taken by the health, social or other welfare services; or
- participating in mediation or other forms of dispute resolution. This may be most appropriate to decisions on the day-to-day care or welfare of a person.

If all attempts to resolve a dispute fail, it may be appropriate to apply to the Court of Protection for a ruling on what particular decision or course of action is in P's best interests. The *Code of Practice* states at para.5.15:

"Any staff involved in the care of a person who lacks capacity should make sure a record is kept of the process of working out the best interests of that person for each relevant decision, setting out:

- how the decision about the person's best interests was reached
- what the reasons for reaching the decision were
- who was consulted to help work out best interests, and
- what particular factors were taken into account.

This record should remain on the person's file."

Best interests and medical treatment

As the approach taken in this section is founded on the common law, an account of com- **1–037** mon law rules relating to best interests in the context of the provision of medical treatment is set out below.

A patient's best interests are not limited to best medical interests (*Re M.B. (Medical Treatment)* [1997] 2 F.L.R. 426, CA); they encompass "medical, emotional and all other welfare issues" (*per* Butler-Sloss P. in *A (Mental Patient: Sterilisation)*, Re [2000] 1

F.L.R. 549 at 555). *Re MB* was applied in *Trust A v H (An Adult Patient)* [2006] EWHC 1320 (Fam); (2006) 9 C.C.L.R 474, where Potter P. said at paras 25–26:

"In English law 'best interests' are not confined to best medical interests and the court is not tied to the clinical assessment of what is in the patient's best interests, being itself obliged to take into account a broad spectrum of medical, social, emotional and welfare issues before reaching its own conclusion on the basis of a careful consideration of the evidence.

When considering those best interests the court assesses the advantages and disadvantages of various treatment and management options, the viability of each such option, and its likely effect on the patient and the enjoyment of his or her life. Any likely benefit of the treatment has to be balanced and considered in the in the light of any additional suffering such treatment might entail."

In *Y (Mental Patient: Bone Marrow Donation), Re* [1996] 2 F.L.R. 787, Connell J. held that it was in the best interests of an incompetent patient to donate bone marrow to her gravely ill sister. Having heard evidence that the death of the sister would have a particularly adverse effect upon the mother, with whom the patient enjoyed a very close relationship, and, in particular, would significantly handicap her ability to visit the patient, his Lordship held that the procedure would be to the patients "emotional, psychological and social benefit".

The sanctity of life is a fundamental principle and there is a very strong presumption in favour of a course of action which will prolong life (*B (A Minor) (Wardship: Medical Treatment), Re* [1981] 1 W.L.R. 1421). Lord Goff said in Airedale *NHS Trust v Bland* [1993] 1 All E.R. 821, at 865–866:

". . . the fundamental principle is the principle of the sanctity of human life - a principle long recognised not only in our own society but also in most, if not all, civilised societies throughout the modern world, as is indeed evidenced by its recognition both in Art.2 of the European Convention on Human Rights and in Art. 6 of the International Covenant on Civil and Political Rights

But this principle, fundamental though it is, is not absolute We are concerned with circumstances in which it may be lawful to withhold from a patient medical treatment or care by means of which his life may be prolonged. But here too there is no absolute rule that the patient's life must be prolonged by such treatment or care, if available, regardless of the circumstances."

This approach is illustrated by the case of *D (Medical Treatment: Mentaly Disabled Patient), Re* [1998] 2 F.L.R. 22 where Sir Stephen Brown P. granted a declaration that "notwithstanding the [patient's] inability to consent to or refuse medical treatment, it is lawful as being in the best interests of the patient that the [NHS Trust] do not impose haemodialysis upon him in circumstances in which, in the opinion of the medical practitioners responsible for such treatment, it is not reasonable practicable so to do". This was a case where it had proved to be impossible to treat a gravely ill, physically protesting, incompetent patient. The doctors had sought a declaration to protect themselves from any liability arising from a failure to carry out the treatment.

In *W Healthcare NHS Trust v H* [2004] EWCA Civ 1324, reference was made to the following passage from para.1.2 of the BMA's "Withholding and Withdrawing Life Prolonging Medical Treatment: Guidance for decision making" (2000):

"Where, however, the disability is so profound that individuals have no or minimal levels of awareness of their own existence and no hope of recovering awareness the question arises as to whether continuing to provide treatment aimed at prolonging that life would provide a benefit to them."

Brooke L.J. said at para.30:

"English law, as it stands at present, places a very heavy burden on those who are advocating a course which would lead inevitably to the cessation of a human life."

In *R (on the application of Burke) v The General Medical Council* [2005] EWCA Civ 1003; [2005] H.R.L.R. 35, Lord Phillips M.R. said at para.33:

"The courts have accepted that where life involves an extreme degree of pain, discomfort or indignity to a patient, who is sentient but not competent and who has manifested no wish to be kept alive, these circumstances may absolve the doctors of the positive duty to keep the patient alive. Equally the courts have recognised that there may be no duty to keep alive a patient who is in a persistent vegetative state. In each of these examples the facts of the individual case may make it difficult to decide whether the duty to keep the patient alive persists."

In *Re J (A Minor) (Wardship: Medical Treatment)* [1991] Fam 33, Lord Donaldson M.R. said in a case where two NHS trusts sought declarations that it would be lawful not to provide further aggressive treatment to a gravely ill child:

"We know that the instinct and desire for survival is very strong. We all believe in and assert the sanctity of human life . . . even very severely handicapped people find a quality of life rewarding which to the unhandicapped may seem manifestly intolerable. People have an amazing adaptability. But in the end there will be cases in which the answer must be that it is not in the interests of the child to subject it to treatment which will cause increased suffering and produce no commensurate benefit, giving the fullest possible weight to the child's, and mankind's desire to survive."

The Lord Chancellor said at the second reading of the Bill in the House of Lords that "in some cases it will be in the best interests of the person to withhold treatment or to give palliative care that might incidentally shorten life" (*Hansard*, HL Vol.668, col.15). In support of this approach, he quoted from the Roman Catholic Archbishop of Cardiff who had said:

". . . it is not the church's position that life must be sustained at all costs. On the contrary, one can quite reasonably, and consistently with one's responsibilities for oneself and others, decide to refuse treatment—even life sustaining treatment—which one judges burdensome or futile, knowing that forgoing the treatment will shorten one's life."

In *Re A*, above, Thorpe L.J. said at 560:

"[T]he first instance judge with the responsibility to make an evaluation of the best interests of a claimant lacking capacity should draw up a balance sheet. The first entry should be of any factor or factors of actual benefit Then on the other sheet the judge should write any counterbalancing dis-benefits to the applicant Then the judge should enter on each sheet the potential gains and losses in each instance making some estimate of the extent of the possibility that the gain or loss might accrue. At the end of that exercise the judge should be better placed to strike a balance between the sum of the certain and possible gains against the sum of the certain and possible losses. Obviously, only if the account is in relatively significant credit will the judge conclude that the applicant is likely to advance the best interests of the claimant."

Adopting this "balance sheet" approach is recommended for practitioners who are faced with particularly difficult or contentious decisions.

In *Re A*, the question whether third party interests, such as the interests of potential sexual partners of the patient, should ever be considered in a case concerned with the best interests of a patient was left open. During the Bill's passage through Parliament, the BMA sought assurances that it would be possible to conduct a diagnostic test on an incapacitated person primarily for the benefit of a family member in the case of genetic diseases, or to a nurse or doctor if a needlestick accident had occurred during the person's treatment. The Minister of State responded to these concerns as follows:

"[T]he Bill will allow for acts whose primary purpose is to benefit a third party, provided that those acts are in P's best interests. I reassure the House that the interpretation of best interests could be broader than P's medical best interests. I can confirm that the Bill will not prevent a genetic test for a familial cancer, for example, that might not be essential to P's medical care but would provide considerable benefit to some other family member. Similarly, HIV testing would be lawful if there were a needlestick injury to a nurse involved in P's care and if a timely diagnosis of HIV status would be in P's best interests, so that treatment could be started.There is the ability for a medical professional in those circumstances - if they reasonably think that a person might have HIV /AIDS or hepatitis C and they might have been affected by it - to request a test so that treatment of P could start" (*Hansard*, HC Vol.428, col.1601).

Although it is likely that a court would confirm the lawfulness of the assurances given by the Minister, the best interests principle would not be satisfied in a situation where the procedure in question resulted in no tangible or intangible benefit to P. It could be argued in a situation where the primary purpose of the intervention is to benefit a third party that an intangible benefit would be the desire of P, had he or she been capable, to be seen to be "a normal decent person, acting in accordance with contemporary standards of morality" (*C (Spinster and Mental Patient), Re* [1991] 3 All E.R. 866, *per* Hoffmann J. at 870).

Where there is no alternative treatment available for a mentally incapacitated patient and the disease is progressive and fatal, it is reasonable to consider experimental treatment with unknown benefits and risks, but without significant risks of increased suffering to the patient, in cases where there is some chance of benefit to the patient (*Simms v Simms* [2002] EWHC Fam 2734; [2003] 1 All E.R. 669) Butler-Sloss P. said at para.57: "A patient who is not able to consent to pioneering treatment ought not to be deprived of the chance in circumstances where he would be likely to consent if he had been competent". Her Ladyship stressed, at para.64, that in such cases the views of the family of the patient about the proposed treatment would carry great weight in the wider considerations of the best interests test.

Although, in the absence of an appropriate lasting power of attorney, the next of kin of a mentally incapable patient has no legal right either to consent or to refuse treatment on behalf of the patient, it is not necessarily undesirable for such consent to be sought if the interests of the patient will not be adversely affected by any consequential delay. This is because "contact with the next of kin may reveal that the patient has made an anticipatory choice which, if clearly established and applicable in the circumstances—two major 'ifs'— would bind the practitioner (*NHS Trust v T (Adult Patient: Refusal of Medical Treatment)*, above, *per* Lord Donaldson M.R. at 649).

Where a clinician concludes that a treatment that has been requested by a relative of the patient is inimical to the patient's best interests and his professional conscience, intuition or hunch confirms that view, he may refuse to act and cannot be compelled to do so, though he should not prevent another from so acting, should that clinician feel able to do so (*Re Wyatt* [2005] EWHC 2293 (Fam); [2005] 4 All E.R. 1325, para.36).

The General Medical Council describes the best interests' principle in *Seeking patients' consent: the ethical considerations*,1999, at para.25:

"In deciding what options may be reasonably considered as being in the best interests of a patient who lacks capacity to decide, [the treating doctor] should take into account:

- options for treatment or investigation which are clinically indicated;
- any evidence of the patient's previously expressed preferences, including an advance statement;
- your own and the health care team's knowledge ofthe patient's background, such as cultural, religious, or employment considerations;
- views about the patient's preferences given by a third party who may have other knowledge of the patient, for example the patient's partner, family, carer, or a person with parental responsibility;

- which option least restricts the patient's future choices, where more than one option (including non treatment) seems reasonable in the patient's best interest."

In the absence of a valid and applicable advance decision, the supposed view of the patient, as identified by relatives, will be no more than a factor to be taken into account in determining where his or her best interests lie.

Subsection (1)

Although the Government resisted an amendment to insert an anti-discrimination prin- **1–038** ciple in s.1 for technical reasons and because it "would be inconceivable that giving someone less favourable treatment because of his disability, sex, age, race or sexual orientation could ever be considered to be in his best interests" (*per* the Parliamentary Under-Secretary of State (*Hansard*, HL Vol.668, col.1194)), the question of including some form of anti-discrimination or equal consideration provision in the Bill was a recurrent theme in the Parliamentary debates. The Government's response to this concern was to amend this provision at report stage in the House of Lords to "make sure that no one began a best interests determination with unjustified assumptions or prejudices. [The provision now] makes it clear that decision-making must start from a blank slate. People cannot say, 'She is very old so it is not necessary to give her this treatment' or, 'He has very severe physical disabilities, so it is obviously not in his best interests to have an operation'. Instead there must be a full and objective best interests assessment in every situation", *per* Baroness Andrews (*Hansard*, HL Vol.670, col.1320).

A PERSON'S BEST INTERESTS. The best interests criterion does not apply to advance decisions: see the note on s.1(5).

APPEARANCE. This covers "visible medical problems, disabilities, the colour of someone's skin, religious dress, and so on", *per* Baroness Andrews, above.

CONDITION. The condition, which might relate to either a mental or physical disorder, could be temporary.

Subsection (2)

ALL THE RELEVANT CIRCUMSTANCES. In the Bill as originally drafted, this phrase read "all the **1–039** circumstances appearing to him to be relevant". The amendment, together with the addition of subs.(11), were made in order to emphasise the objective nature of the best interests test (*Hansard*, HC Vol.428, col.1631).

IN PARTICULAR. None of the considerations set out in the indicative "checklist" contained in subss.(3)–(7) take precedence over any other consideration. The Government's view is the "any prioritising of factors within the best interests checklist would have the effect of unnecessarily fettering the application of all factors in the checklist. We believe that the checklist as it is in the draft Bill is sufficiently flexible to allow the factors to be applied to any particular individual in their particular circumstances" (*The Government Response to the Scrutiny Committee's Report on the draft Mental Incapacity Bill*, (Cm.6121)).

Subsection (3)

If the person is likely to regain his or her capacity at some point in the future, the decision **1–040** should be postponed until then if such a delay is consistent with the person's best interests. Paragraph 5.28 of the *Code of Practice* identifies "some factors which may indicate that a person may regain or develop capacity in the future". They "are:

- the cause of the lack of capacity can be treated, either by medication or some other form of treatment or therapy

- the lack of capacity is likely to decrease in time (for example, where it is caused by the effects of medication or alcohol, or following a sudden shock)
- a person with learning disabilities may learn new skills or be subject to new experiences which increase their understanding and ability to make certain decisions
- the person may have a condition which causes capacity to come and go at various times (such as some forms of mental illness) so it may be possible to arrange for the decision to be made during a time when they do have capacity
- a person previously unable to communicate may learn a new form of communication."

Subsection (4)

1–041   This provision complements the principle contained in s.1(3). The decision-maker might wish to seek the help of others when complying with this obligation to involve the person to the fullest practicable extent in both the decision-making process and the consequences of the decision.

REASONABLY PRACTICABLE. This is an objective requirement. "[T]here will always be cases where, for urgent or non-emergency reasons, it would be inappropriate and not in a person's best interests to delay acting, which is why the words 'reasonably practicable' are in clause 4(4). It is also unrealistic to expect all people affected by the Bill to be able to participate in decisions. The Bill applies to people in a coma, as well as to those who are seriously distressed or who need urgent care. While in some cases it would be possible to wait until the person is capable of making the decision themselves, in other cases it clearly would not", *per* the Parliamentary Under-Secretary of State, St. Comm. A, col.92.

IMPROVE HIS ABILITY TO PARTICIPATE. Using communication support where this is appropriate.

Subsection (5)

1–042   This provision was inserted at the Committee stage in the House of Lords in an attempt to respond to the concern of those who considered that decisions concerning life-sustaining treatment could lead to euthanasia by omission. Its purpose is to "make it absolutely clear that no person, whether doctor, attorney, deputy or court, can, when making a best interests determination, have the motive of causing death, regardless of what would be in his best interests" (Joint Committee on Human Rights, Fourth Report, Session 204–2005, Appendix 4, para.41). The Joint Committee expressed its concern that proving the motive of a person making a best interests determination will in practice "be extremely difficult" (para.4.42). This concern was shared by some members of the House of Lords who drew a distinction between intent, which can be objectively identified by examining the act, and motive, which is a state of mind which cannot be objectively verified: see, for example, Lord St John of Fawsley (*Hansard*, HL Vol.668, cols 1167–1170).

The Parliamentary Under-Secretary of State said that this provision "does not change the law as it stands at the moment. But it does put it beyond doubt. All that matters is that the decision maker considers the range of treatment options available and the patient's objective best interests in respect of those treatments. [Subsection (5)] cannot be interpreted to mean that doctors are under an obligation to provide, or to continue to provide, life-sustaining treatment where that treatment is not in the best interests of the patients.That is the case even when the patient's death is foreseen" (*Hansard*, H.C. Vol.670, cols.1293–1294). Medical treatment that is judged to be in the best interests of P because, for example, it would provide effective pain control can therefore be given even if one of the adverse consequences of the treatment would be to shorten P's life.

If there is any ambiguity in either an advance decision or a lasting power of attorney about a purported refusal of life-sustaining treatment, the treatment should be provided.: see s.11(8) and *HE v A Hospital NHS Trust* [2003] EWHC 1017 (Fam); [2003] 2 F.L.R.

408, noted under s.24. Also see *W Healthcare NHS Trust v H* [2004] EWCA Civ 1324, above.

LIFE-SUSTAINING TREATMENT. Is defined in subs.(10).

Subsection (6)

The factors set out in this provision cannot determine the decision: they must be con- **1–043** sidered by the decision-maker and weighed against other factors. In the absence of a written record, it may be difficult to establish whether the decision-maker has taken these factors into account when reaching a decision.

In *Ashan v University Hospitals Leicester NHS Trust* [2006] EWHC 2624 (QB), Judge Hegarty QC held that a patient who has been left in a persistent vegetative state following elective surgery should be cared for at home by her family rather than at a specialist private nursing and rehabilitation centre funded by the Trust. The patient's "immediate family are devout Muslims. They firmly believe that she should be cared for at home in a Muslim environment where they could pray together in her presence and ensure the proper observance of Muslim traditions and practices" (para.43). The judge concluded that "the wishes and beliefs of [the patient's] family and, so far they can properly be attributed to her, those which she herself would have held had she continued to have the capacity to do so, are factors which can and should be taken into account in determining whether it is reasonable for her to be cared for at home, even though no tangible benefits, whether physical or emotional, are likely to flow from a recognition of those wishes and beliefs in view of her profound mental incapacity and lack of awareness" (para.56). The judge said, at para.54, that this approach "appears to be entirely consistent" with this provision and subs.(7)(b).

Paragraph (a)

"Wishes and feelings" about a particular issue can be expressed orally, in writing, or **1–044** through behaviour. The past or present wishes and feelings of the person would normally carry substantial weight in the determination of that person's best interests, especially if they are well thought out, written down and signed. The person's present wishes and feelings about a particular issue might be expressed in the form of a "crisis card" that the person might carry on his or her person.

Although the person may lack mental capacity, he or she may be able to indicate present wishes and feelings or preferences through expressions of pleasure or distress. These indications, which might be accessed through the use of psychological techniques, should be given serious consideration by the decision maker. As the incapacity might have the effect of altering the person's perception about what he or she might find acceptable, where past wishes and feelings conflict with present wishes and feelings, greater weight should be given to the latter.

The person's ascertainable wishes and feelings must be considered by the decision-maker who could be faced with the task of balancing a person's wishes and feelings against a contrary course of action which is objectively believed to be in that person's best interests. For example, the person could have been subject to significant psychological strain when the wishes and feelings were expressed. The *Code of Practice* states at para.5.38: "[The person's] wishes and feelings, beliefs and values will not necessarily be the deciding factor in working out their best interests. Any such assessment must consider past and current wishes and feelings, beliefs and values alongside all other factors, but the final decision must be based entirely on what is in the person's best interests."

There will clearly be occasions when, having undertaken the consultations set out in subs.(7), it would be difficult for the decision-maker to establish whether the person's past expression of wishes and feelings as reported by others represent that person's actual wishes and feelings expressed at that time. This situation could occur when the reporter has a vested interest in the decision. It is also important for the decision-maker to be alert to the possibility of the person's expression of his or her past or present wishes and feelings having been subject to the undue influence of another (see the note on s.1(3)).

The context within which the wishes and feelings were expressed should be carefully examined, e.g. a person might have expressed a desire not to live at a time when he or she was clinically depressed or was ignorant about the true prognosis of an illness or of the treatment that could be offered. The person might also have been misinformed about a crucial component of an issue that was being considered. It is also the case that a person's wishes and feelings can undergo dramatic shifts due to a change of personal perspective. One disabled witness to the Joint Committee wrote that she had had a settled wish that she wanted to die "that lasted about ten years, and during the first five of those years I made serious suicide attempts several times. I was saved only because my friends refused to accept my view that my life had no value, and made sure I received emergency treatment in hospital, which was given against my will. Then I was extremely angry with them; now I am eternally grateful. What has changed is not my medical condition, but my outlook on life. If advance decisions had been legally binding then, I have no doubt that I would have written one" (Alison Davis, Oral and written evidence, Ev 359).

RELEVANT WRITTEN STATEMENT. The purpose of the words in parenthesis "is to clarify that if someone with capacity has written down their wishes and feelings in respect of a matter, including positive preferences, those must be explicitly taken into account in a best-interests determination", *per* the Parliamentary Under-Secretary of State (*Hansard*, HC Vol.670, col.1442). In the context of medical treatment, where someone has sought to make a written advance decision that does not qualify under ss.24 and 25, but there is a reasonable belief that the written statement is an expression of the person's wishes, it must be taken into account under this provision. Also see the note on "advance statements" in the General Note to s.24.

Paragraph (b)

1–045   Beliefs and values may be evidenced by factors such as the person's cultural background, religious and/or political affiliation, memberships of societies, subscriptions to charitable causes and known past behaviour and expressions of conviction. If P has never had capacity, it will be extremely difficult to ascertain his or her beliefs and values. In this situation, it is suggested that an assumption should be made that P would be "a normal decent person, acting in accordance with contemporary standards of morality" (*C (Spinster and Mental Patient), Re* [1991] 3 All E.R. 866, *per* Hoffmann J. at 870).

Paragraph (c)

1–046   OTHER FACTORS. Such as emotional bonds, family obligations or concern for others.

Subsection (7)

1–047   The purpose of the consultation is to seek information which would assist the decision-maker in making the best interests determination. As the procedure set out in this section has to be followed in respect of every decision that is taken on behalf of an incapacitated person, it is likely that the decision-maker would conclude that it would not be "appropriate" to consult where trivial decisions have to be made.

The decision-maker must bear in mind P's right to confidentiality when undertaking the consultation(s). Disclosure in confidence can be made to someone who has a proper interest in having the information in question (*R (on the application of S) v Plymouth City Council* [2002] EWCA Civ 388; [2002] M.H.L.R. 118, para.49) if such disclosure is the best interests of P. It is likely that appropriate consultees would have such an interest.

If there is no-one apart from a paid carer in the categories set out in this provision with whom it would be appropriate to consult about P's best interests, an independent mental capacity advocate must be consulted in the situations set out in ss.37–39. The decision-maker must bear in mind P's right to confidentiality when undertaking the consultation(s).

The decision-maker must *consider* consulting the persons listed. Such persons may be able to assist with providing information relevant to the issues set out in subs.(6).The consultations might also disclose the existence of an advance decision made by P. Whether it is "practicable and appropriate" to undertake the consultation will depend upon a number of factors including the urgency and nature of the decision. The views of the consultees about P's best interests may differ from P's own views as identified under subs.(6)(a).

A decision-maker must be able to justify a decision that it was not "practicable and appropriate" to consult someone identified in this provision. It is important not to equate "practicable" with "possible" (*Owen v Crown House Engineering* [1973] 3 All E.R. 618, 622 NIRC). In *Dedman v British Building and Engineering Appliances Ltd* [1974] 1 W.L.R. 171, 179, CA, Scarman L.J. said:

> "The word 'practicable' is an ordinary English word of great flexibility: it takes its meaning from its context. But, whenever used, it is a call for the exercise of common sense, a warning that sound judgment will be impossible without compromise. Sometimes the context contemplates a situation rarely to be achieved though much to be desired: the word then indicates one must be satisfied with less than perfection . . . [S]ometimes . . . what the context requires may have been possible, but may not for some reason have been 'practicable'. Whatever its context, the quality of the word is that there are circumstances in which we must be content with less than 100 per cent: and it calls for judgment to determine how much less."

Given this interpretation, although reasonable steps should be taken in an attempt to make contact with the persons named in this provision, the decision-maker would not be required either to act as a private detective in order to discover a person's whereabouts or to use a disproportionate amount of time in the attempt.

The weight to be given to the views expressed by the consultees will depend on a number of factors including the extent of their knowledge of P, the amount of contact that they have with P, whether they have a vested interest in the decision to be taken and their relationship with P. It is unlikely that it would be "appropriate" to consult with a person who has a history of ill-treating or neglecting P.

It should be noted that studies have shown that relatives' perception of the patient's likely views often differ substantially from the patient's own wishes; see, for example, A.B. Seckler *et al*, "Substituted judgment: how accurate are proxy predictions?"(1991) 115(9) Ann. Intern. Med. 743. Studies on social comparison processes suggest that "we are not particularly good at assessing other people's opinions, abilities, or future behaviour" and that the "dominant view is that we tend to be egocentric", i.e. people judge others in the same way that they judge themselves. (N. Harvey, M. Twyman and C. Harries "Making Decisions for other People: The Problem of Judging Acceptable Levels of Risk" (Jan, 2006) 7(1) *Forum: Qualitative Social Research* (On-line Journal) Art.26, para.21, available at: *www.qualitative-research.net/fqs-texte/1-06/06-1-26-e.htm*.

Paragraph (b)

Carers UK in its evidence to the Joint Committee expressed concern that this provision **1–048** gives "equal decision-making weight to both professionals and to carers" (Oral and written evidence, Ev 338). It should be noted in this context that there have been occasions when the sustained opposition of family carers to the firmly held views of professionals about the care needs of an incapacitated person has been proved to have been correct; see, for example, the "Report on an Investigation into Complaint No.02/C/17068 against Bolton Metropolitan Borough Council" (November 2004).

INTERESTED IN HIS WELFARE. The decision-maker should consider the nature of the interest and its motivation before consulting persons in this category. The Parliamentary Under-Secretary of State for Constitutional Affairs said that an advocate could fall into this category (St. Comm. A, col.100).

ANYONE ENGAGED IN CARING FOR THE PERSON. The carer identified in this provision need not be a relative of P. "Care" is not defined. It is suggested that the approach that should be adopted when determining whether a person qualifies as a carer under this provision should mirror the approach that the Court of Appeal took in *Re D (Mental patient: habeas corpus)* [2000] 2 F.L.R. 848 when explaining the meaning of the term "cared for" in s.26(4) of the Mental Health Act 1983. Having described the phrase as containing clear and everyday words, the court held that in order to justify a finding that a relative is caring for the patient, the services provided must be more than minimal and they need not have been provided in the long term. The court was asked to consider the situation of a relative who assisted the patient in managing his financial affairs, checked whether he was eating appropriately and took away his soiled clothing and bed clothes. In finding that the relative was caring for the patient, the court said that there "was more than sufficient evidence to pass the 'cared for' test, wherever one sets the threshold of services amounting to 'cared for'. In other words, the services were not merely minimal. They were services which were substantial and sustained." It is clear from this case that a person may be engaged in caring for P even if they do not share the same residence.

Subsection (8)

1–049   This applies the duties contained in this section to the following situations: (1) any decision made by a donee acting under a lasting power of attorney; and (2) where the person concerned does not in fact lack capacity but where the decision-maker reasonably believes the person lacks capacity.

Subsection (9)

1–050   If the decision-maker, having satisfied the requirements of subss.(1)–(7) reasonably believes that what has been done or decided is in the best interests of the P, he or she will have complied with this section. Reasonable belief is an objective test and the decision-maker will therefore need to identify objective reasons to support the contention that he or she believed that the decision was in the P's best interests.

Subsection (10)

1–051   This provision was subject to a Government amendment to delete the word "his" before "life" because "in the case of a pregnant woman we want to ensure that the life of the baby, not only the life of the mother, must be considered", *per* the Parliamentary Under-Secretary of State (*Hansard*, HL Vol.668, col.1184).

The nature of life sustaining treatment is considered in the *Code of Practice* at para.5.30:

"Whether a treatment is 'life-sustaining' depends not only on the type of treatment, but also on the particular circumstances in which it may be prescribed. For example, in some situations giving antibiotics may be life-sustaining, whereas in other circumstances antibiotics are used to treat a non-life-threatening condition. It is up to the doctor or healthcare professional providing treatment to assess whether the treatment is life-sustaining in each particular situation."

Subsection (11)

1–052   This provision recognises that the decision-maker might not be aware of all of the circumstances of P, or of the decision in question.

Acts in connection with care or treatment

1–053   **5.**—(1) If a person ("D") does an act in connection with the care or treatment of another person ("P"), the act is one to which this section applies if—

    (a) before doing the act, D takes reasonable steps to establish whether P lacks capacity in relation to the matter in question, and

    (b) when doing the act, D reasonably believes—

   (i) that P lacks capacity in relation to the matter, and

   (ii) that it will be in P's best interests for the act to be done.

(2) D does not incur any liability in relation to the act that he would not have incurred if P—

  (a) had had capacity to consent in relation to the matter, and

  (b) had consented to D's doing the act.

(3) Nothing in this section excludes a person's civil liability for loss or damage, or his criminal liability, resulting from his negligence in doing the act.

(4) Nothing in this section affects the operation of sections 24 to 26 (advance decisions to refuse treatment).

GENERAL NOTE

The aim of this section is to clarify aspects of the common law principle of necessity **1–054** which enable decisions to be taken for people who lack capacity. It does not create any new powers of intervention or duties to act, but offers protection against civil and criminal liability for certain acts done in connection with the care or treatment of P and which would normally require that persons consent, e.g. helping P to dress, wash or to eat, entering P's house, moving P from his own home to a care home, taking P to the dentist, and providing P with medical treatment. Such acts, which could be performed by a range of professional and lay people, are not limited to "day to day" or emergency situations, as they could include, for example, performing a serious planned operation on P. Without the protection of this section, such acts could amount to civil wrongs, such as trespass, or crimes, such as assault. Liability for negligent acts is unaffected (subs.(3)). Subject to the limitations set out in s.6, this section enables steps to be taken on behalf of P by family members, carers, and health and care professionals without the need for any formal authority or involvement of the Court of Protection as long as the steps are in the P's best interests. Some decisions cannot be made without the involvement of an independent mental capacity advocate (see s.25 *et seq.*). Section 27 lists those decisions that can never be made on behalf of a person who lacks capacity.

There is no requirement for decisions taken to be documented or for any person or body to be informed of the decisions taken. The protection will apply in any setting where P is being cared for or where services are being provided to him or her, e.g. at P's home, a care home, a day centre or a hospital. As one person does not have power to act to the exclusion of others, it is likely that a number of persons will be acting under the powers contained in this section during the course of a day. It is surely unrealistic to expect lay carers, the majority of whom are unlikely to have received any training on this Act, to undertake a capacity assessment and a best interests determination in respect of the decisions that they need to make in respect of P.

The established common law position that no-one has the power to make decisions on behalf of a mentally incapacitated person is unchanged (*F v West Berkshire HA* [1989] 2 All E.R. 545, HL) as this section does not confer power on anyone to make substitute decisions on behalf of the person or to give substitute consent. As a large number of people are unlikely to have made provision for their incapacity through creating lasting powers of attorney, the "operational reality of [this section] is likely to be crucial" (Joint Committee, para.103).

If P is subject to guardianship under the Mental Health Act 1983, D should not take decisions or act in a manner which conflicts with the exercise of the statutory powers of the guardian (see s.8 of the 1983 Act) as such decisions or acts could constitute the offence of obstruction under s.129 of that Act.

A decision made by either a donee under a lasting power of attorney or a deputy appointed by the court will take priority over any action that might be taken under this section (s.6(6)).

The point at which it would be unwise to rely on the protection provided by this section, and when an application should be made to the Court of Protection for an order or to have a deputy appointed is unclear.

Paragraph 6.18 of the *Code of Practice* states that the Court of Protection must be asked to make decisions relating to:

"• the proposed withholding or withdrawal of artificial nutrition and hydration (ANH) from a patient in a permanent vegetative state (PVS)
• cases where it is proposed that a person who lacks capacity to consent should donate an organ or bone marrow to another person
• the proposed non-therapeutic sterilisation of a person who lacks capacity to consent (for example, for contraceptive purposes)
• cases where there is a dispute about whether a particular treatment will be in a person's best interests."

Consideration should also be given to making an application to the court for a declaration if the legality of the proposed action is in doubt.

This provision does not provide any procedural safeguards aimed at preventing the inappropriate use of "section 5 acts". If there is concern about the manner in which P is being cared for, consideration could be given to invoking the multi-agency adult protection procedure. In extreme cases, the offence of ill-treatment or wilful neglect might be committed under s.44.

Subsection (1)

1–055   Paragraph (a) emphasises the Act's "ethos of empowerment and personal autonomy, and the key obligation of all carers to support and maximise the decision-making capacity of the person who lacks capacity", *per* the Parliamentary Under-Secretary of State for Constitutional Affairs, St. Comm. A, col.107.

The *Code of Practice*, at para.6.5, states that actions that might be covered by this section include:

"Personal care

• helping with washing, dressing or personal hygiene
• helping with eating and drinking
• helping with communication
• helping with mobility (moving around)
• helping someone take part in education, social or leisure activities
• going into a person's home to drop off shopping or to see if they are alright
• doing the shopping or buying necessary goods with the person's money
• arranging household services (for example, arranging repairs or maintenance for gas and electricity supplies)
• providing services that help around the home (such as homecare or meals on wheels)
• undertaking actions related to community care services (for example, day care, residential accommodation or nursing care). . .
• helping someone to move home (including moving property and clearing the former home).

Healthcare and treatment

• carrying out diagnostic examinations and tests (to identify illness, condition or other problem)
• providing professional medical, dental and similar treatment
• giving medication
• taking someone to hospital for assessment or treatment
• providing nursing care (whether in hospital or in the community)
• carrying out any other necessary medical procedures (for example, taking a blood sample) or therapies (for example, physiotherapy or chiropody)

- providing care in an emergency."

A healthcare professional is not authorised under this section to provide medical treatment to P if he or she is aware that the treatment in question is specified in a valid and applicable advance decision that has been made by P: see s.26.

A PERSON. Including a person who instructs another to act. This Act does not specify who has the authority to take a particular decision or to undertake a particular act.

DOES AN ACT. Acting on a reasonable belief that P lacks capacity, and having concluded that there are reasonable grounds for believing that the decision or act is in P's best interests. The steps taken to establish the reasonableness of the belief and the reasonableness of the grounds will reflect the status of the decision-maker and the significance of the decision being taken: a healthcare professional would be expected to adopt a more rigorous approach than a lay carer, and a routine care intervention would require less investigation than a serious medical decision. It will also be the case that the urgency of the action required, for example, the provision of emergency medical treatment, will dictate the extent of the steps that can be taken.

CARE. This term is not defined. Payment for something that is arranged for P's care or treatment is provided for by s.8.

TREATMENT. Includes a diagnostic or other procedure (s.64(1)).

REASONABLY BELIEVES. Formal assessments of capacity will rarely be required with most day to day decisions, but D must be able to identify objective reasons to explain why he or she believes P lacks capacity. A formal capacity assessment should be undertaken where a decision is either contentious, significant or is likely to be challenged. Professional assistance should be sought by a lay carer in these circumstances. The starting point is a presumption of capacity (s.1(2)). The other relevant principles set out in s.1 should also be applied.

LACKS CAPACITY. In relation to the particular decision that needs to be made. Many of those who will be making a judgment about P's capacity, using the test set out in s.3, will be lay people.

BEST INTERESTS. The checklist contained in s.4 must be followed, and the least restrictive principle contained in s.1(6) should be applied. The amount of time devoted to ascertaining the best interests of P will, in non-urgent cases, depend upon the significance of the decision under consideration.

Subsection (3)
Consent is not a defence to a claim in the tort of negligence and there are some criminal **1–056** offences, such as manslaughter, which depend on a finding of negligence as defined in civil law. This provision therefore makes it clear that liability for negligence is unaffected by this section.

Subsection (4)
A valid and applicable advance decision relating to the person's healthcare is unaffected **1–057** by this section which gives no protection from liability if the decision is not followed.

Section 5 acts: limitations
6.—(1) If D does an act that is intended to restrain P, it is not an act to which **1–058** section 5 applies unless two further conditions are satisfied.

(2) The first condition is that D reasonably believes that it is necessary to do the act in order to prevent harm to P.

(3) The second is that the act is a proportionate response to—

(a) the likelihood of P's suffering harm, and

(b) the seriousness of that harm.

(4) For the purposes of this section D restrains P if he—

(a) uses, or threatens to use, force to secure the doing of an act which P resists, or

(b) restricts P's liberty of movement, whether or not P resists.

(5) But D does more than merely restrain P if he deprives P of his liberty within the meaning of Article 5(1) of the Human Rights Convention (whether or not D is a public authority).

(6) Section 5 does not authorise a person to do an act which conflicts with a decision made, within the scope of his authority and in accordance with this Part, by—

(a) a donee of a lasting power of attorney granted by P, or

(b) a deputy appointed for P by the court.

(7) But nothing in subsection (6) stops a person—

(a) providing life-sustaining treatment, or

(b) doing any act which he reasonably believes to be necessary to prevent a serious deterioration in P's condition,

while a decision as respects any relevant issue is sought from the court.

DEFINITIONS

1–059   "the Human Rights Convention": s.64(1)

"public authority": s.64(1)

"lasting power of attorney": s.64(1)

"deputy": s.64(1)

"the court": s.64(1)

"life-sustaining treatment": s.64(1)

GENERAL NOTE

1–060   This section sets two important limitations to the protection from liability given to "section 5 acts".

The first (subss.(1) to (5)) relates to restraint, which is defined in subs.(4). Restraint can only be used when: (1) the person using it reasonably believes that it is necessary to prevent harm to P and; (2) its use is proportionate both to the likelihood and seriousness of the harm. The restraint must also be in P's best interests (s.1(5)). Restraint that does not meet these conditions is unlawful.The practical result of this is that only the minimum amount of restraint for the shortest duration should be used to prevent the harm occurring. This reflects the "least restrictive option" principle in s.1(6).

This section, together with s.5, provides authority for taking P to hospital and providing P with treatment at the hospital, even if taking P to the hospital and the subsequent treatment involves restricting P's liberty (subs.(4)(b)). The use of restraint which results in P being deprived of his or her liberty would constitute a violation of P's rights under Art. 5 of the European Convention of Human Rights: see subs.(5) and *HL v United Kingdom* (2005) 40 E.H.R.R. 32, ECHR. Depriving a person of their liberty for a short period in order to respond to an emergency does not constitute a violation of Art.5 (*X v United Kingdom* (1982) 4 E.H.R.R. 188, para.41). Deprivations of liberty which do not result in the person being subject to an application for detention under the Mental Health Act 1983 must be authorised by the Court of Protection in order to comply with Art.5. The Government has set out proposals in Part 2 of the Mental Health Bill, which was presented to Parliament on November 16, 2006, which would amend this Act by providing a procedure to authorise the deprivation of the liberty of mentally incapacitated compliant persons in both hospitals and care homes. The nature of a "deprivation of liberty" is considered in the notes to s.28.

Although this provision does not provide for the restraint of P in order to prevent harm to others, such action is authorised under common law powers to prevent a breach of the peace. In *Albert v Lavin* [1981] 3 All E.R 878, the House of Lords confirmed that under common law "every citizen in whose presence a breach of the peace is being, or reasonably appears to be about to be, committed has the right to take reasonable steps to make the person who is breaking or threatening to break the peace refrain from doing so; and those reasonable steps in appropriate cases will include detaining him against his will" (*per* Lord Diplock at 880). A breach, which can take place in public or on private property, occurs when "harm is actually done or is likely to be done to a person or in his presence to his property or a person is in fear of being so harmed through an assault, an affray, a riot, an unlawful assembly or other disturbance" (*R. v Howell* [1981] 3 All E.R. 383, *per* Watkins L.J. at 389). Restraining P from causing harm to others could be justified under this provision if it was considered that P's actions would provoke a reaction that would cause harm to P. If there is concern about the manner in which a donee of a lasting power of attorney or a court appointed deputy is restraining P, a complaint may be made to the Public Guardian (s.58(1)(h)).

The second limitation (subss.(6) and (7)) is that a valid decision by a donee or a deputy takes priority over any action which might be taken under s.5. There is an important proviso to this limitation. If there is a dispute as to whether a decision of a donee or deputy either prevents life-sustaining treatment being given to P or might cause a serious deterioration of Ps condition, action can be taken to sustain life or prevent serious deterioration while the dispute is referred to the Court of Protection.

Subsection (1)

RESTRAIN. Acts of restraint could include steadying P's shaking arm to enable an injection **1–061** to be given safely, holding P down whilst administering a sedative, using reasonable force to take P to hospital to receive necessary treatment, using barriers to prevent P from falling out of bed, preventing P from running into the road, putting a car seatbelt on P, telling P that he will be restrained if he persists in a particular activity, securing the external doors of a care home to prevent P from leaving, assisting P to undress, and preventing P from harming himself.

The Government did not adopt the recommendation of the Joint Committee on Human Rights that the use or threat of force or other restrictions of liberty of movement be expressly confined to emergency situations for the following reason:

"Sometimes it is not always in a person's best interests for matters to be left until it is an urgent situation. For example, restraint may be necessary in order to undertake a diagnostic procedure. If such a procedure is left until there is an urgent need or an emergency, then the resulting harm to the person may be worse. If a person needs treatment for a bad tooth, it will generally be in that person's best interests to be restrained, and to have the tooth treated, rather than to wait until it is so bad as to count as an emergency requiring intervention" (Letter from the Parliamentary-Under Secretary of State to the Chair of the Committee, December 16, 2004, Annex, para.4).

Subsection (2)

REASONABLY BELIEVES. D must be able to identify objective reasons to justify the necessity **1–062** of acting to prevent P from suffering harm.

Harm. This term, which is not defined, is not confined to physical harm. It could include preventing P from causing financial harm to him or her self by, for example, restraining P from ripping up bank notes or from spending money recklessly. It could also include the prevention of psychological harm by, for example, restraining P from acting in a manner which could result in him or her suffering verbal abuse from members of the public.

The *Code of Practice*, at para.6.45, provides the following examples of harmful situations:

"• a person with leaning disabilities might run into a busy road without warning, if they do not understand the dangers of cars
 • a person with dementia may wander away from home and get lost, if they cannot remember where they live
 • a person with manic depression might engage in excessive spending during a manic phase, causing them to get into debt
 • a person may also be at risk of harm if they behave in a way that encourages others to assault or exploit them (for example, by behaving in a dangerously provocative way)."

Subsection (3)

1–063   Proportionate response. In terms of both the degree and duration of the restraint. It follows that (a) the minimum amount of restraint should be used in order to prevent harm occurring, and (b) the level of restraint used should diminish as the risk of harm diminishes. The *Code of Practice* provides the following example at para.6.47:

"[A] carer may need to hold a person's arm while they cross the road, if the person does not understand the dangers of roads. But it would not be a proportionate response to stop the person going outdoors at all. It may be appropriate to have a secure lock on a door that faces a busy road, but it would not be a proportionate response to lock someone in a bedroom all the time to prevent them from attempting to cross the road."

In the context of restraint used in the provision of medical treatment, the following decisions were made prior this Act coming into force:

(i) The extent of force or compulsion that may become necessary in ensuring that medical treatment is provided to a mentally incapacitated patient can only be judged in each individual case and by health professionals. It may become for them a balance between continuing treatment that is forcibly opposed and deciding not to continue with it (*Re M.B. (Medical Treatment)* [1997] 2 F.L.R. 426, CA, at 439).

(ii) It is lawful "to overcome non-co-operation of a resisting patient by sedation and a moderate and reasonable use of restraint" in order to provide treatment if such treatment "is in the patient's best interests. The lawfulness of such restraint has to be carefully considered when assessing the balance of benefit and disadvantage in the giving of the proposed medical treatment and where the best interest of the patient truly lies. A patient . . . has . . . the right not to be subjected to degrading treatment under Article 3 of the European Convention on Human Rights" (*Trust A v H (an Adult patient)* [2006] EWHC 1230; (2006) 9 C.C.L.R. 474, *per* Sir Mark Potter P. at para.27).

(iii) In *R. (on the application of Wilkinson) v The Responsible Medical Officer Broadmoor Hospital* [2001] EWCA 1545; [2002] 1 W.L.R. 419, para.64, Hale L.J. said that where a mentally incapacitated patient is "actively opposed to a course of action, the benefits which it holds for him will have to be carefully weighed against the disadvantages of going against his wishes, especially if force is required to do this."

The Department of Health and Department of Education and Skills has issued "Guidance on restrictive physical interventions for people with learning disabilities and autistic spectrum disorder, in health, education or social care settings" (July 2002). This guidance was issued under s.7 of the Local Authority Social Services Act 1970 (c.42).

Subsection (4)

The definition contained in this provision includes verbal restraint, such as threatening P **1–064** with the use of force, and locking P in a room even if P does not indicate any objection to the confinement.

RESTRICTS P'S LIBERTY. But not deprive P of his or her liberty (subs.(5)). Restrictions on P's liberty are not confined to emergency situations as P could be subjected to restrictions of his or her liberty for an indefinite period without such restrictions constituting a deprivation of his or her liberty.

Subsection (5)

This provision was added to the Bill at the report stage in the House of Lords because the **1–065** Fourth Report of the Joint Committee on Human Rights, at para.4.9, wanted the Bill to confirm expressly that actions amounting to the deprivation of liberty do not fall within the definition of "restraint".

This Act cannot be used to subject P to a deprivation of liberty, as neither s.5 nor s.6 satisfy the requirements of Art.5 of the European Convention on Human Rights. However, Art.5 is not violated if a person is deprived of his or her liberty for a short period in order to respond to an emergency (*X v United Kingdom*, above). The distinction between a deprivation of liberty and a mere restriction of liberty is not always easy to determine: see the General Note to s.28.

Subsection (6)

If a carer or doctor wishes to challenge a decision made by a donee or deputy on the **1–066** ground that the decision of the donee or deputy is not in P's best interests, an application could be made to the Court of Protection to determine the issue. In the absence of such action, the decision of the donee or deputy must be respected as a failure to do so would be unlawful.

DOES AN ACT. It is submitted that this phrase includes an instruction to another to do an act.

Subsection (7)

This provision does not apply where a complaint has been made to the Public Guardian **1–067** under s.58(1)(h) about the decision of the donee or deputy.

LIFE-SUSTAINING TREATMENT. Is defined in s.4(10).

Payment for necessary goods and services

7.—(1) If necessary goods or services are supplied to a person who lacks **1–068** capacity to contract for the supply, he must pay a reasonable price for them.

(2) "Necessary" means suitable to a person's condition in life and to his actual requirements at the time when the goods or services are supplied.

GENERAL NOTE

In general, a contract entered into by a person who lacks capacity (P) is voidable and can **1–069** be set aside if the other person knew or must be taken to have known of the lack of capacity. Under s.3(2) of the Sale of Goods Act 1979 (c.54), this rule does not apply if "necessaries" are supplied and P must pay a"reasonable price" for the goods. There is also a matching common law rule about "necessary" services. This section combines these rules to set out a single statutory rule to cover "necessary" goods and services. Subsection (2) repeats the established legal definition of what is "necessary". Thus, for example, a cleaner who carries on cleaning the house of P, who has a progressive dementia, can expect to be paid. As P lacks the capacity both to order or to pay for necessaries, ss.5 and 8 allows for a carer to do both.

At the committee stage in the House of Lords, the Government resisted an amendment to extend the existing powers to set aside a contract made by a person who lacks capacity to a situation where: (1) the other party was not aware of the incapacity; and (2) the contract can be set aside without loss to the other party, or where the person lacking capacity has been persuaded to enter into a plainly disadvantageous contract. However, the Government committed itself "to carrying out scoping research work to assess whether there is a problem arising from the current law and, if so, the extent of that problem. This will take into account people who lack capacity and the broader group of vulnerable consumers more generally. The Department of Constitutional Affairs will also commit to working with the Department of Trade and Industry as part of the implementation strategy of the Bill to ensure that policy on consumer strategy, credit and indebtedness is sensitive to the needs of consumers who lack capacity", *per* the Parliamentary Under-Secretary of State (*Hansard*, HL Vol.670, cols 1471–1472).

Subsection (2)

1–070   CONDITION IN LIFE. This means the living circumstances of P, in particular the standard of life that P enjoys. The *Code of Practice* states, at para.6.58, that the aim of this provision "is to make sure that people can enjoy a similar standard of living and way of life to those they had before lacking capacity. For example, if a person who now lacks capacity previously chose to buy expensive designer clothes, these are still necessary goods—as long as they can still afford them. But they would not be necessary for a person who always wore cheap clothes, no matter how wealthy they were". Deciding whether goods and services are "necessary" can therefore depend upon a identifying a number of subtle factors that shape a person's lifestyle.

Expenditure

1–071   **8.**—(1) If an act to which section 5 applies involves expenditure, it is lawful for D—

(a) to pledge P's credit for the purpose of the expenditure, and

(b) to apply money in P's possession for meeting the expenditure.

(2) If the expenditure is borne for P by D, it is lawful for D—

(a) to reimburse himself out of money in P's possession, or

(b) to be otherwise indemnified by P.

(3) Subsections (1) and (2) do not affect any power under which (apart from those subsections) a person—

(a) has lawful control of P's money or other property, and

(b) has power to spend money for P's benefit.

DEFINITIONS

1–072   "property": s.64(1)

GENERAL NOTE

1–073   If D, acting under s.5, arranges something for P's care or treatment that costs money then D can either promise that P will pay (i.e. D may pledge the credit of P), use money which P has in his possession, pay himself back from P's money in his possession or consider him or herself owed by P. Nothing in this section allows D to gain access to P's funds where they are held by a third party such as a bank or building society. Such funds cannot be accessed until formal steps are taken, such as registering a relevant power of attorney, or making an application to the Court of Protection for a deputy to be appointed or for a single order to be made. This section does not authorise D to sell any of P's property or to gain access to any of P's assets other than cash that is in P's possession.

D cannot make a decision that conflicts with a decision made by either a donee of a lasting power of attorney ("LPA") or a deputy (s.6(6)).

D could be appointed under reg.33 of the Social Security (Claims and Payments) Regulations 1987 (SI 1987/1968) to be the "appointee" to act on behalf of P. Appointeeship is considered in the Introduction and General Note to this Act.

Although there is no requirement placed on D to keep records of the financial transactions undertaken on behalf of P, given the potential for allegations of financial abuse to be made it would clearly be sensible for D to do so.

Subsection (2)

INDEMNIFIED. If D cannot be compensated by cash that is in the possession of P, an application should be made to the court if it is not possible to claim reimbursement from a donee of a LPA or a deputy who has been granted appropriate powers by the court. **1–074**

Subsection (3)

This recognises that people may have control over P's money or property by other routes, for example by virtue of being appointed as P's appointee. A donee or a deputy appointed by the court could also have lawful control over P's money. **1–075**

Lasting powers of attorney

Lasting powers of attorney

9.—(1) A lasting power of attorney is a power of attorney under which the donor ("P") confers on the donee (or donees) authority to make decisions about all or any of the following— **1–076**

(a) P's personal welfare or specified matters concerning P's personal welfare, and

(b) P's property and affairs or specified matters concerning P's property and affairs, and which includes authority to make such decisions in circumstances where P no longer has capacity.

(2) A lasting power of attorney is not created unless—

(a) section 10 is complied with,

(b) an instrument conferring authority of the kind mentioned in subsection (1) is made and registered in accordance with Schedule 1, and

(c) at the time when P executes the instrument, P has reached 18 and has capacity to execute it.

(3) An instrument which—

(a) purports to create a lasting power of attorney, but

(b) does not comply with this section, section 10 or Schedule 1, confers no authority.

(4) The authority conferred by a lasting power of attorney is subject to—

(a) the provisions of this Act and, in particular, sections 1(the principles) and 4 (best interests), and

(b) any conditions or restrictions specified in the instrument.

DEFINITIONS
  "property": s.64(1)

1–077

GENERAL NOTE

1–078   A power of attorney is a legal document under which one person (the "donor") empowers another person (the "attorney" or "donee") or persons to act in his or her stead, either generally or for specific purposes. An act done by a donee can be treated as an act done by the donor, so as to affect the donor's relations with third parties. Prior to the Enduring Powers of Attorney Act 1985 (c.29), a power of attorney would be automatically revoked if the donor lost mental capacity. That Act introduced Enduring Powers of Attorney ("EPA") which enabled donors to continue to act on behalf of the donor's property and affairs after the donor ceased to have capacity if certain formalities were satisfied. This section, together with ss.10–14, creates a new form of power of attorney, a "lasting power of attorney" ("LPA"). These replace the EPA and the 1985 Act is repealed by Sch.7. A key distinction between an EPA and a LPA is that the former were confined to the donor's property and affairs, while the latter can also extend to personal welfare matters, which can include health care decisions (s.11(7)(c)). The legal effect of existing EPAs is preserved and integrated into the scheme of this Act by s.66(3) and Sch.4. A person with mental capacity who has made an EPA before this Act comes into force can either destroy it and then make a LPA, or can do nothing. An EPA cannot be made after this Act has come into force (s.66(3)). The power to make an ordinary power of attorney under the Powers of Attorney Act 1971(c.27) is unaffected by this Act.

A LPA can only be executed by a mentally capable adult (subs.(2)(c)), and it will only be valid if it complies with s.10, and the instrument conferring the authority is made in the prescribed form and registered with the Public Guardian in accordance with Sch.1 (subss.(2)(a)(b),(3)). There is nothing to prevent a person who is detained under the Mental Health Act 1983 from executing a LPA as long as he or she has the capacity to do so. Publicly funded legal advice through the Legal Help scheme cannot be provided to assist an individual to create a LPA (Access to Justice Act 1999, Sch.2, para.1(ea)). The Public Guardian is required to establish and maintain a register of LPAs (s.58(1)(a)), and will receive reports from donees (s.58(1)(f)).

Decisions made by the donee must be in P's best interests and he or she must act in accordance with the principles set out in s.1 (subs.(4)(a)). The donee must also comply with any conditions or restrictions that P has put in the LPA (subs.(4)(b)). If the donee is granted the power to refuse consent to life sustaining treatment, his or her decision must not be motivated by a desire to bring about the donor's death (ss.4(5),11(8)). The donee, who acts as the agent of P (see the General Notes to s.10), is subject to the restrictions on restraint set out in s.6 (s.11(1)–(6)), and to any advance decision made by P (s.11(7)(b); but see s.25(2)(b)). The Public Guardian can investigate a complaint about the way in which a donee is exercising his or her powers (s.58(1)(h)). This function can be discharged in co-operation with other persons who are involved in the care of treatment of P(s.58(2)). The Public Guardian can direct a Court of Protection Visitor to investigate the complaint and report to him (s.58(1)(d)). The Public Guardian could then report to the court which could decide to revoke the LPA (s.22(4)(b)).

By making an LPA, the donor (P), confers on the donee or donees authority to make decisions about P's personal welfare and/or property and affairs or specified matters concerning those areas. The authority to make decisions includes, where appropriate, the authority to act on decisions made (s.64(2)). The LPA must include authority for the donee/s to make decisions when P no longer has capacity to make those decisions (subs.(1)).

If P wishes, a LPA relating to P's property and affairs can operate as an "ordinary" power of attorney while P has mental capacity as long as it will continue to have effect after P loses capacity. Section 11(7)(a) prevents a personal welfare LPA having similar effect: it can only be used once the donor has lost capacity.

Separate LPAs can be created for welfare and financial matters. In her evidence to the Joint Committee, the Health Minister acknowledged the need, in some cases, to appoint different donees in relation to different types of decision:

"From the health care side it may be that people might want different attorneys for different decisions. Somebody that you trust with your finances may not be the same as somebody that you wanted to make decisions about your health and welfare" (Q754).

The Joint Committee expressed its concern about evidence that it has received "indicating that financial abuse occurs in approximately 10–15% of cases involving EPAs. Further evidence estimated that that abuse was as high as 20%" (para.138). These figures relate to unethical conduct. It is estimated that 2%–3% of cases involve criminal conduct (Oral and written evidence, Ev 188). This Act attempts to reduce the risk of financial abuse by requiring an LPA to be executed and registered before it can be used (see subs.(2)), thereby reducing the difficulties associated with the monitoring of EPAs. A report prepared for the Public Guardianship Office, "The role of the Public Guardianship Office in safeguarding vulnerable adults against financial abuse" (undated) by Hilary Brown *et al*, suggests that further action will be required to tackle the financial abuse of incapacitated persons who are subject to LPAs. There are also potential conflicts of interest between P and the donee in relation to welfare matters. For example, a decision by the donee to authorise the placement of P in a care home might have the effect of diminishing the potential inheritance of the donee. The powers of the Court of Protection in relation to LPAs are set out in ss.22 and 23. They include the power to revoke a LPA if the donee is not acting in P's best interests (s.22(3)(4)). The Public Guardian can receive reports from donees (s.58(1)(f)).

Baroness Andrews outlined the manner in which the Act can be utilised to prevent financial abuse by donees:

"[D]onors of financial LPAs will be advised that they can, if they so choose, stipulate in their financial LPA that they wish the [donee] to provide annual accounts to the Public Guardian or to any other third party for checking. That is a front-line defence. Therefore, the Public Guardian can check accounts not only if he is asked to do so but also if someone raises a concern. Concerns can be raised by different sorts of objectors at all stages. If an objector raises concerns about a prospective [donee] at the registration stage, the Court may add a requirement for the [donee] to lodge accounts if that would alleviate the concerns of the objector. That is a second line of defence.

Anyone can raise a concern with the Office of the Public Guardian if they fear that [a donee] of a registered LPA is not acting properly. The Court will then be able to direct that the [donee] should lodge accounts. We believe that is robust. They could be 'one-off' accounts or annual accounts. They could be lodged with the Court, a solicitor, an accountant or, indeed, a third party.

In the broader context the *Code of Practice* makes it clear to financial [donees] that they should keep accounts. We intend to issue guidance to reinforce that message" (*Hansard*, HL Vol.669, cols 771–772).

The House of Lords Select Committee on Medical Ethics in its comments on proxy decision-making on healthcare matters, observed that, "whilst the idea of the patient appointed proxy is in many ways attractive, it is vulnerable to the same problems as advance directives, and indeed to a greater degree" (HL Paper 21–1, para.268). The Committee observed that personal relationships are not immutable, and that the choice of proxy might soon become out of date. The Committee also noted the practical difficulties of ascertaining what choice the patient would have made, that previous statements of preference form an unreliable basis for future decisions, and the difficulty in ensuring the objectivity of the proxy (even when acting in good faith).

Subsection (1)

DONOR. See subs.(2)(c). Only individuals can make LPAs. There is no provision for joint **1–079** LPAs to be made by, for example, a husband and wife. The donor is not required to live in England or Wales.

ALL OR ANY. An LPA can relate to personal welfare matters, to property and affairs, or to both. A donee will be provided with protection by ss.5 and 6 for acts done outside the scope of the LPA.

Subsection (1)(a)

1–080 PERSONAL WELFARE. The donee has no power to act under the authority of a welfare LPA if the donor has the mental capacity to make the decision in question (s.11(7)(a)). The *Code of Practice*, at para.7.21, states that personal welfare LPAs might include decisions about:

"• where the donor should live and who they should live with
• the donor's day-to-day care, including diet and dress
• who the donor may have contact with
• consenting to or refusing medical examination and treatment on the donor's behalf
• arrangements needed for the donor to be given medical, dental or optical treatment
• assessments for and provision of community care services
• whether the donor should take part in social activities, leisure activities, education or training
• the donor's personal correspondence and papers
• rights of access to personal information about the donor, or
• complaints about the donor's care or treatment."

A welfare LPA which gives general powers to the donee would include all of the above powers. A welfare LPA which is not drafted in general terms can either specify the powers that the donee is granted, or can specify the types of decisions that the donee is not empowered to make.

There is a potential overlap between financial and welfare LPAs. For example, a decision that it would be in the best interests of P to live in a care home, which is a welfare decision, would require a financial decision to be made in that the care home fees would need to be paid. If the LPA provides for separate donees for financial and welfare matters, this could lead to the decision of the welfare donee being thwarted by the refusal of the financial donee to pay the fees. In such a situation, both donees must act in the best interests of P. If the dispute cannot be resolved, a complaint should be made to the Public Guardian who can require a Court of Protection Visitor to report to him on the matter (s.58(1)(d)).

The implications of providing healthcare decision making powers to a donee are considered in the General Note to s.11.

Subsection (1)(b)

1–081 PROPERTY AND AFFAIRS. Means "business matters, legal transactions and other dealing of a similar kind" (*F v West Berkshire HA* [1989] 2 All E.R. 545, HL, *per* Lord Brandon at 554). The *Code of Practice*, at para.7.36, states that financial LPAs might include decisions about:

"• buying or selling property
• opening, closing or operating any bank, building society or other account
• giving access to the donor's financial information
• claiming, receiving and using (on the donor's behalf) all benefits, pensions, allowances and rebates (unless the Department for Work and Pensions has already appointed someone and everyone is happy for this to continue)
• receiving any income, inheritance or other entitlement on behalf of the donor
• dealing with the donor's tax affairs
• paying the donor's mortgage, rent and household expenses
• insuring, maintaining and repairing the donor's property
• investing the donor's savings
• making limited gifts on the donor's behalf . . .
• paying for private medical care and residential care or nursing home fees

- applying for any entitlement to funding for NHS care, social care or adaptations
- using the donor's money to buy a vehicle or any equipment or other help they need
- repaying interest and capital on any loan taken out by the donor."

A financial LPA may grant the donee general powers, in which case the donee will be authorised to undertake any of the acts set out above. As an alternative, the donor might wish to grant the donee specific powers, or could specify the types of decisions the donee is not empowered to make.

Subsection (2)(b)

REGISTERED. The donor could either register the instrument straight away, or could leave it **1–082** with the proposed donee with a request that it be registered when he or she believes that the donor has lost the capacity to make the decision to register. In both cases, the LPA cannot be used until the Public Guardian has registered it.

Subsection (2) (c)

REACHED 18. This ensures that there is no overlap with the Children Act 1989 or the ward- **1–083** ship jurisdiction of the High Court.

Subsection (2)(c)

CAPACITY. The donor must have the capacity to execute the instrument at the time when it **1–084** is executed. In *Re K, Re F* [1998] 1 All E.R. 358, a case on the 1985 Act, Hoffman J. held that the donor should be able to understand:

1. If such be the terms of the power, that the donee will be able to assume complete authority over the donor's affairs.
2. If such be the terms of the power, that the donee will in general be able to do anything with the donor's property which he himself could have done.
3. That the authority will continue if the donor should be or become mentally incapable.
4. That if he should be or become mentally incapable, the power will be irrevocable without confirmation by the court.

This test, which was described by Sir Christopher Staughton in the Court of Appeal in *Re W* [2001] 4 All E.R. 88, 92, as a "sound indication of what the donor must understand if the power is to be valid", is a broader test than that set out in Sch.1, para.2(1)(e).

Subsection (3)

CONFERS NO AUTHORITY. Note, however, that the court can declare an instrument that is not **1–085** in the prescribed form to be treated as if it were, if it is satisfied that the person executing the instrument intended it to create a LPA (Sch.1, para.3(2)).

Subsection (4)

BEST INTERESTS. The donee must therefore apply the s.4 check list before any decision is **1–086** made on behalf of P.

ANY CONDITIONS OR RESTRICTIONS. Even if the condition or restriction, viewed objectively, does not serve the best interests of P. The scope of a donee's power is also limited by the fact that he or she acts as the agent of P: see the General Note to s.10.

Appointment of donees

10.—(1) A donee of a lasting power of attorney must be— **1–087**
(a) an individual who has reached 18, or
(b) if the power relates only to P's property and affairs, either such an individual or a trust corporation.

(2) An individual who is bankrupt may not be appointed as donee of a lasting power of attorney in relation to P's property and affairs.

(3) Subsections (4) to (7) apply in relation to an instrument under which two or more persons are to act as donees of a lasting power of attorney.

(4) The instrument may appoint them to act—

(a) jointly,

(b) jointly and severally, or

(c) jointly in respect of some matters and jointly and severally in respect of others.

(5) To the extent to which it does not specify whether they are to act jointly or jointly and severally, the instrument is to be assumed to appoint them to act jointly.

(6) If they are to act jointly, a failure, as respects one of them, to comply with the requirements of subsection (1) or (2) or Part 1 or 2 of Schedule 1 prevents a lasting power of attorney from being created.

(7) If they are to act jointly and severally, a failure, as respects one of them, to comply with the requirements of subsection (1) or (2) or Part 1 or 2 of Schedule 1—

(a) prevents the appointment taking effect in his case, but

(b) does not prevent a lasting power of attorney from being created in the case of the other or others.

(8) An instrument used to create a lasting power of attorney—

(a) cannot give the donee (or, if more than one, any of them) power to appoint a substitute or successor, but

(b) may itself appoint a person to replace the donee (or, if more than one, any of them) on the occurrence of an event mentioned in section 13(6)(a) to (d) which has the effect of terminating the donee's appointment.

DEFINITIONS

1–088   "lasting power of attorney": s.64(1)

"property": s.64(1)

"trust corporation": s.64(1)

"bankrupt": s.64(3)

GENERAL NOTE

1–089   This section sets out requirements relating to the appointment of donees and how they should act. An individual donee must be an adult and, if the LPA relates to property and affairs, not be a bankrupt (subss.(1)(a),(2)). A trust corporation, as well as an individual, can be appointed as donee to a LPA that relates only to property and affairs (subs.(1)(b)). Apart from where a trust corporation is appointed, the appointment of a donee is personal. This contrasts with the appointment of a deputy who can be the holder of an office or position (s.19(2)). If an individual is appointed, it is important for the donor to be confident that the chosen donee would be likely to act in his or her best interests when performing functions under this Act. The Act does not place an obligation on a donee to accept appointment.

A donee acts as the agent of the donor. Under the law of agency, an act of an agent done within the scope of his authority binds his principal, in this case P. As an agent the donee is bound by a number of common law duties toward P, including the duty to act with due care and skill, to act in good faith, not to delegate his or her functions to another, to keep the donor's affairs confidential apart from where the disclosure of information is allowed by the LPA or is otherwise required, to keep accounts of monies received and paid on P's behalf, and not to permit his or her own interests to conflict with the duties owed to P.

The relationship of the donee to the patient is that of a fiduciary and like all fiduciaries the donee should not benefit from the relationship (*Bunting v W* [2005] EWHC 1274 (Ch), para.31). The donee also has a duty to act within the scope of the LPA (s.9(4)(b)) although he or she has implied authority to do what is necessary for or incidental to the effective execution of the powers granted. The donee also has a duty to act in the donor's best interests, to be guided by the best principals set out in s.1, to have regard to the *Code of Practice* (s.42(4)(a)), and to comply with any directions that the Court of Protection might make. The duties of an agent are described in the *Code of Practice* at paras 7.58–7.68. For a comprehensive account of the law of agency, see Francis M.B. Reynolds, *Bowstead and Reynolds on Agency*, (18th ed., Sweet & Maxwell, London, 2006).

In this Act references to making decisions, in relation to a donee, include, where appropriate, acting on decisions made (s.64(2)).

Any concerns about the way in which the donee in undertaking his or her functions, including a concern that the donee might lack mental capacity, should be reported to the Public Guardian or, if criminal behaviour is suspected, the police. The Public Guardian may decide to direct a Court of Protection Visitor to visit P and/or the donee (s.58(1)(d)). In serious cases, the Public Guardian will refer the matter to the court. Also see the note on adult protection procedures in s.44.

The *Code of Practice*, at para.7.70, states that signs that a donee may be exploiting the donor (or failing to act in the donor's best interests) include:

"• stopping relatives or friends contacting the donor – for example, the attorney may prevent contact or the donor may suddenly refuse visits or telephone calls from family and friends for no reason
• sudden unexplained changes in living arrangements (for example, someone moves in to care for a donor they've had little contact with)
• not allowing healthcare or social care staff to see the donor
• taking the donor out of hospital against medical advice, while the donor is having necessary medical treatment
• unpaid bills (for example, residential care or nursing home fees)
• an attorney opening a credit card account for the donor
• spending money on things that are not obviously related to the donor's needs
• the attorney spending money in an unusual or extravagant way
• transferring financial assets to another country."

A number of witnesses to the Joint Committee expressed their concern about the situation that could arise when a donee who is a close relative of P appears not to be acting in the best interests of the P because of a conflict of interest. This difficulty was said to be "not common but neither is it rare" (Oral and written evidence, Ev 472). An example of how such a conflict can arise has been given by Baroness Finlay:

"A lady aged 59 was very ill. Her family appeared to be very concerned about her pain and constantly asked for her diamorphine to be increased. However, we remained unconvinced that her pain was really that severe. In fact, the patient declined increasing doses of diamorphine. Her 60th birthday arrived and was passed with minimal celebration, after which the family visited very little. She became depressed and spoke to one of the night nurses, explaining that the problem was that on her 60th birthday, her fixed-term life insurance policy expired. The family would not now inherit what they thought they would if she had died, and if her drugs had been duly increased" (*Hansard*, HL Vol.642, col.766).

Donees who are close relatives might not accurately reflect P's wishes as studies have shown that relatives' perception of the patient's likely views often differ substantially from the patient's own wishes; see, for example, A.B. Seckler *et al*, "Substituted judgment: how accurate are proxy predictions?" (1991) 115(9) Ann. Intern. Med. 743; also see the studies cited in R. Schiff *et al*, "Living wills and the Mental Capacity Act: a postal questionnaire survey of UK geriatricians" (2006) 35 *Age and Ageing* 116 and the notes to s.4(7).

In its "*Response to the Scrutiny Committee's Report on the draft Mental Incapacity Bill*" (Cm.6121), the Government recognised "that there may be potential for conflict of interest in an LPA" and agreed "that donors should be given information about this and more generally about the seriousness of making an LPA".

Subsection (1)

1–090   INDIVIDUAL. A professional donee, such as an accountant or a solicitor, must be referred to by name. For example, it is not possible to refer to "a partner in Sue, Grabit and Run".

TRUST CORPORATION. Is defined in the Trustee Act 1925 (c.19), s.68(1) as "the Public Trustee or a corporation either appointed by the court in any particular case to be a trustee, or entitled by rules made under s.4(3) of the Public Trustee Act 1906 (c.55), to act as custodian trustee." A trust corporation is "often parts of banks or other financial institutions" (*Code of Practice*, para.7.9).

Subsection (2)

1–091   The Parliamentary Under-Secretary of State announced that the Government had "decided that the Office of the Public Guardian will check to see if prospective financial attorneys are bankrupt when an LPA is registered" (*Hansard*, HL Vol.668, col.1417). If the donee is bankrupt, then the LPA will be invalid. There is nothing to prevent a bankrupt from being appointed to act as a donee of a welfare LPA.

Subsection (4)

1–092   This provides that where two or more people are appointed as donees, they may be appointed either to act jointly (so that they must all join together in any decision), or to act jointly and severally (which means that they can act either independently or all together) or to act jointly in respect of some matters and jointly and severally in respect of others. The donor therefore "has all possible options when wanting to appoint more than one donee", *per* the Parliamentary Under-Secretary of State (*Hansard*, HL Vol.670, col.1473). If the donor does not specify, it will be assumed that the donees were appointed jointly (subs.(5)).

Subsection (6)

1–093   For joint donees, any breach by one of them of the requirements concerning how LPAs are made will prevent a LPA from being created.

Subsection (7)

1–094   Where donees are appointed jointly and severally, a breach by one of them of the requirements concerning how LPAs are made will only prevent the appointment taking affect in his or her case; a valid LPA is created in respect of the other donee(s).

Subsection (8)

1–095   This enables a donor to provide in the LPA for the replacement of the donee(s) on the occurrence of an event mentioned in s.13(6)(a)–(d) which would normally terminate a donee's powers. One of these events is the death of the donee. It would therefore be possible, for example, for a donor to appoint his spouse as donee, but nominate his child as a replacement donee. Under para.(a), a donee cannot be given power by the LPA to choose a successor.

Lasting powers of attorney: restrictions

1–096   **11.**—(1) A lasting power of attorney does not authorise the donee (or, if more than one, any of them) to do an act that is intended to restrain P, unless three conditions are satisfied.

(2) The first condition is that P lacks, or the donee reasonably believes that P lacks, capacity in relation to the matter in question.

(3) The second is that the donee reasonably believes that it is necessary to do the act in order to prevent harm to P.

(4) The third is that the act is a proportionate response to—

(a) the likelihood of P's suffering harm, and

(b) the seriousness of that harm.

(5) For the purposes of this section, the donee restrains P if he—

(a) uses, or threatens to use, force to secure the doing of an act which P resists, or

(b) restricts P's liberty of movement, whether or not P resists,

or if he authorises another person to do any of those things.

(6) But the donee does more than merely restrain P if he deprives P of his liberty within the meaning of Article 5(1) of the Human Rights Convention.

(7) Where a lasting power of attorney authorises the donee (or, if more than one, any of them) to make decisions about P's personal welfare, the authority—

(a) does not extend to making such decisions in circumstances other than those where P lacks, or the donee reasonably believes that P lacks, capacity,

(b) is subject to sections 24 to 26 (advance decisions to refuse treatment), and

(c) extends to giving or refusing consent to the carrying out or continuation of a treatment by a person providing health care for P.

(8) But subsection (7)(c)—

(a) does not authorise the giving or refusing of consent to the carrying out or continuation of life-sustaining treatment, unless the instrument contains express provision to that effect, and

(b) is subject to any conditions or restrictions in the instrument.

DEFINITIONS

"lasting power of attorney": s.64(1)   **1–097**

"the Human Rights Convention": s.64(1)

"treatment": s.64(1)

"life-sustaining treatment": s.64(1)

GENERAL NOTE

Subsections (1)–(6) place restrictions on the use of restraint by donees similar to those **1–098** that apply to "section 5 acts" (see s.6) and deputies (see s.20). Reference should be made to the notes on s.6.

A donee has no power to bring or defend legal proceedings on behalf of the donor. The authority of the court could be sought for the donee to act as the donor's litigation friend.

Under subs.(7), a personal welfare LPA:

(i) can only take effect after P loses capacity. Decision making will therefore fluctuate between the donor and donee in cases where the donor has fluctuating capacity. It is also the case that P could be capable of making some simple personal welfare decisions, but not other, more complex, decisions. This could give rise to considerable practical difficulties. A healthcare professional who is proposing to provide medical treatment for P must also assess P's capacity. Any dispute between donee and the professional about the assessment of P's capacity that remains unresolved should be referred to the Court of Protection for a declaration under s.15(1)(a);

(ii) is generally subject to any advance decision that P has made: see the note on subs.(7)(b), below; and

(iii) can authorise the donee to give or refuse consent to the carrying out or continuation of health care for P. This power is subject to any conditions or restrictions in the LPA and to subs.(8) which prohibits the donee from refusing life-sustaining treatment for

P unless the LPA expressly allows for this. A LPA does not provide the donee with a power to demand that a specific form of medical treatment be provided to P.

In order to make a healthcare decision on behalf of P, the donee should have received the same information about the nature of the treatment being proposed and its consequences as P would have received had he or she had been mentally capable. The power to make a LPA which enables the donee to make healthcare decisions has been criticised on the ground that patients' views about the medical treatment that they would wish to receive are not fixed; they adapt to circumstances (see further the note on s.25(4)(c)). An application to the Court of Protection should be made if the donee is asked to consent to a non-therapeutic treatment, such as an organ donation, if such treatment is not specified in the LPA.

The fact that the donee has the power to refuse medical treatment on behalf of P represents a significant change in the doctor patient relationship in that a non-medical donee can override the doctor's clinical judgment as to what treatment his or her patient should receive. If a doctor wishes to challenge a decision made by a donee not to consent to treatment for P, the doctor could consider making an application to the Court of Protection for on order overriding the donee's decision on the ground that the donee was not acting in P's best interests. But as the briefing note on the Mental Capacity Bill by the Catholic Bishops' Conference of England and Wales (July 2004, at para.24) notes, how many doctors "will have the time, energy and motivation to ask a court to override a[donee] whose determination of best interests appears to them to be defective or questionable?" If the decision of the donee to refuse treatment either stops the doctor from providing life-sustaining treatment or would be likely to lead to a serious deterioration in P's condition, the treatment can continue until the decision of the court is made (s.6(6), (7)).

A donee cannot refuse the provision of basic care for P, such as the provision of hydration and nutrition by non-artificial means and keeping P clean, because the cessation of such care would never be in P's best interests.

A healthcare professional who treats P despite the existence of a LPA which provides for a donee to make the decision in question will be protected from legal liability by virtue of s.5 unless, at the time, he is satisfied that such a LPA exists. If an urgent healthcare decision needs to be taken in respect of P and there is no time to contact the donee, the healthcare professional should proceed to treat P in his or her best interests and then report to the donee.

Subsection (6)

1–099   See the note to s.6(5).

Subsection (6) para.(a)

1–100   REASONABLY BELIEVES. The donee must be able to satisfy this objective test by identifying the grounds that he or she had for believing that P lacked capacity.

1–101   *Subsection (6) para.(b)*

Generally, a LPA is subject to the terms of an advance decision. However, if the LPA is made after the advance decision it overrides the advance decision if it confers on the donee the power to refuse treatments specified in the advance decision (s.25(2)(b)).

Subsection (6) para.(c)

1–102   The LPA does not provide a donee with the power to require that a particular medical treatment be given to P if such treatment is not considered by healthcare professionals to be in the best interests of P.

Subsection (7)

1–103   MAKE DECISIONS. See s.64(2).

Subsection (8)

The power of a donee to prevent life-sustaining treatment to be given to P, which is sub- **1–104** ject to the restriction contained in s.4(5), was the subject of considerable criticism during the Bill's passage through Parliament. For example, Earl Howe said:

"In very many cases—perhaps the majority—the doctor and the [donee] will be in agreement about what is in the patient's best interests, and no problem will therefore arise. The problems arise when doctor and [donee] are in disagreement.

Both of them are required under the Bill to work in the patient's best interests. But the interpretation of 'best interests' is open to difference. What the Bill is saying is that, in the worst case, [a donee] with no medical knowledge whatever can take it on himself to gainsay a doctor whose professional advice is that the patient whose life is at stake should receive certain treatment. It might be perfectly possible for the [donee] to maintain, with some justification, that his decision to refuse consent was taken in the best interests of P. But the doctor, who had close knowledge and experience of the treatment, might not think that a fair and reasonable view of best interests.

What happens then? The Bill allows the doctor to seek a ruling from the Court [of Protection] where there is such disagreement. But let us take the example of a doctor who has no previous knowledge of the patient and who is confronted by a [donee] with no medical expertise and articulates his views plausibly and forcefully. Are we going to imagine that every doctor in that position will have the strength of purpose and the degree of self-belief to refer the matter to the Court? I find that unlikely. Doctors are professional people, but they are also human. I very much fear that some will be browbeaten into agreeing to a course of action that runs contrary to their better judgment" (*Hansard*, HLVol.670, col.1484).

This provision is compatible with Art.2 of the European Convention on Human Rights which provides for a"right to life" because the donee is chosen by a competent adult and can only act under this Act in the best interests of that person.

Scope of lasting powers of attorney: gifts

12.—(1) Where a lasting power of attorney confers authority to make decisions **1–105** about P's property and affairs, it does not authorise a donee (or, if more than one, any of them) to dispose of the donor's property by making gifts except to the extent permitted by subsection (2).

(2) The donee may make gifts—

(a) on customary occasions to persons (including himself) who are related to or connected with the donor, or

(b) to any charity to whom the donor made or might have been expected to make gifts,

if the value of each such gift is not unreasonable having regard to all the circumstances and, in particular, the size of the donor's estate.

(3) "Customary occasion" means—

(a) the occasion or anniversary of a birth, a marriage or the formation of a civil partnership, or

(b) any other occasion on which presents are customarily given within families or among friends or associates.

(4) Subsection (2) is subject to any conditions or restrictions in the instrument.

DEFINITIONS

"lasting power of attorney": s.64(1)   **1–106**

"property": s.64(1)

GENERAL NOTE

1–107   This section limits the power of a donee of a financial LPA to dispose of P's property by making gifts. Only gifts coming within the categories set out in subs.(2) are allowed. The donee must also act in accordance with any conditions or restrictions on his or her power to make gifts which are specified in the LPA, and satisfy the best interests criterion (s.9(4)(a)). If the donee wishes to make a gift which exceeds his or her authority under the LPA, an application should be made to the court under s.18(1)(b). The court has power to authorise gifts that are more substantial than those permitted by subs.(2) if satisfied that these would be in P's best interests (s.23(4)).

Subsection (2)

1–108   NOT UNREASONABLE. This is for the donee to determine. The donee is not required to obtain consent from anyone before making the gift. The authorisation of the Court of Protection should be obtained if it is proposed to make a substantial gift in order to reduce P's tax liability.

Subsection (3)

1–109   ANY OTHER OCCASION. Taking into account P's past and present wishes and feelings (s.4(6)(a)).

Revocation of lasting powers of attorney etc

1–110   **13.**—(1) This section applies if—

   (a) P has executed an instrument with a view to creating a lasting power of attorney, or

   (b) a lasting power of attorney is registered as having been conferred by P,

and in this section references to revoking the power include revoking the instrument.

   (2) P may, at any time when he has capacity to do so, revoke the power.

   (3) P's bankruptcy revokes the power so far as it relates to P's property and affairs.

   (4) But where P is bankrupt merely because an interim bankruptcy restrictions order has effect in respect of him, the power is suspended, so far as it relates to P's property and affairs, for so long as the order has effect.

   (5) The occurrence in relation to a donee of an event mentioned in subsection (6)—

   (a) terminates his appointment, and

   (b) except in the cases given in subsection (7), revokes the power.

   (6) The events are—

   (a) the disclaimer of the appointment by the donee in accordance with such requirements as may be prescribed for the purposes of this section in regulations made by the Lord Chancellor,

   (b) subject to subsections (8) and (9), the death or bankruptcy of the donee or, if the donee is a trust corporation, its winding-up or dissolution,

   (c) subject to subsection (11), the dissolution or annulment of a marriage or civil partnership between the donor and the donee,

   (d) the lack of capacity of the donee.

   (7) The cases are—

   (a) the donee is replaced under the terms of the instrument,

   (b) he is one of two or more persons appointed to act as donees jointly and severally in respect of any matter and, after the event, there is at least one remaining donee.

(8) The bankruptcy of a donee does not terminate his appointment, or revoke the power, in so far as his authority relates to P's personal welfare.

(9) Where the donee is bankrupt merely because an interim bankruptcy restrictions order has effect in respect of him, his appointment and the power are suspended, so far as they relate to P's property and affairs, for so long as the order has effect.

(10) Where the donee is one of two or more appointed to act jointly and severally under the power in respect of any matter, the reference in subsection (9) to the suspension of the power is to its suspension in so far as it relates to that donee.

(11) The dissolution or annulment of a marriage or civil partnership does not terminate the appointment of a donee, or revoke the power, if the instrument provided that it was not to do so.

DEFINITIONS
    "lasting power of attorney": s.64(1)   **1–111**
    "property": s.64(1)
    "bankrupt": s.64(3)
    "trust corporation": s.64(1)

GENERAL NOTE
    This section identifies the way in with an LPA can be revoked, whether before or after **1–112** registration.

P can revoke an LPA at any time while he or she has capacity to do so (subs.(2)). P's bankruptcy will revoke a LPA that relates to P's property and affairs, but not a personal welfare LPA or that part of a LPA giving authority to make personal welfare decisions (subs.(3)). An interim bankruptcy restrictions order merely suspends a financial LPA (subs.(4)).

The events relating to the donee which are set out in subs.(6) terminate his or her appointment and also revoke the LPA, apart from when the terms of the LPA replace the donee or where the donee is acting jointly and severally with others and, after the event, there is at least one remaining donee (subs.(7)).

The Public Guardian should be informed if a LPA is revoked as this would enable him to cancel the registration (Sch.1, para.17).

Subsection (2)
    P might have the capacity to revoke the power by, for example, saying "I don't want X **1–113** deciding things for me any more", but not have the capacity to make the decision in question. This power can be exercised during a period of temporary capacity.

Subsection (3)
    BANKRUPTCY. See s.64(3) and (4).   **1–114**

Subsection (4)
    BANKRUPTCY RESTRICTIONS ORDERS. These are provided for in Sch.4A of the Insolvency Act **1–115** 1986 (c.45).

Subsection (6)
    BANKRUPTCY OF THE DONEE. But see subss.(8)–(10).   **1–116**

    DISSOLUTION OR ANNULMENT OF A MARRIAGE, OR CIVIL PARTNERSHIP. But see subs.(11). A civil partnership is a registered relationship between two people of the same sex which ends only on death, dissolution or annulment, as provided for in the Civil Partnership Act 2004.

LACK OF CAPACITY OF THE DONEE. Although the matter is not free from doubt, it is submitted that a temporary incapacity of the donee would not revoke the LPA.

Protection of donee and others if no power created or power revoked

1–117   **14.**—(1) Subsections (2) and (3) apply if—

(a) an instrument has been registered under Schedule 1 as a lasting power of attorney, but

(b) a lasting power of attorney was not created,

whether or not the registration has been cancelled at the time of the act or transaction in question.

(2) A donee who acts in purported exercise of the power does not incur any liability (to P or any other person) because of the non-existence of the power unless at the time of acting he—

(a) knows that a lasting power of attorney was not created, or

(b) is aware of circumstances which, if a lasting power of attorney had been created, would have terminated his authority to act as a donee.

(3) Any transaction between the donee and another person is, in favour of that person, as valid as if the power had been in existence, unless at the time of the transaction that person has knowledge of a matter referred to in subsection (2).

(4) If the interest of a purchaser depends on whether a transaction between the donee and the other person was valid by virtue of subsection (3), it is conclusively presumed in favour of the purchaser that the transaction was valid if—

(a) the transaction was completed within 12 months of the date on which the instrument was registered, or

(b) the other person makes a statutory declaration, before or within 3 months after the completion of the purchase, that he had no reason at the time of the transaction to doubt that the donee had authority to dispose of the property which was the subject of the transaction.

(5) In its application to a lasting power of attorney which relates to matters in addition to P's property and affairs, section 5 of the Powers of Attorney Act 1971 (c. 27) (protection where power is revoked) has effect as if references to revocation included the cessation of the power in relation to P's property and affairs.

(6) Where two or more donees are appointed under a lasting power of attorney, this section applies as if references to the donee were to all or any of them.

DEFINITIONS

1–118   "lasting power of attorney": s.64(1)
"purchaser": s.64(1)
"property": s.64(1)

GENERAL NOTE

1–119   This section provides legal protection to donees and others who act on invalid LPAs.

Subsection (1) outlines the situations to which subss.(2) and (3) apply. It gives protection to donees and others who rely on registered LPAs which later turn out to be invalid. The protection applies whether or not the registration has been cancelled. Broadly, both donees and third parties will be protected from legal liability if they were unaware that the LPA was invalid.

Subsections (4) and (5) deal with property. If either para.(a) or (b) of sub.(4) is satisfied, a purchaser of property from a donee of an invalid LPA will be protected unless the purchaser was aware of the invalidity.

General powers of the court and appointment ofdeputies

Power to make declarations

15.—(1) The court may make declarations as to—   **1–120**
  (a) whether a person has or lacks capacity to make a decision specified in the declaration;
  (b) whether a person has or lacks capacity to make decisions on such matters as are described in the declaration;
  (c) the lawfulness or otherwise of any act done, or yet to be done, in relation to that person.
  (2) "Act" includes an omission and a course of conduct.

DEFINITIONS
  "the court": s.64(1)   **1–121**

GENERAL NOTE

This section provides the Court of Protection with the power to make declarations about **1–122** whether an individual has mental capacity, and whether an act or proposed act was or would be lawful. A declaration may be refused on the ground that no such declaration is needed. For example, in *H (Mental Patient: Diagnosis), Re* (1993)1 F.L.R. 28, the judge held that a C.T. scan for a schizophrenic patient with a suspected brain tumour was not one of those cases where it was either necessary or desirable to grant a declaration. He did not wish to "send a signal" that this and similar procedures should be delayed pending a costly application to the court.

The power to make declarations regarding a person's capacity is likely to be exercised where: (a) healthcare professionals cannot resolve a dispute about a person's capacity to make a serious decision regarding the provision of medical treatment; or (b) there is a dispute as to whether a person was mentally capable when either an advance decision or a lasting power of attorney was made. Declarations regarding the lawfulness of an act are likely to be made most frequently in cases involving controversial or particularly serious decisions regarding the provision of care or medical treatment for the incapacitated person. Subsection (2) confirms that the court can be asked to make declarations on an omission to act (for example, the withholding or withdrawing of medical treatment), as well as on a course of conduct. As a superior court of record, the Court of Protection has the same powers as the High Court (see s.45(1)).

The inherent jurisdiction of the High Court to make declarations relating to adults (see below) is not ousted by this Act. In *Re SA (Vulnerable Adult with Capacity: Marriage)* [2005] EWHC 2942 (Fam); [2006] 1 F.L.R. 867, Munby J. held, following *G (an Adult) (Mental Capacity: Court's Jurisdiction), Re*, below, that in certain circumstances the inherent jurisdiction can be exercised for the protection of vulnerable adults who do not lack capacity to make the decision in question. His Lordship said at para.79:

"The inherent jurisdiction can be invoked wherever a vulnerable adult is, or is reasonably believed to be, for some reason deprived of the capacity to make the relevant decision, or disabled from making a free choice, or incapacitated or disabled from giving or expressing a real and genuine consent. The cause may be, but is not for this purpose limited to, mental disorder or mental illness. A vulnerable adult who does not suffer from any kind of mental incapacity may nonetheless be entitled to the protection of the inherent jurisdiction if he is, or is reasonably believed to be, incapacitated from making the relevant decision by reason of such things as constraint, coercion, undue influence or other vitiating factors."

His Lordship elaborated by stating that (1) "constraint" involved "some significant curtailment of the freedom to do those things which in this country free men and women are entitled to do"; (2) undue influence occurs "where a vulnerable adult's capacity or will to decide has been sapped or overborne by the improper influence of another"; and (3) other disabling circumstances include "circumstances that may so reduce a vulnerable adult's understanding and reasoning powers as to prevent him from forming or expressing a real and genuine consent, for example, the effects of deception, misinformation, physical disability, illness, weakness (physical, mental or moral), tiredness, shock, fatigue, depression, pain or drugs" (para.78). A vulnerable adult is "someone who, whether or not mentally incapacitated, and whether or not suffering from any mental illness or mental disorder, is or may be unable to take care of him or herself, or unable to protect him or herself against significant harm or exploitation, or who is deaf, blind or dumb, or who is substantially handicapped by illness, injury or congenital deformity. This, I emphasise, is not and is not intended to be a definition. It is descriptive, not definitive; indicative rather than prescriptive" (para.82).

The Declaratory Jurisdiction of the High Court

1–123   As the Court of Protection's jurisdiction to make declarations is founded on the inherent jurisdiction of the High Court to make declarations, an account of the development of this jurisdiction in so far as it relates to personal welfare matters is given below.

The question of the lawfulness of treating patients who are incapable of giving consent because they are unconscious in circumstances where the operation or other treatment cannot safely be delayed until consciousness is recovered or because they are deemed to be mentally incapable of making a decision whether to receive treatment was considered in the House of Lords in *F v West Berkshire HA* [1989] 2 All E.R. 545. Their Lordships held that:

1.   Under the common law doctrine of necessity a doctor can lawfully operate on, or give other treatment to, adult patients who are incapable, for one reason or another, of consenting to his doing so, provided that the operation or other treatment concerned is the best interests of such patients. The operation or other treatment will be in the best interests of patients if, but only if, it is carried out in order either to save their lives or ensure improvement or prevent deterioration in their physical or mental health. Lord Brandon said at 551: "in many cases it will not only be lawful for doctors, on the grounds of necessity, to operate on or give other medical treatment to adult patients disabled from giving their consent: it will be their common law duty to do so."

2.   A doctor will be deemed to have acted in the best interests of a mentally incapable patient and will be immune from liability in trespass to the person if he establishes that he acted in accordance with a practice accepted at the time as proper by a responsible body of medical opinion skilled in the particular form of treatment in question (*Bolam v Friern Hospital Management Committee* [1957] 2 All E.R.118 applied).

3.   Special considerations apply in the case of an operation for the sterilisation of an adult woman who is physically perfectly healthy because such treatments cannot be considered to be either curative or prophylactic. No court now has jurisdiction either by statute or derived from the Crown as parens patriae to give or withhold consent to such operations in the case of a mentally incapable adult. However, the High Courtdoes have jurisdiction to make a declaration that the proposed operation is lawful on the ground that in the circumstances it is in the best interests of the patient. Although a declaration is not necessary to establish the lawfulness of the operation, in practice the court's jurisdiction should be invoked prior to the operation taking place, since a declaration would establish by judicial process whether the proposed operation was in the best interests of the patient and therefore lawful.

The purpose of the declaratory jurisdiction was explained by Sir Thomas Bingham MR in *S (Hospital Patient: Court's Jurisdiction) (No.1), Re* [1996] Fam. 1 at 18:

"[I]n cases of controversy and cases involving momentous and irrevocable decisions, the courts have treated as justiciable any genuine question as to what the best interests of a patient require or justify. In making these decisions the courts have recognised the desirability of informing those involved whether a proposed course of conduct will render them criminally or civilly liable; they have acknowledged their duty to act as a safeguard against malpractice, abuse and unjustified action; and they have recognised the desirability, in the last resort, of decisions being made by an impartial independent tribunal."

In *R (on the application of Burke) v The General Medical Council* [2005] EWCA Civ 1003; [2005] H.R.L.R 35, para.80, the Court of Appeal, having considered the decision of the European Court of Human Rights in *Glass v United Kingdom* [2004] 1 F.L.R 1019, held that:

1. A declaration does not "authorise" treatment that would otherwise be unlawful. The court makes a declaration whether or not proposed treatment or the withdrawal of treatment will be lawful.
2. Good practice may require medical practitioners to seek such a declaration where the legality of proposed treatment is in doubt. This is not, however, something that they are required to do as a matter of law.

Subsequent to the decision in *F*, the courts have held that declarations relating to the medical treatment of mentally incapable patients should also be applied for in the following circumstances: where it is proposed to withdraw artificial feeding from a patient in a persistent vegetative state (*Airedale NHS Trust v Bland* [1993] 1 All E.R. 821, HL), where there is doubt about the mental capacity of the patient (*St George's Healthcare NHS Trust v S* [1998] 3 All E.R. 673), where it was anticipated that force might have to be used to administer an anaesthetic to a patient who required a CT scan (*Doncaster and Bassetlaw Hospitals NHS Trust v C* [2004] EWHC 1657 (Fam Div)), and where it is proposed to harvest bone marrow from the patient (*Y (Mental Patient: Bone Marrow Donation), Re* [1996] 2 F.L.R. 787). Declarations have been applied for in a number of cases where it was proposed to sterilise a mentally incompetent patient. The test for making an application for a declaration in such cases was established by Sir Stephen Brown P. in *GF (Medical Treatment), Re* [1992] 1 F.L.R. 293 when he said at 294:

"I take the view that no application for leave to carry out [a sterilisation] operation need be made in cases where two medical practitioners are satisfied that the operation is (1) necessary for therapeutic purposes, (2) in the best interests of the patient, and (3) there is no practicable, less intrusive means of treating the condition."

In *LC (Medical Treatment: Sterilisation), Re* [1997] 2 F.L.R. 258, Thorpe J. held that leave to perform the sterilisation operation could not be justified upon the basis of some vague and unsubstantiated fear that the patient would be exposed to the risks of pregnancy from which she is presently protected. A similar approach was taken in *S (Medical Treatment: Adult Sterilisation, Re* [1998] 1 F.L.R. 994, where Johnson J. refused to grant a declaration on an application by the patient's mother in "the absence of any risk [of pregnancy] that can be called identifiable rather than speculative". A sterilisation can be in the best interests of the patient even if the risk of pregnancy is small (*W (An Adult: Mental Patient) (Sterilisation), Re* [1993] 1 F.L.R. 381).

In *An NHS Trust v D* [2003] EWHC 2793 (Fam Div), Coleridge J. considered the following question: when should an NHS Trust make an application to the High Court for a declaration that the proposed termination of the pregnancy of a mentally incapacitated patient is lawful? His Lordship held that where there is any doubt as to either the mental capacity of the patient or whether the termination would be in her best interests, an application to the court should be made. In particular, the following circumstances would ordinarily warrant the making of an application:

1. Where there is a dispute as to capacity, or where there is a realistic prospect that the patient will regain capacity, following a response to treatment, within the period of her pregnancy or shortly thereafter;
2. Where there is a lack of unanimity amongst the medical professionals as to the best interests of the patient;
3. Where the procedures under s.1 of the Abortion Act 1967 (c.87) have not been followed (i.e. where two medical practitioners have not provided a certificate);
4. Where the patient, members of her immediate family, or the foetus's father have opposed, or expressed views inconsistent with, a termination of the pregnancy; or
5. Where there are other exceptional circumstances (including where the termination may be the patient's last chance to bear a child).

If any case is considered to fall anywhere near the boundary line in relation to any of the above criteria, it should for the avoidance of doubt be referred to the court (*S (Adult Patient: Sterilisation: Patient's Best Interests), Re* [2001] Fam.15, *per* Thorpe L.J. at 32).

It is essential for protocols to be put in place to deal with the possible termination of the pregnancy of patients in psychiatric hospitals. Such protocols should be designed to address the issue in good time and should ensure that the patient is referred at an early stage to independent legal advice whether from the Official Solicitor or from the solicitor who represented her at the Mental Health Review Tribunal (*SS (Medical Treatment: Late Termination), Re* [2002] 1 F.L.R. 445).

Declarations can be applied for in respect of treatment in the future (*NHS Trust v T (Adult Patient: Refusal of Medical Treatment)* [2004] EWHC 1279 (Fam Div); [2005] 1 All E.R. 387). In this case Charles J. confirmed that an interim declaration could be made pursuant to CPR Part 25.1(1)(b). His Lordship said, at para.45, that when the court is faced with an emergency situation where treatment cannot be delayed because of an imminent high risk to life the court should make every effort to ensure that the person who it is proposed should be treated in reliance of any declaration has an opportunity to make representations (either directly or indirectly) to the court (and thus in cases of emergency out of hours to the Duty Judge). It would then be for the Judge to decide on capacity and then if appropriate on best interests by applying the normal civil standard on the best evidence then available. It is submitted that in extreme emergencies where there is no time to seek the assistance of the court, any doubt that may exist about the patient's capacity must be resolved in favour of society's interest in upholding the concept that all human life is sacred and that it should be preserved if at all possible.

In *Re Wyatt* [2005] EWHC 2293 (Fam); [2005] 4 All E.R. 1325, Hedley J. held that, in exceptional circumstances, a declaration can be used to resolve a future dispute which can be clearly identified and reasonably anticipated. This finding was upheld on appeal, although the Court of Appeal expressed reservations about judges making open-ended declarations which they may have to re-visit if circumstances change (*Wyatt v Portsmouth Hospital NHS Trust* [2005] EWCA Civ 1181, para.118).

In *G (An Adult) (Mental Capacity: Court's Jurisdiction), Re* [2004] EWHC 2222 (Fam Div), an incapacitated young woman had been made the subject of interim declarations to protect her from the actions of her father. The evidence was that after a period of being subject to the interim declarations the daughter would regain her mental capacity and her mental health would improve, but that once the protection of the court was withdrawn the daughter's mental health would deteriorate and she would lose her mental capacity. Bennett J. held that in these circumstances he had jurisdiction to make declarations to ensure that the continuing protection of the court was not withdrawn simply because the daughter had regained her mental capacity, given the likely consequences if the court withdrew its protection. The judge said, at para.104, that if the declarations sought were in the daughter's best interests, the court, by intervening, far from depriving her of her right to make decisions, will be ensuring that her now stable and improving mental health is sustained, that she has the best possible chance of continuing to be mentally capable, and of ensuring a quality of life that prior to the court's intervention she was unable to enjoy.

A declaration will not be used to require a doctor to act against his or her clinical judgment. In *National Health Service Trust v D* [2000] 2 F.L.R. 677, Cazalet J. said at 686:

"[I]t is well-established that there can be no question of the court directing a doctor to provide treatment which he or she is unwilling to give and which is contrary to that doctor's clinical judgment."

In recent years declarations have been made to regulate the care of mentally incapable adults in cases where there is a dispute about the care that the adult either is receiving or will receive in the future. It is now possible for the High Court to make declarations as to the lawfulness of proposed actions in relation to the adult in circumstances where the issue in question cannot be resolved by recourse to the Mental Health Act 1983. In *Local Authority v Health Authority (Disclosure: Restriction on Publication)* [2003] EWHC 2746 (Fam Div); [2004] 1 All E.R. 480, para.96, Butler-Sloss P. said that the granting of declarations is "a flexible remedy and adaptable to ensure the protection of a person who is under a disability". Caselaw has extended the jurisdiction to the extent that "in cases of controversy and cases involving momentous and irrevocable decisions, the courts have treated as justiciable any genuine question as to what the best interests of a patient require or justify" (*S (Hospital Patient: Court's Jurisdiction) (No.1), Re*), above, *per* Sir Thomas Bingham M.R. at 18). By using this jurisdiction the High Court is able to effectively resolve disputes such as who should have responsibility for the future care of the adult, who the adult should have contact with and under what circumstances, and the powers that staff can use when providing the adult with care, including the use of restraint and detention.

In *F (Adult: Court's Jurisdiction), Re* [2000] 2 F.L.R. 512, CA, the local authority was concerned that T, an 18 year old with an intellectual age of 5–8 years, who was being accommodated in one of the authority's specialist establishments contrary to her mother's wishes, would be at risk of neglect and exposure to sexual exploitation if she were to return to her home. As T was not mentally impaired within the meaning of s.1(2) of the Mental Health Act 1983, the local authority was unable to protect T by making her the subject of a guardianship application under that Act. The authority therefore sought declarations from the High Court, the effect of which were to keep T in the accommodation and to restrict and supervise her contact with her family. In determining the question of the jurisdiction of the High Court to make such declarations, the Court held that:

(i) the application of the common law doctrine of necessity (see *F v West Berkshire HA*, above), is not limited to medical and similar matters; it embraces the problems that arose in this case;

(ii) the doctrine, which can be invoked by both an authority and an individual, may properly be invoked side by side with the 1983 Act (*R. v Bournewood Community and Mental Health NHS Trust Ex p. L* [1998] 3 All E.R. 289, HL);

(iii) the jurisdiction of the High Court under its inherent jurisdiction to grant relief by way of declarations was therefore not excluded by the 1983 Act;

(iv) the jurisdiction will only be invoked if there is a serious justiciable issue; and

(v) in making a declaration the judge will be guided by the patient's best interests on an application of a welfare test analogous to that applied in wardship cases.

Sedley L.J. said at 529: "[N]either the mother nor the (imaginary) sister nor the local authority possesses by virtue of their status any power to detain T. Nor, however, does T have the capacity to choose one of them as an appropriate carer. If the role of carer is contested, it is the court alone which has the power—and in my judgment the duty—to make that choice in T's best interests. From the choice will follow the exercise of care; and from the exercise of care, if absolutely necessary, some restraint may follow."

The nature of the High Court's declaratory jurisdiction over mentally incompetent adults was reviewed by Munby J. in *A (A Patient) v A Health Authority* [2002] EWHC 18 (Fam Div/Admin); [2002] Fam 213. His Lordship held that:

(i)   the jurisdiction could be invoked by anyone whose past or present relationship with the incompetent adult, whether formal or informal, gave him or her a genuine and legitimate interest in obtaining a decision, rather than being a stranger or officious busybody. Thus proceedings can be brought by a relative, a carer, a local authority or a NHS Trust;

(ii) the jurisdiction may regulate all that conduces to the incompetent adult's welfare and happiness, including companionship and his or her domestic and social environment;

(iii) the jurisdiction, which extended no further than the parens patriae jurisdiction in relation to children, extended not merely to declaratory relief but also to the grant of injunctive relief - at least interlocutory injunctive relief to preserve or regulate the status quo;

(iv) cases which involved only issues of public law should be litigated by way of an application in the Administrative Court for judicial review. Private law cases about the best interests of the adult were to be litigated in the Family Division notwithstanding the fact that issues of public law might be involved; and

(v)   if the task facing the judge was to come to a decision for and on behalf of an incompetent adult then the welfare of that person had to be the paramount consideration. If the task of the judge was to review the decision of the public authority taken in the exercise of some statutory power then the governing principles were those of public law.

In *A Local Authority v BS* [2003] EWHC 1909 (Fam Div); [2003] 2 F.L.R.1235, a case where it was alleged that a mentally incapacitated adult had been struck by her father, interim declarations were made on a without notice basis rendering it lawful for the local authority to (1) place the adult in a residential placement; (2) to prohibit her father from removing her from that placement; and (3) to limit the contact between the adult and her father to supervised contact. Wall J. said, at para.21, that although in a field as complex as care for the mentally disabled, a high degree of pragmatism is inevitable, in each case there are four essential building blocks. First, is mental incapacity established? Secondly, is there a serious justicable issue relating to welfare? Thirdly, what is it? Fourthly, with the welfare of the incapable adult as the court's paramount consideration, what are the balance sheet factors which must be drawn up to decide which course of action is in his or her best interests? His Lordship said at, para.18, that in certain circumstances, the court will have to make findings of fact about disputed historical matters but that this would only be necessary if they are required to determine the identification of the incapable person's best interests. There will plainly be cases which are very fact specific. There will be others in which the principle concern is the future, and the relative suitability of the plans which each party can put forward for both the short term and the long term care of the mentally incapable adult.

The inherent jurisdiction was invoked in *A London Borough Council v T and T B*, November 1, 2001, where detailed declarations and injunctions were made by the court on the application of the local authority in a situation where there had been a breakdown of trust between a mentally incapacitated adult's mother and the authority which had led to the parties becoming polarised in their positions. The judge found that "there have been occasions where the mother has behaved either in an illogical fashion or in a fashion which can perhaps be most aptly described as not constructive". The relief was designed to provide for the care of the adult by the authority for the foreseeable future and for regulating contact between the mother and her daughter. Constant and relentless complaints by the mother resulted in the judge approving the appointment of an independent non-legal advocate for the client who would provide a channel "for the time to be investigated and dealt with". A penal notice was added to some of the orders because of the past breaches of the undertakings that the mother had given to the court.

In *S (Adult Patient) (Inherent Jurisdiction; Family Life), Re* [2002] EWHC 2278; [2003] 1 F.L.R. 292, above, the jurisdiction was used to determine a dispute between the local authority and the father of a mentally incapacitated adult about the future place of residence of the adult. Munby J. described at, para.6, the court's role in this case, a case which fell entirely within the confines of private law, as acting as "a surrogate decision maker on behalf of [the adult]". His Lordship said at para.20:

"[T]he doctrine of necessity enables [the parents of a mentally incapacitated adult] not merely to assume the responsibility for the day-to-day care of their child, with all the routine decision-making which that entails, but also to decide, no doubt, where appropriate, in conjunction with suitable professional advisors, more important matters such as where their child should live, who he should see, what services offered by public authorities he should make use of, what medication he should take and what nursing, dental and medical treatment he should receive. [Cases should only come before the court] if disputes erupt between those seeking to care for the patient."

His Lordship reminded himself of the following point made by Lord Goff in *F v West Berkshire HA*, above, at 566:

"officious intervention cannot be justified by the principle of necessity. So intervention cannot be justified when another more appropriate person is available and willing to act."

The jurisdiction was invoked in *Re S.* because there is no presumption of the right of contact between a parent and an adult child, even one under a disability (*D-R (Adult: Contact), Re* [1999] 1 F.L.R.1161, *per* Butler-Sloss L.J. at 1165), and neither the local authority nor the father had the legal authority to decide where the adult should live. The judge had to weigh the father's rights under Art.8 of the European Convention on Human Rights against the son's Art.8 rights. Munby J. held, at para.39, that where there is a conflict between these rights, the State, in the form of the local authority, may have a positive obligation to intervene, even at the risk of detriment to the father's family life, if such intervention is necessary to ensure respect for the son's Art.8 rights. His Lordship further held that in proceedings under the inherent jurisdiction concerning mentally incapable adults:

(i) there is nothing analogous to the threshold requirements contained in ss.31 and 100 of the Children Act 1989 requiring the State to establish, before intervention takes place, either the risk of significant harm and/or parenting which falls short of the reasonable;

(ii) although there is no presumption that mentally incapacitated adults are better off with their families, other things being equal, the parent, if he or she is willing and able, is the most appropriate person to look after such an adult; not some public authority, however well meaning and seemingly well equipped to do so; and

(iii) the Court has jurisdiction to identify a third party (a "surrogate decision maker") as the most appropriate person to be responsible not merely for the adult's care but also for taking important decisions about his life.

A noteworthy feature arising from the cases noted above is that the threshold for removing a mentally incapable adult from the parental home is substantially lower than that required to remove a child in that there is no requirement to establish that the adult is either suffering, or is likely to suffer significant harm. All that is required is that the balance sheet exercise identified by Thorpe L.J. in *Re A*, above, indicates that removal is in the adult's best interests.

In *City of Sunderland v PS and CA* [2007] EWHC 623 (Fam), para.22, Munby J. said that "proper compliance with s.6 of the Human Rights Act 1998 requires the judges to mould and adapt the inherent jurisdiction so that it is compatible with the requirement of Art.5 [of the European Convention on Human Rights], as well as Art.8". Applying this principle to cases where it was in the best interests of mentally incapable adults to be detained in care homes, his Lordship said, at para.23, that the following minimum requirements must be satisfied in order to comply with Art.5:

1. The detention must be authorised by the court on application made by the local authority and *before* the detention commences.
2. Subject to the exigencies of urgency or emergency the evidence must establish unsoundness of mind of a kind or degree warranting compulsory confinement. In other words, there must be evidence establishing at least a prima facie case that the individual lacks capacity and that confinement of the nature proposed is appropriate.
3. Any order authorising detention must contain provision for an adequate review at reasonable intervals, in particular with a view to ascertaining whether there still persists unsoundness of mind of a kind or degree warranting compulsory confinement.

His Lordship also held that the power under s.37 of the Supreme Court Act 1981 for the court to appoint a receiver could be invoked by the court in the exercise of the inherent jurisdiction even though there was an available statutory remedy under Pt VII of the Mental Health Act 1983. His Lordship said at para.34:

"It is necessary for PS's interests for her income and savings to be put under proper control, but it would be an unnecessary burden and, in my judgment, wholly disproportionate to the very modest amounts involved, to condemn the parties to the trouble and expense of separate proceedings in the Court of Protection. In the circumstances it seemed to me that the appropriate course was for me to appoint an appropriate officer of the local authority to be PS's receiver."

In *A Local Authority v Z* [2004] EWHC 2817 (Fam Div); [2005] H.R.L.R. 2, Hedley J. considered the extent of the duty owed by a local authority when the welfare of a vulnerable adult (who may or may not be mentally incapacitated) in their area is threatened by the criminal (or other wrongful) act of another. In this case a husband was intending to assist his severely disabled wife in her desire to commit suicide. Assisting the suicide of another is a crime (Suicide Act 1961 (c.60) , s.2(1)). His Lordship held that in such a case the local authority incurred the following duties:

1. To investigate the position of a vulnerable adult to consider what was her true position and intention.
2. To consider whether she was legally competent to make and carry out her decision and intention.
3. To consider whether any other (and if so, what) influence may be operating on her position and intention and to ensure that she has all the relevant information and knows all the available options.
4. To consider whether to invoke the inherent jurisdiction of the High Court so that the question of competence could be judicially investigated and determined.
5. In the event of the adult not being competent, to provide all such assistance as may be reasonably required both to determine and give effect to her best interests.
6. In the event of the adult being competent, to allow her in any lawful way to give effect to her decision although that should not preclude the giving of advice or assistance in accordance with what are perceived to be in her best interests.
7. Where there are reasonable grounds to suspect that the commission of a criminal offence may be involved, to draw that to the intention of the police.
8. In very exceptional circumstances, to invoke the jurisdiction of the court under s.222 of the Local Government Act 1972 (c.70) in order to seek an injunction to restrain a criminal act.

Although a local authority can invoke the inherent jurisdiction in order to determine whether a mentally vulnerable adult has the capacity to marry, the High Court has no jurisdiction to determine whether it is in the best interests of that adult to marry a particular person (*Sheffield City Council v E* [2004] EWHC 2808 (Fam Div); [2005] Fam 326).

Butler-Sloss P. invoked the inherent jurisdiction to grant an injunction to prevent the publication of a report that had been prepared by a local authority subsequent to its decision to remove a number of foster children and vulnerable adults from the home of their foster mother (*Local Authority v Health Authority (Disclosure: Restriction on Publication)*), above). Her Ladyship found that the publication of the report would be "deeply damaging and detrimental" to the welfare of the mentally incapacitated adults.

In *NHS Trust v Bland*, above, Lord Goff at 864–865 reiterated his opinion that declaratory relief was justified, while recognising:

"that strong warnings have been given against the civil courts usurping the function of the criminal courts, and it has been authoritatively been stated that a declaration as to the lawfulness or otherwise of future conduct is 'no bar to criminal prosecutions, no matter the authority of the court which grants it': see *Imperial Tobacco Ltd v Attorney General* [1980] 1 All E.R. 866."

The court has jurisdiction to grant whatever relief in declaratory form is necessary to safeguard and promote the incapacitated adult's welfare and interests (*S (Adult Patient) (Inherent Jurisdiction: Family Life), Re*, above, para.50). This can include injunctive relief, including interlocutory injunctive relief, the making of tipstaff orders (location orders, collection orders and passport orders) and orders enabling third parties to take protective steps in relation to an incapacitated adult: see *Re SA*, above, paras 84–95. Guidance on the making of without notice applications to the court was provided by Charles J. in *B Borough Council v Mrs S and Mr S (by the Official Solicitor)* [2006] EWHC 2584 (Fam), at paras 38–43, 158.

The wardship jurisdiction of the High Court should be invoked if the individual that needs protecting is a child and intervention under the Children Act 1989 is either not possible or inappropriate (*F (Mental Health Act: Guardianship), Re* [2000] 1 F.L.R. 192).

Subsection (1) para.(a)
WHETHER A PERSON HAS OR LACKS CAPACITY. The court will apply the tests set out in ss.2 and **1–124** 3. In *Masterman-Lister v Brutton & Co* [2002] EWCA Civ 1889; [2003] 3 All E.R.162, para.29, Kennedy L.J. said that the "conclusion that in law capacity depends on time and context means that inevitably a decision as to capacity in one context does not bind a court which has to consider the same issue in a different context". This case is also authority for the proposition that although the final decision as to capacity rests with the court, in almost every case "the court will need medical evidence to guide it" (*ibid.*).

Subsection (1) para.(c)
A declaration cannot be used to authorise what would otherwise be unlawful, nor can it **1–125** render unlawful that which would otherwise be lawful (*R (on the application of Burke) v General Medical Council*, above, para.71).

On the basis of the caselaw set out above, the *Code of Practice* states, at para.8.18, that cases involving any of the following decisions should be brought before the court:

"• decisions about the proposed withholding or withdrawal of artificial nutrition and hydration (ANH) from patients in a permanent vegetative state (PVS)
• cases involving organ or bone marrow donation by a person who lacks capacity to consent
• cases involving the proposed non-therapeutic sterilisation of a person who lacks capacity to consent to this (e.g. for contraceptive purposes) and
• all other cases where there is a doubt or dispute about whether a particular treatment will be in a person's best interests."

Powers to make decisions and appoint deputies: general

16.—(1) This section applies if a person (P) lacks capacity in relation to a mat- **1–126** ter or matters concerning—
  (a) P's personal welfare, or

(b) P's property and affairs.

(2) The court may—

(a) by making an order, make the decision or decisions on P's behalf in relation to the matter or matters, or

(b) appoint a person (a deputy) to make decisions on P's behalf in relation to the matter or matters.

(3) The powers of the court under this section are subject to the provisions of this Act and, in particular, to sections 1(the principles) and 4(best interests).

(4) When deciding whether it is in P's best interests to appoint a deputy, the court must have regard (in addition to the matters mentioned in section 4) to the principles that—

(a) a decision by the court is to be preferred to the appointment of a deputy to make a decision, and

(b) the powers conferred on a deputy should be as limited in scope and duration as is reasonably practicable in the circumstances.

(5) The court may make such further orders or give such directions, and confer on a deputy such powers or impose on him such duties, as it thinks necessary or expedient for giving effect to, or otherwise in connection with, an order or appointment made by it under subsection (2).

(6) Without prejudice to section 4, the court may make the order, give the directions or make the appointment on such terms as it considers are in P's best interests, even though no application is before the court for an order, directions or an appointment on those terms.

(7) An order of the court may be varied or discharged by a subsequent order.

(8) The court may, in particular, revoke the appointment of a deputy or vary the powers conferred on him if it is satisfied that the deputy—

(a) has behaved, or is behaving, in a way that contravenes the authority conferred on him by the court or is not in P's best interests, or

(b) proposes to behave in a way that would contravene that authority or would not be in P's best interests.

DEFINITIONS

1–127   "property": s.64(1)
   "the court": s.64(1)

GENERAL NOTE

1–128   This section sets out the core jurisdiction of the Court of Protection, which is to make substitute decisions for persons lacking the required mental capacity to make decisions for themselves about either their personal welfare or their property and affairs, or to appoint a deputy to do so if this is in their best interests. The court does not have jurisdiction to supply consent to any matter on behalf of P. Sections 17 and 18 indicate to extent of the court's powers with regard to the personal welfare and the property and affairs of P. A decision of the court is to be preferred to the appointment of a deputy who, if appointed, should be granted powers as limited in scope and duration as is reasonable practicable (subs.(4)). This requirement is consistent with the least restrictive intervention principle set out in s.1(6). The deputy's appointment can be revoked or his or her powers varied if the court considers that the deputy's past, present or future actions will not serve P's best interests (subs.(8)). The court has power to act on its "own motion" to make whatever order is in P's best interests (subs.(6)), and can vary or discharge existing orders (subs.(7)). When exercising this jurisdiction, the court must make decisions which are in the best interests of the mentally incapacitated person (subs.(3)). The court can make any order or appointment which is in the best interests of P, regardless of the nature of the application made to it.

The Public Guardian is required to establish and maintain a register of orders appointing deputies, and to supervise deputies (s.58(1)(b) and (c)), and will receive reports from deputies (s.58(1)(f)). The Public Guardian can investigate a complaint about the way in which a deputy is exercising his or her powers (s.58(1)(h)). Ultimately the matter could be referred to the court which has power to either discharge the order appointing the deputy or to vary the deputy's powers (subs.(7)). The supervision and investigatory functions of the Public Guardian can be discharged in co-operation with other persons who are involved in the care of treatment of P (s.58(2)).

Subsection (2)

Making an order. The *Code of Practice* states at paras 8.27–8.28:   **1–129**

"In some cases, the court must make a decision, because someone needs specific authority to act and there is no other route for getting it. These include cases where:

- there is no EPA or property and affairs LPA in place and someone needs to make a financial decision for a person who lacks capacity to make that decision (for example, the decision to terminate a tenancy agreement), or
- it is necessary to make a will, or to amend an existing will, on behalf of a person who lacks capacity to do so.

Examples of other types of cases where a court decision might be appropriate include cases where:

- there is genuine doubt or disagreement about the existence, validity or applicability of an advance decision to refuse treatment . . .
- there is a major disagreement regarding a serious decision (for example, about where a person who lacks capacity to decide for themselves should live)
- a family carer or a solicitor asks for personal information about someone who lacks capacity to consent to that information being revealed (for example, where there have been allegations of abuse of a person living in a care home)
- someone suspects that a person who lacks capacity to make decisions to protect themselves is at risk of harm or abuse from a named individual (the court could stop that individual contacting the person who lacks capacity)."

Article 8 of the European Convention on Human Rights may impose on a local authority not merely the power but in appropriate circumstances the duty to apply to the court for an order if that is necessary to protect a vulnerable adult from possible harm at the hands of his family. In *S (Adult Patient) (Inherent Jurisdiction; Family Life), Re* [2002] EWHC 2278; [2003] 1 F.L.R. 292, para.39, Munby J. said:

". . . as *Botta v Italy* [(1998) 26 E.H.R.R. 241] shows, the State, even in this sphere of relations between purely private individuals, may have positive obligations to adopt measures which will ensure effective respect for the son's private life. Thus the State, in the form of the local authority, may have a positive obligation to intervene, even at the risk of detriment to the father's family life, if such intervention is necessary to ensure respect for the son's Article 8 rights. And the State, in the form of the High Court, has a positive obligation to act in such a way as to ensure respect for those rights."

Appoint a person. The appointment of deputies is governed by s.19. A deputy's power to make decisions on behalf of P is limited to the matters specified by the court (para.(b)). Where possible, the court will seek to make a single order (subs.(4)(a)). Given the terms of s.5, it is likely that the appointment of a deputy to make personal welfare decisions in relation to P will be made rarely. The Government said its response to recommendation 54 of the Joint Committee's Report (Cm.6121):

"We would only expect deputies to be given healthcare powers in rare cases, for example, where there is a dispute between family members as to who has the patient's best interests at heart and where the patient has chronic and/or degenerative health problems calling for repeated assessments and decisions by doctors and carers."

In these circumstances, the "court is unlikely to appoint as a deputy someone who is unknown to the person. Appointing someone who has no particular insight into the person's wishes, feelings, values or healthcare needs would not be in the person's best interests. The court must appoint a deputy only if that appointment would be in the best interests of the person lacking capacity under [s.16(3)]", *per* the Parliamentary Under-Secretary of State, St. Comm. A, para.195.

The *Code of Practice* states at paras 8.38–8.39:

"Deputies for personal welfare decisions will only be required in the most difficult cases where:

- important and necessary actions cannot be carried out without the court's authority, or
- there is no other way of settling the matter in the best interests of the person who lacks capacity to make particular welfare decisions.

Examples include when:

- someone needs to make a series of linked welfare decisions over time and it would not be beneficial or appropriate to require all of those decisions to be made by the court. For example, someone (such as a family carer) who is close to a person with profound and multiple learning disabilities might apply to be appointed as a deputy with authority to make such decisions
- the most appropriate way to act in the person's best interests is to have a deputy, who will consult relevant people but have the final authority to make decisions
- there is a history of serious family disputes that could have a detrimental effect on the person's future care unless a deputy is appointed to make necessary decisions
- the person who lacks capacity is felt to be at risk of serious harm if left in the care of family members. In these rare cases, welfare decisions may need to be made by someone independent of the family, such as a local authority officer. There may even be a need for an additional court order prohibiting those family members from having contact with the person."

The need for a deputy to be appointed to manage the person's property and affairs is likely to arise in the same circumstances that governed the appointment of receivers under Pt VII of the Mental Health Act 1983, in particular when property needs to be sold or if the person has financial resources that the court considers requires management by a deputy. The Public Accounts Committee stated that for "a receivership to be successful [under the 1983] Act, it is crucial that the receiver appointed is trustworthy and reliable. It is also important that the receiver is competent to manage the patient's affairs and should take an active interest in the patient's welfare" (House of Commons, Session 1993–1994, Thirty-ninth Report, para.5). The following cases decided under the 1983 Act on the position of receivers are relevant to the position of deputies under this Act:

1. As well as establishing that the receiver acts as the patient's agent (see the note on s.19), the case of *EG, Re* [1914] 1 Ch. 927 established that a solicitor instructed by the receiver in connection with the patient's affairs is the solicitor of the patient and not that of the receiver.
2. The effect of an appointment of a receiver is not to create a liability to a third party that would not otherwise exist. A receiver's duty to satisfy a patient's legal liabilities is entirely dependent on there being such liabilities in existence (*Bell v Todd* [2002] Lloyd's L.R.12, para.22).
3. A person who has been rendered a patient as the result of the actions of a tortfeasor is entitled to require the tortfeasor to bear the costs of the receiver as part of the damages (*Cassel v Riverside HA* [1992] P.I.Q.R. Q168).

See the General Note, above. **1–130**

Subsection (4) para. (b)
LIMITED IN SCOPE AND DURATION. This provision reflects the fact that many disabled people **1–131** have capacity to take many day-to-day decisions and would only require the assistance of a deputy in relation to a limited range of matters.

Subsection (5)
If a deputy considers that the powers conferred by the court are insufficient to carry out **1–132** the necessary duties toward the person lacking capacity, he or she should apply to the court either to vary the powers in the order of appointment, or for the court to make a particular decision itself.The court "will be able to grant powers to the deputy on condition that it first obtains the Public Guardian's consent for certain actions. It is important that deputies are, of course, properly supervised, but it would be disproportionately burdensome and costly to require them to apply to the court all the time for authority to act. That supervisory role should properly be undertaken by the Public Guardian", *per* the Parliamentary Under-Secretary of State (*Hansard*, HL Vol.670, col.1474).

Subsection (7)
See s.18(5). **1–133**

Subsection (8)
This provides the court with similar powers to those it has with respect to donees: see **1–134** s.22(3),(4).

Section 16 powers: personal welfare

17.—(1) The powers under section 16 as respects P's personal welfare extend **1–135** in particular to—
  (a) deciding where P is to live;
  (b) deciding what contact, if any, P is to have with any specified persons;
  (c) making an order prohibiting a named person from having contact with P;
  (d) giving or refusing consent to the carrying out or continuation of a treatment by a person providing health care for P;
  (e) giving a direction that a person responsible for P's health care allow a different person to take over that responsibility.
  (2) Subsection (1) is subject to section 20 (restrictions on deputies).

DEFINITIONS
  "treatment": s.64(1) **1–136**
  "deputy": s.64(1)

GENERAL NOTE
This section sets out in subs.(1) the types of personal welfare matters that, under s.16, the **1–137** Court of Protection may either determine itself or appoint a deputy to make decisions about on P's behalf. The power of deputies to make decisions is subject to the restrictions set out in s.20 (subs.(2)) and is limited to the matters specified by the court (s.16(2)(b)).

The list in subs.(1) which is indicative, not exhaustive, is based on matters that have been dealt with by the High Court in the exercise of its inherent jurisdiction to make declarations: see the General Note to s.15. It is not a list of decisions that must always go the court for determination; rather it provides examples of decisions that could go to the court for determination if it would be appropriate to do so.

If the court makes an order which has the effect of depriving P of his or her liberty, the order should make provision for regular and independent reviews of the detention if it is to satisfy the requirements of Art.5(4) of the European Convention on Human Rights as set out in *HL v United Kingdom* (2005) 40 E.H.R.R. 32, ECHR, at para.135.

Subsection (1) (a)

1–138 As the court only has power to make any decision that P could have made, this power cannot be used to override the provisions of either s.47 of the National Health Service and Community Care Act 1990 (c.19), which provides for the assessment by a local authority of a person's need for community care services (which includes the provision of accommodation), or the National Assistance Act (Choice of Accommodation) Directions 1992.

Subsection (1) (c)

1–139 A restraining order could be made where the named person presents a risk of abuse, or where continued contact with that person will harm or distress P. The power restrain a named person cannot extend to any interference with other rights of that person, such as the right to occupy property.

Subsection (1) (d)

1–140 In the consultation paper *"Who Decides"* (Cm.3803 at 7.26), the Government expressed its concern that a deputy "might have less prior knowledge of a patient's wishes regarding treatment than the patient's doctor". The fact that a deputy has the power to refuse treatment on behalf of P represents a significant change in the doctor patient relationship in that a non-medical deputy can override the doctor's clinical judgment as to what medical treatment his or her patient should receive; see further the General Note to s.11. This power is subject to the limitation set out in s.20(5).

The deputy does not have the power to direct that a different person should take over responsibility for P's health care (s.20(2)(b)). Neither does the deputy have the power to require a doctor to provide treatment which is not considered to be in P's best interests. This is because if P were capable, he or she would not have such a power.

Subsection (1) (e)

1–141 This allows for the court to order that the responsibility for P's healthcare be transferred to another doctor where P's doctor has a conscientious or clinical objection to a treating P.

Section 16 powers: property and affairs

1–142 **18.**—(1) The powers under section 16 as respects P's property and affairs extend in particular to—

(a) the control and management of P's property;

(b) the sale, exchange, charging, gift or other disposition of P's property;

(c) the acquisition of property in P's name or on P's behalf;

(d) the carrying on, on P's behalf, of any profession, trade or business;

(e) the taking of a decision which will have the effect of dissolving a partnership of which P is a member;

(f) the carrying out of any contract entered into by P;

(g) the discharge of P's debts and of any of P's obligations, whether legally enforceable or not;

(h) the settlement of any of P's property, whether for P's benefit or for the benefit of others;

(i) the execution for P of a will;

(j) the exercise of any power (including a power to consent) vested in P whether beneficially or as trustee or otherwise;

(k) the conduct of legal proceedings in P's name or on P's behalf.

(2) No will may be made under subsection (1)(i) at a time when P has not reached 18.

(3) The powers under section 16 as respects any other matter relating to P's property and affairs may be exercised even though P has not reached 16, if the court considers it likely that P will still lack capacity to make decisions in respect of that matter when he reaches 18.

(4) Schedule 2 supplements the provisions of this section.

(5) Section 16(7) (variation and discharge of court orders) is subject to paragraph 6 of Schedule 2.

(6) Subsection (1) is subject to section 20 (restrictions on deputies).

DEFINITIONS
"property": s.64(1)   **1–143**

GENERAL NOTE

This section, which is supplemented by Sch.2, provides a non-exhaustive, indicative list **1–144** of the matters relating to P's property and affairs that come within the jurisdiction of the Court of Protection under s.16. The Court may either determine the matter itself or appoint a deputy to make decisions on P's behalf. The power of deputies to make decisions is subject to the restrictions set out in s.20 (subs.(6)) and is limited to the matters specified by the court (s.16(2)(b)).

Like s.17, subs.(1) does not contain a list of matters which must always be referred to the court; it provides an indication of the types of order the court might make if an application is made.

It is submitted that the court may make an order if the provisions of a financial LPA do not enable P's best interests to be satisfied: see *Re C*, Rattee J., unreported, January 23, 1996.

If P's sole source of income is social security benefits, the Department of Work and Pensions can appoint an "appointee" to receive and deal with the benefits on P's behalf: see the Introduction and General Note to this Act under the heading "Appointees".

Subsection (1)

This largely reproduces the list which applied to the Court of Protection under s.96 of the **1–145** Mental Health Act 1983.

Paragraph (a)

PROPERTY. This includes papers held by the Official Solicitor in an action in which he acts **1–146** as the patient's litigation friend (*E (Mental Health Patient), Re* [1985] 1 All E.R. 609, CA). In *E* the court held that the parents of a patient had no absolute right to see such papers, although they were the patient's property, but must obtain the authority of the Court of Protection to order disclosure of them as necessary or expedient for the benefit of the patient.

Paragraph (b)

GIFT. The court will adopt the stance that it takes to the making of wills: see *C, Re* and *S,* **1–147** *Re*, noted under para.(i), below. Although it is proper to propose a gift where one of the objectives is to reduce liability for tax, this should not be the sole objective (*CWM, Re* [1951] 2 K.B. 714).

Any view expressed by the P about a gift can be taken into account by the court but cannot be regarded as determinative. The court will be concerned to establish whether P has been subjected to the undue influence of the proposed recipient of the gift. The criteria for capacity to make a gift were set out in *Beaney (Deceased), Re* [1978] 2 All E.R. 595 at 601:

> "The degree or extent of understanding required in respect of any instrument is relative to the particular transaction which it is to effect Thus, at one extreme, if the subject-matter and value of a gift are trivial in relation to the donor's other assets, a low degree of understanding will suffice. But, at the other, if its effect is to dispose of the donor's only asset of value and thus, for practical purposes, to pre-empt the devolution of his estate under [the donor's] will or intestacy, then the degree of understanding required is as high as that required for a will, and the donor must understand the claims of all potential donees and the extent of the property to be disposed of."

DISPOSITION OF P'S PROPERTY. Provisions relating to the preservation of interests in property disposed of on behalf of P are contained in paras 8 and 9 of Sch.2.

Paragraph (h)

1–148   Paragraphs 5 and 6 of Sch.2 are concerned with the making of settlements on behalf of P. Settlements are likely to be created, with or without the appointment of a deputy, where P has been awarded substantial damages for personal injury.

In *L(WJG), Re* [1966] Ch. 135, at 144 and 145, Cross J. considered the approach to be adopted by a judge in determining whether and how he should exercise his discretion in regard to the making of a settlement where one of the objects of the exercise was to save death duties. His Lordship said: "As the state had maintained [P] free of charge for many years, it would be a little shabby to deprive it of the chance of recouping some of that expenditure by way of death duties."

Paragraph (i)

1–149   Paragraphs 2 to 4 of Sch.2 apply to the making of a will on behalf of P.

P must be an adult before a will can be made (subs.(2)). In *D(J), Re* [1982] 2 All E.R. 37 at 42 and 43, Megarry V-C. identified five considerations which the court should have in mind when deciding on what provisions should be inserted in a will made under a similar jurisdiction under the Mental Health Act 1959. They are:

1. It is to be assumed that the patient is having a brief lucid interval at the time when the will was made.
2. During the lucid interval the patient has full knowledge of the past and a full realisation that as soon as the will is executed he will relapse into the actual mental state that previously existed, with the prognosis as it actually is.
3. It is the actual patient who has to be considered and not a hypothetical patient.
4. During the hypothetical lucid interval, the patient is to be envisaged as being advised by competent solicitors.
5. In all normal cases, the patient is to be envisaged as taking a broad brush to the claims on his bounty, rather than an accountant's pen.

In *C (Spinster and Mental Patient), Re* [1991] 3 All E.R. 866, Hoffmann J. held that in the case of a person who has never enjoyed a rational mind the court when called upon to interpret the phrase "the patient might be expected to provide" in s.95(1)(c) of the 1983 Act should assume that the patient would have been a normal decent person who would have acted in accordance with contemporary standards of morality. In appropriate cases this could result in the patient making charitable gifts and bequests. *Re C* was considered in *S (Gifts by Mental Patient), Re* [1997] 1 F.L.R. 96, 99 where Ferris J. said on the question of dispositions to charity: "It seems to me that I ought not authorise the making of dispositions to charity except to the extent that I have a reasonable degree of confidence that not only is it objectively reasonable but that it is something which the patient herself would have wished to be done if she were of full capacity and aware ofthe circumstances."

The court will not make a new will under this provision unless it is satisfied that there are grounds for making a change. In *Re S*, above, Ferris J. said at 99:

"[M]y approach gives weight to the undesirability of the court exercising its jurisdiction in such a way as to change the existing position in circumstances where it is not fully satisfied that the change is something which the patient herself would have desired."

The court has no jurisdiction to determine the validity of an existing will and, in particular, whether P had the required mental capacity when he made it. The test for testamentary capacity (the capacity required to make a will) was set out by the Court of Appeal in *Banks v Goodfellow* (1870) L.R. 5 Q.B. 549:

"It is essential that a testator shall understand the nature of the act and its effects; shall understand the extent of the property of which he is disposing; shall be able to comprehend and appreciate the claims to which he ought to give effect; and, with a view to the latter object, that no disorder of mind shall poison his affections, pervert his sense of right, or prevent the exercise of his natural faculties - that no insane delusion shall influence his will in disposing of his property and bring about a disposal of it which, if the mind had been sound, would not have been made."

Paragraph (k)
The conduct of legal proceedings need not be confined to proceedings relating either to **1–150** P's personal welfare or his property and affairs *(W (EEM), Re* [1971] Ch.123).

Subsection (3)
This provision enables the court to take a long term view where a brain damaged child **1–151** has been awarded a large sum of damages and there is no prospect of the child ever gaining the capacity to manage that money.

Appointment of deputies
   19.—(1) A deputy appointed by the court must be—   **1–152**
  (a) an individual who has reached 18, or
  (b) as respects powers in relation to property and affairs, an individual who has reached 18 or a trust corporation.
   (2) The court may appoint an individual by appointing the holder for the time being of a specified office or position.
   (3) A person may not be appointed as a deputy without his consent.
   (4) The court may appoint two or more deputies to act—
  (a) jointly,
  (b) jointly and severally, or
  (c) jointly in respect of some matters and jointly and severally in respect of others.
   (5) When appointing a deputy or deputies, the court may at the same time appoint one or more other persons to succeed the existing deputy or those deputies—
  (a) in such circumstances, or on the happening of such events, as may be specified by the court;
  (b) for such period as may be so specified.
   (6) A deputy is to be treated as P's agent in relation to anything done or decided by him within the scope of his appointment and in accordance with this Part.
   (7) The deputy is entitled—
  (a) to be reimbursed out of P's property for his reasonable expenses in discharging his functions, and

(b) if the court so directs when appointing him, to remuneration out of P's property for discharging them.

(8) The court may confer on a deputy powers to—

(a) take possession or control of all or any specified part of P's property;

(b) exercise all or any specified powers in respect of it, including such powers of investment as the court may determine.

(9) The court may require a deputy—

(a) to give to the Public Guardian such security as the court thinks fit for the due discharge of his functions, and

(b) to submit to the Public Guardian such reports at such times or at such intervals as the court may direct.

DEFINITIONS
1–153   "deputy": s.64(1)
"the court": s.64(1)
"property": s.64(1)
"trust corporation": s.64(1)
"Public Guardian": s.64(1)

GENERAL NOTE
1–154   A deputy appointed by the Court of Protection must be an adult who consents to the appointment, with the exception that a trust corporation can be appointed in respect of P's property and affairs (subss.(1) and (3)). Most deputies are likely to be a member of P's family. When appointing a deputy, the court will exercise its discretion so as to satisfy the best interests of P(s.1(5)). The spouse of P has no right to be appointed (*Davy (Laura), Re* [1892] 3 Ch. 38). The court will decide the extent of the powers to be conferred on the deputy (s.16(5)). The powers will be subject to the restrictions contained in s.20. The deputy's powers can be varied by the court, which can also revoke the appointment (s.16(8)). A deputy will be provided with protection by ss.5 and 6 for acts done outside the scope of the appointment. There is no time limit attached to the appointment.

Those applying to become deputies would need to demonstrate why an appointment is necessary. There is no requirement for the court to be satisfied as to the suitability of an individual for appointment by, for example, investigating any actual or potential conflict of interest, although the Public Guardian is required to supervise deputies (s.58(1)(c)). Unlike a donee under a lasting power of attorney, the deputy can be the holder of a specified office, such as a Director of Adult Services (subs.(2)). Where there is more than one deputy, they can be appointed to act either jointly or jointly and severally, i.e. they must either act together with the agreement of all donees (jointly), or each donee can act independently of the other (severally). As an alternative, the donees can be appointed to act jointly in respect of some matters and jointly and severally in respect of others (subs.(4)). When making the appointment, the court has the power to appoint a successor or successors to the original appointee(s) and to specify the circumstances under which this could occur (subs.(5)). The *Code of Practice* states at para.8.44:

"Appointment of a successor deputy might be useful if the person appointed as deputy is already elderly and wants to be sure that somebody will take over their duties in the future, if necessary."

A deputy can claim reasonable expenses and, if the court directs, the deputy can be paid for his or her services. Both expenses and the payments will be made out of P's property (subs.(7)). The deputy can be provided with the power to deal with all matters concerning the control and management of P's property, including being able to invest (subs.(8)). The court will be able to require a deputy to give the Public Guardian security against misbehaviour and to direct the deputy to file reports with the Public Guardian at specified intervals (subs.(9)). Although case law has established that receivers appointed Court of Protection under Pt VII of the Mental Health Act 1983 are statutory agents of the person who lacks capacity (*EG, Re* [1914] 1 Ch. 927), it was considered "helpful to make statutory provision to that effect in relation to dputies" (Explanatory Notes, para.73). This is done in subs.(6). An act of an agent, done within the scope of his authority binds his principal, in this case P. As as agent the deputy is bound by a number of common law duties toward P, including the duty to act with due care and skill, to act within the scope of the authority granted by the court, to act in good faith, not to delegate his or her functions to another without authority, to keep the affairs of P confidential, to keep accounts of monies recieved and paid on P's behalf, and not to permit his own interests to conflict with his duties to P. The duties of an agent are set out in the *Code of Practice* at paras 8.55–8.67. In addition to these duties, the deputy is required to act in P's best interests (s.20(6)) to apply the principles set out in s.1 and to have regard to the *Code of Practice* (s.42(4)(b)). *EG, Re* is authority for the propositions that the property of P does not vest in the deputy (at 933), and that the deputy is not personally liable for the costs of those he or she employs in the course of acting for P (at 935). The deputy should notify any third party with whom he is dealing of the fact that he is acting as deputy for P, as it is a general principle of the law of agency that an agent is personally liable on any contract made in his own name on behalf of a principal where the name or existence of the principal (P) is undisclosed at the time of contracting. Also see the comment on the law of agency in the General Note to s.10.

Any concerns about the manner in which a deputy is performing his or her functions should be reported to the Public Guardian who is responsible for supervising the activities of deputies (s.58(1)(c)). The Public Guardian may decide to direct a Court of Protection Visitor to visit P and/or the deputy. Allegations of serious criminal conduct, such as physical or sexual abuse, should be reported directly to the police, and the Public Guardian informed. Also see the note on adult protection procedures in s.44.

The "Court of Protection and Office of the Public Guardian Fees" Consultation Paper CP 23/06 (DCA, September 2006) states at pp.18–19:

"Most deputies will be supervised through a range of activities that reflect the need for 'light touch' supervision characterised by:

- training and coaching opportunities for new deputies to undertake their role;
- support for deputies from easily-accessible customer support and advice service;
- a requirement to provide some form of annual account or report (if directed by the court) in a format determined by the Office of the Public Guardian;
- confirmation of security bonding as directed by the court; and
- providing short term advice and assistance regarding case specific queries.

Where the assessment process determines that a greater degree of supervision is appropriate, a higher level of activity will be undertaken comprising:

- more support for the deputies in the greater supervision category;
- a requirement to provide an annual account or report (if directed by the court) in a format determined by the Office of Public Guardian;
- an initial visit followed by an assessment of the need for further visits;
- confirmation of security bonding as directed by the court;
- other records may be requested as set out in the Act; and
- additional financial assessments may take place during the initial period of accounting.

These cases will be subject to periodic review by the Office of the Public Guardian. . . . Where someone wishes to complain that the supervision level that the Office of the Public Guardian has decided to apply is not appropriate, they will be able to apply to the Office of the Public Guardian for a review via a new review process."

In this Act references to making decisions, in relation to a deputy, include, where appropriate, acting on decisions made (s.64(2)).

Subsection (6)

1–155 "A key principle governing deputies is that they cannot do more than the person could do if he or she had capacity", *per* the Parliamentary Under-Secretary of State, St. Comm. A, para.191.

AGENT. The duties of an agent are set out above.

Subsection (9)

1–156 SECURITY. For example, a guarantee bond.

Restrictions on deputies

1–157 **20.**—(1) A deputy does not have power to make a decision on behalf of P in relation to a matter if he knows or has reasonable grounds for believing that P has capacity in relation to the matter.

(2) Nothing in section 16(5) or 17 permits a deputy to be given power—

(a) to prohibit a named person from having contact with P;

(b) to direct a person responsible for P's health care to allow a different person to take over that responsibility.

(3) A deputy may not be given powers with respect to—

(a) the settlement of any of P's property, whether for P's benefit or for the benefit of others,

(b) the execution for P of a will, or

(c) the exercise of any power (including a power to consent) vested in P whether beneficially or as trustee or otherwise.

(4) A deputy may not be given power to make a decision on behalf of P which is inconsistent with a decision made, within the scope of his authority and in accordance with this Act, by the donee of a lasting power of attorney granted by P (or, if there is more than one donee, by any of them).

(5) A deputy may not refuse consent to the carrying out or continuation of life-sustaining treatment in relation to P.

(6) The authority conferred on a deputy is subject to the provisions of this Act and, in particular, sections 1 (the principles) and 4 (best interests).

(7) A deputy may not do an act that is intended to restrain P unless four conditions are satisfied.

(8) The first condition is that, in doing the act, the deputy is acting within the scope of an authority expressly conferred on him by the court.

(9) The second is that P lacks, or the deputy reasonably believes that P lacks, capacity in relation to the matter in question.

(10) The third is that the deputy reasonably believes that it is necessary to do the act in order to prevent harm to P.

(11) The fourth is that the act is a proportionate response to—

(a) the likelihood of P's suffering harm, or

(b) the seriousness of that harm.

(12) For the purposes of this section, a deputy restrains P if he—

(a) uses, or threatens to use, force to secure the doing of an act which P resists, or

(b) restricts P's liberty of movement, whether or not P resists,

or if he authorises another person to do any of those things.

(13) But a deputy does more than merely restrain P if he deprives P of his liberty within the meaning of Article 5(1) of the Human Rights Convention (whether or not the deputy is a public authority).

DEFINITIONS **1–158**
  "deputy": s.64(1)
  "property": s.64(1)
  "lasting power of attorney": s.64(1)
  "life-sustaining treatment": s.64(1)
  "the Human Rights Convention": s.64(1)
  "public authority": s.6(1)

GENERAL NOTE

This section sets out a number of limitations on the powers of deputies, who must always **1–159** act in P's best interests (subs.(6)).

Subsection (1) specifies that a deputy cannot act where P is able to act for himself. The Explanatory Notes state at para.75:

"In some cases the person may have fluctuating capacity, for example as a result of mental health problems, and it is not acceptable for a deputy to carry on making substitute decisions when the person concerned has in fact recovered."

As it is can be difficult to determine whether a person with fluctuating mental capacity is enjoying a lucid interval, the deputy should consider seeking professional assistance if he suspects that P is able to act for himself.

Subsections (2) and (3) list matters which must always be dealt with by the court, not a deputy.

Subsection (4) provides that a deputy cannot be given power to override a valid decision made by a donee under P's LPA. If there is concern or a dispute about the way the donee is carrying on his or her responsibilities under the LPA, the court must use its powers under ss.22 and 23 rather that seeking to appoint a deputy.

Subsection (5) prevents deputies from refusing consent to the carrying out or continuation of life-sustaining treatment.

Subsections (7)–(13) impose limitations on a deputy's power to restrain P. They match those imposed in relation to "section 5 acts" by s.6 and on donees by s.11, and reference should be made to the notes on s.6. The deputy will have to be acting within the scope of an authority expressly conferred on him by the court (subs.(8)).

Subsection (2) (a)

If a deputy is concerned about someone's conduct toward P, he or she can apply to the **1–160** court for a relevant order to be made, or apply for a non-molestation order under Pt IV of the Family Law Act 1996 (c.27) as P's litigation friend.

Subsection (6)

All deputies, both professional and lay, will need to be familiar with the principles set out **1–161** in s.1 and with the "checklist" approach used in best interest determinations made under s.4.

Subsection (11)

There appears to be a drafting error in this provision. To make it consistent with ss.6(3) **1–162** and 11(4)(a), "or" should read "and".

Subsection (13)

See the notes to s.6(5). **1–163**

Transfer of proceedings relating to people under 18

21.—[(1)] The [Lord Chief Justice, with the concurrence of the Lord **1–164** Chancellor] may by order make provision as to the transfer of proceedings relating to a person under 18, in such circumstances as are specified in the order—

(a) from the Court of Protection to a court having jurisdiction under the Children Act 1989 (c. 41), or

(b) from a court having jurisdiction under that Act to the Court of Protection.

[(2) The Lord Chief Justice may nominate any of the following to exercise his functions under this section—

(a) the President of the Court of Protection;

(b) a judicial office holder (as defined in section 109(4) of the Constitutional Reform Act 2005).]

AMENDMENTS

1–165   The amendments to this section were made by SI 2006/1016, art.2, Sch.1, para.31.

GENERAL NOTE

1–166   Generally speaking, this Act is concerned with people aged 16 and over who lack capacity (s.2(5); but see s.18(3)), while the Children Act 1989 is mainly concerned with people under the age of 18. This section deals with any overlap between the two jurisdictions by providing the Lord Chancellor with a power to make transfer of proceedings orders. The Parliamentary Under-Secretary of State gave the following example of the need for a transfer:

> "[I]f the parents of a 17 year-old who has profound learning difficulties are in dispute with each other about residence or contact, it might be more appropriate for the Court of Protection to deal with that, since a s.8 order made under the Children Act 1989 would expire on the child's eighteenth birthday at the latest" (*Hansard*, HL Vol.668, col.1485).

Powers of the court in relation to lasting powers of attorney

Powers of court in relation to validity of lasting powers of attorney

1–167   **22.**—(1) This section and section 23 apply if—

(a) a person (P) has executed or purported to execute an instrument with a view to creating a lasting power of attorney, or

(b) an instrument has been registered as a lasting power of attorney conferred by P.

(2) The court may determine any question relating to—

(a) whether one or more of the requirements for the creation of a lasting power of attorney have been met;

(b) whether the power has been revoked or has otherwise come to an end.

(3) Subsection (4) applies if the court is satisfied—

(a) that fraud or undue pressure was used to induce P—

　(i) to execute an instrument for the purpose of creating a lasting power of attorney, or

　(ii) to create a lasting power of attorney, or

(b) that the donee (or, if more than one, any of them) of a lasting power of attorney—

　(i) has behaved, or is behaving, in a way that contravenes his authority or is not in P's best interests, or

　(ii) proposes to behave in a way that would contravene his authority or would not be in P's best interests.

(4) The court may—

(a) direct that an instrument purporting to create the lasting power of attorney is not to be registered, or

(b) if P lacks capacity to do so, revoke the instrument or the lasting power of attorney.

(5) If there is more than one donee, the court may under subsection (4)(b) revoke the instrument or the lasting power of attorney so far as it relates to any of them.

(6) "Donee" includes an intended donee.

DEFINITIONS
    "lasting power of attorney": s.64(1)   **1–168**
    "the court": s.64(1)

GENERAL NOTE
    This section and s.23 set out the powers of the Court of Protection where a person has **1–169** drawn up a document (an "instrument") which is either intended to be registered as a lasting power of attorney (LPA) at some time in the future, or has already been registered as a LPA. The court is provided with a power to determine questions about the validity and revocation of LPAs (subs.(2)), and can direct that the instrument should not be registered, or where it has been registered and P lacks capacity, that it should be revoked if any of the grounds in subs.(3) are satisfied (subs.(4)). This section also provides that where there is more than one donee, the court may revoke the instrument or the LPA so far as it relates to any of them provided that P lacks capacity (subss.(5),(6)).

Subsection (3)
    UNDUE PRESSURE. It is likely that the court will have regard to the caselaw on "undue influ- **1–170** ence" when considering this term. In *Re T (Adult: Refusal of Medical Treatment)* [1992] 4 All E.R. 649, 662, CA, Lord Donaldson said that, while it is acceptable for a patient to receive advice or for the patient to have been subject to the strong persuasion of others in reaching a decision, such persuasion must not "overbear the independence of the patient's decision". His Lordship identified the real question in each case as being:

> "does the patient really mean what he says or is he merely saying it for a quiet life, to satisfy someone else or because the advice and persuasion to which he has been subjected is such that he can no longer think and decide for himself? In other words, it is a decision expressed in form only, not in reality?"

His Lordship identified two aspects of the effect of outside influence that could be of "crucial importance": the strength of will of the patient and the relationship of the "persuader" to the patient. With regard to the former, a patient who is "very tired, in pain or depressed will be much less able to resist having his will overborne than one who is rested, free from pain and cheerful". With regard to the relationship between the persuader and the patient, his Lordship spoke of the potential strength of the parental and marital relationship, especially with regard to arguments based on religious belief. These factors should make the doctor alert to the possibility that the patient may not mean what he or she says. Other outside influences that could vitiate a patient's consent include fraud, misrepresentation and duress.

Powers of court in relation to operation of lasting powers of attorney

    23.—(1) The court may determine any question as to the meaning or effect of a **1–171** lasting power of attorney or an instrument purporting to create one.

(2) The court may—

(a) give directions with respect to decisions—

    (i) which the donee of a lasting power of attorney has authority to make, and

    (ii) which P lacks capacity to make;

(b) give any consent or authorisation to act which the donee would have to obtain from P if P had capacity to give it.

(3) The court may, if P lacks capacity to do so—

(a) give directions to the donee with respect to the rendering by him of reports or accounts and the production of records kept by him for that purpose;

(b) require the donee to supply information or produce documents or things in his possession as donee;

(c) give directions with respect to the remuneration or expenses of the donee;

(d) relieve the donee wholly or partly from any liability which he has or may have incurred on account of a breach of his duties as donee.

(4) The court may authorise the making of gifts which are not within section 12(2) (permitted gifts).

(5) Where two or more donees are appointed under a lasting power of attorney, this section applies as if references to the donee were to all or any of them.

DEFINITIONS

1–172   "the court": s.64(1)
"lasting power of attorney": s.64(1)

GENERAL NOTE

1–173   This section provides the Court of Protection with powers to decide any questions about the "meaning or effect"of a LPA or an instrument purporting to create one (subs.(1)), to give directions to donees where P lacks capacity (subs.(2)(a)), and to give any consent or authorisation which P might have given had he or she not lacked capacity (subs.(2)(b)). If P is incapacitated, the court also has power to give the donee directions in relation to producing reports, accounts, records and information, determining a donee's remuneration and expenses, and relieving a donee from some or all of the liabilities arising from a breach of his or her duties as donee (subs.(3)). The Court may also authorise the making of gifts beyond the scope of what is permitted by s.12(2) (subs.(4)).

Subsection (1)

1–174   MEANING OR EFFECT. This gives the court power to determine any point of construction arising on the LPA, and whether a donee has power to carry out a particular act.

Subsection (2)

1–175   The purpose of para.(b) was explained by the Parliamentary Under-Secretary of State:

"[Donees] are in law regarded as agents and are therefore affected by the law of agency as well as the provisions of the Bill. [Under the law of agency] it is sometimes necessary for the [donee] to give the consent or authorisation of the donor before they can act. The obvious example is where the donee would like to purchase the donor's property. The donor would make it a condition of the power of attorney that the [donee] must get their consent. In other words, if I wanted to buy the house of someone for whom I acted as [donee], I would need to get their consent to do so. However, if they lack capacity, I cannot get their consent. Yet, it would be wrong for me to purchase their house without consent. In those circumstances, the court would step in and give the consent. So, it is a protection, but a protection in circumstances where the law of agency applies" (*Hansard*, HL Vol.668, col.1426).

Subsection (3) para.(a)

1–176   As, generally speaking, the court will not exercise any supervision over the conduct of a donee, the giving of directions relating to the production of reports etc is likely to be triggered by concerns being raised by persons who are in close contact with P.

Subsection (3) para.(c)

REMUNERATION. The directions could override a provision for remuneration contained in **1–177** the LPA.

Subsection (3) para.(d)

ANY LIABILITY. Note the breath of this power. Unlike the power to relieve trustees from **1–178** breaches of trust under s.61 of the Trustee Act 1925, there is no requirement for the donee to have acted "honestly and reasonably".

Subsection (4)

This provision could be used to authorise gifts for tax planning purposes. **1–179**

Advance decisions to refuse treatment

Advance decisions to refuse treatment: general

24.—(1) "Advance decision" means a decision made by a person (P), after he **1–180** has reached 18 and when he has capacity to do so, that if—

(a) at a later time and in such circumstances as he may specify, a specified treatment is proposed to be carried out or continued by a person providing health care for him, and

(b) at that time he lacks capacity to consent to the carrying out or continuation of the treatment,

the specified treatment is not to be carried out or continued.

(2) For the purposes of subsection (1)(a), a decision may be regarded as specifying a treatment or circumstances even though expressed in layman's terms.

(3) P may withdraw or alter an advance decision at any time when he has capacity to do so.

(4) A withdrawal (including a partial withdrawal) need not be in writing.

(5) An alteration of an advance decision need not be in writing (unless section 25(5) applies in relation to the decision resulting from the alteration).

DEFINITIONS
   "treatment": s.64(1) **1–181**

GENERAL NOTE

Sections 24–26 deal with advance decisions to refuse medical treatment. As they broadly **1–182** "seek to codify and clarify the current common law rules" relating to advance directives (Explanatory Notes, para.84), a brief account of these rules is set out below. An advance directive made before the commencement of this Act will take effect as an advance decision if it complies with the relevant provisions of this Act. The Government's cautious approach to legislating in this area is illustrated by the following extract from "*Who Decides? Making Decisions on Behalf of Mentally Incapacitated Adults*" (Cm.3803):

> "The Government recognises the strength of feeling on this subject. This was the area of the Law Commission's work which aroused the greatest public concern, and it is clear that this is a matter on which many have deep rooted personal, moral, religious and ethical views. The Government does not believe that it would be appropriate to reach any conclusions in this area in the absence of fresh consultation—not just on the detailed plans put forward by the Law Commission, but also on the need for and the merits of legislation in this area generally" (para.4.2).

This caution was, to a certain extent, explained by the conclusion of the House of Lords Select Committee on Medical Ethics which had commended the development of advance directives, but decided that "it could well be impossible to give advance directives in

general greater legal force without depriving patients of the benefit of the doctor's professional expertise and of new treatments and procedures which may have become
available since the directive was signed" ((1993–94) HL Paper 21–1, para.185).

Advance Directives

1–183   The case of *C (Adult: Refusal of Medical Treatment)*, Re [1994] 1 All E.R. 819, was the
first occasion when an English Court had been invited to rule directly on the legal validity
of an advance directive. Thorpe J. held that a refusal of treatment could take the form of a
declaration of intention never to consent in the future or never to consent in some future
circumstances. The effect of this ruling was that an advance refusal of treatment for either
a physical or mental disorder made when the patient is mentally capable survives any
supervening incapacity, even if the refusal leads to the patient's death. His Lordship
accepted that a patient might have capacity to make a present refusal but lack the capacity
to make an anticipatory refusal.

The criteria required for an advance directive to be valid were identified by Hughes J. in
AK (Adult Patient) (Medical Treatment: Consent), Re [2001] 1 F.L.R.129 (points 1 and 2),
and by Munby J. in *HE v A Hospital NHS Trust* [2003] EWHC 1017 (Fam Div); [2003] 2
F.L.R. 408 (points 3–9). They are:

1. The treating doctor must be satisfied that the patient was mentally capable at the time
   when the patient made it known that he or she would not consent to the treatment in
   question.
2. All the circumstances in which the expression of wishes was given will have to be
   investigated. In particular, care must be taken to (a) ensure that the anticipatory declaration of wishes still represent the wishes of the patient; (b) investigate how long
   ago the expression of wishes was made; and (c) investigate with what knowledge the
   expression of wishes was made.
3. There are no formal requirements for a valid advance directive. An advance directive
   may be oral or in writing.
4. There are no formal requirements for the revocation of an advance directive. An
   advance directive, whether oral or in writing, may be revoked either orally or in writing. A written advance directive or an advance directive executed under seal can be
   revoked orally.
5. An advance directive is inherently revocable. Any condition in an advance directive
   purporting to make it irrevocable, any even self-imposed fetter on a patient's ability
   to revoke an advance directive, and any provision in an advance directive purporting
   to impose formal or other conditions upon its revocation, is contrary to public policy
   and void. So, a stipulation in an advance directive, even if in writing, that it shall be
   binding unless and until it is revoked in writing is void as being contrary to public
   policy.
6. The existence and continuing validity and applicability of an advance directive is a
   question of fact. Whether an advance directive has been revoked or has for some
   other reason ceased to be operative is a question of fact.
7. The burden of proof is on those who seek to establish the existence and continuing
   validity and applicability of an advance directive.
8. Where life is at stake the evidence must be scrutinised with especial care. Clear and
   convincing proof is required. The continuing validity and applicability of the
   advance directive must be clearly established by convincing and inherently reliable
   evidence.
9. If there is doubt that doubt falls to be resolved in favour of the preservation of life.

In *R. (on the application of Burke) v The General Medical Council* [2005] EWCA Civ
1003; [2005] H.R.L.R. 35, the Court of Appeal confirmed that an advance directive provides a competent patient with a right to refuse treatment after he ceased to be
competent; it cannot be used to require that a patient be provided with any form of treatment that he might consider to be in his own best interests.

If a patient makes a valid advance directive to the effect that he or she is not to be resuscitated if he or she is found in an unconscious state after attempting suicide, the directive must be respected *(W (Adult: Refusal of Medical Treatment), Re* [2002] EWHC 901 (Fam Div)). A failure to respect a valid advance directive can result in a claim for battery being made against the clinician *(Airedale NHS Trust v Bland* [1993] 1 All E.R. 821, HL).

For advance directives and psychiatric treatment, see A. Halpern and G. Szmukler, "Psychiatric advance directives: reconciling autonomy and non-consensual treatment" (1997) 21 *Psychiatric Bulletin* 323. Dr A. Treloar identifies major potential problems with the use of advance directives in "Advance directives: limitations upon their application in elderly care" (1999) 14 *International Journal of Geriatric Psychiatry* 1039. A study by T. Thompson, R. Barbour and L. Schwartz found that advance directives are open to widely varying interpretations in that some of the clinicians interviewed justified treatment contrary to an advance directive on the basis of the patient's best interests ("Adherence to advance directives in critical care decision making: vignette study" (2003) 327 *British Medical Journal* 1011). An anonymous postal questionnaire survey of members of the British Geriatrics Society found that the majority of geriatricians who responded were strongly in favour of the use of living wills by older people despite recognising their potential for problems. Over half had cared for patients who has living wills, and most felt positively about the experience (R. Schiff *et al.* "Living wills and the Mental Capacity Act: a postal questionnaire survey of UK geriatricians" (2006) 35 *Age and Ageing* 116). For an analysis of advance directives/advance decisions under common law and under this Act, see Sabine Michalowski, "Advance Refusals of Life-Sustaining Medical Treatment: The Relativity of an Absolute Right" (2005) 68(6) M.L.R. 948.

Advance Decisions

This section defines an advance decision, sometimes referred to as a "living will". The **1–184** person making the advance decision need not refer to it as such. An advance decision can only be made by a mentally capable person aged 18 or over and the decision must specify the treatment that is being refused.The decision could have been made a considerable time before the coming into force of this Act. The effect of an advance decision is to enable the person to refuse the specified treatment when that person loses the capacity to give or refuse consent to that treatment. In other words, an advance decision which is valid and applicable (s.25) is as effective as a contemporaneous decision made by a mentally capable person in that healthcare professionals are bound by it (s.26), even if they or the patient's relatives or carers disagree with it.

Although this section is concerned with refusals of medical treatments and cannot be used to require a doctor to provide a particular form of medical treatment (*R. (on the application of Burke) v The General Medical Council*, above), the person making the advance decision could attempt to achieve this objective by refusing all but the preferred method of treatment for a particular disorder.

The advance decision can specify particular circumstances in which the refusal may apply. Both the treatment and the circumstances may be specified in lay (i.e. non-medical) terms. Section 25(5) and (6) comes into play if the person wishes the advance decision to apply to a refusal of life sustaining treatment. An advance decision cannot be used to give effect to an unlawful act such as euthanasia, which is a deliberate intervention with the express aim of ending life (s.62).

The best interests criterion does not apply to the application of an advance decision as the person concerned has identified his or her best interests when making the advance decision: see the General Note to s.26.

An advance decision can be overridden by the provisions of ss.57, 58 and 63 of the Mental Health Act 1983 (see s.28), so that a decision that refuses a specific treatment for a mental disorder will be rendered ineffective if a person is detained under a section of the 1983 Act which comes within the scope of Pt IV of that Act.

Apart from an advance decision that relates to life-sustaining treatment (see s.25(5),(6)), this Act does not establish any procedures or formalities that must be followed for an advance decision to be made. The advance decision can be oral or written and there is no procedure that must be followed to establish that the person was mentally capable at the time when the advance decision is made. The advanced decision need not be witnessed and can be made without the benefit of professional advice. Publicly funded legal advice through the Legal Help scheme cannot be provided to assist an individual to make an advance decision (Access to Justice Act 1999, Sch.2, para.1(eb)). To avoid possible legal challenge, it would be sensible for advanced decisions to be written, witnessed and to contain a statement that, in the opinion of the witness, the person was mentally capable of making the decision at the time when it was made, together with a confirmation that the medical consequences of the decision have been explained to the person by a named doctor. A written advance decision could be supplemented by a video recording of the person's verbal confirmation of their decision. There is no provision requiring the advance decision to be reviewed over time, although this is clearly desirable. A written advance directive can be withdrawn or altered orally.

It might be very difficult for a treating doctor to be confident that a patient who is said to have made an oral advance decision during the course of a conversation with a relative had the mental capacity to make the decision at that time (the presumption of capacity set out in s.1(2) will apply) and was provided with sufficient information to enable an informed decision to be made (it is difficult to see how appropriate information could be provided without the involvement of a healthcare professional). It might also be difficult to establish whether the person was subject to the undue influence of the relative at the relevant time (see the note on s.1(3)), or had subsequently revoked the advance decision. Indeed, it may be difficult to establish whether the reported conversation took place at all. Disputes about the existence, validity or applicability of an advance decision can be referred to the Court of Protection (s.26(4)). In *HE v A Hospital NHS Trust*, above, Munby J. said at para.34:

> "The absence of anything in writing goes only to the practicability of proof. For it may be difficult to establish the existence of a binding oral advance directive given, first, the need for clear and convincing proof founded on convincing and inherently reliable evidence and, secondly, the need to demonstrate that the patient's expressed views represented a firm and settled commitment and not merely an offhand remark or informally expressed reaction to other people's problems."

The Minister assured members of the Standing Committee which considered the Bill that "including oral decisions does not mean that any casual statement would count as an advance decision. There would be a world of difference between someone remarking casually to a friend that they would never like to be kept alive artificially and someone with Alzheimer's discussing with a doctor charged with their care how they might expect the condition to progress and making an oral decision to refuse certain interventions as their condition worsens. I remind the Committee that the Bill requires tough tests to be passed if an advance decision is to apply. The decision must be specific and made with capacity to be valid and applicable to the treatment in question. Where there is any doubt, a clinician can safely treat someone and receive protection from liability for a claim for damages, tort, criminal liability or assault [see s.26(2)]", *per* the Parliamentary Under-Secretary of State, St. Comm. A, para.225.

The *Code of Practice* states, at para.9.19, that it would be helpful for the following information to be included in a written advance decision:

- "• full details of the person making the advance decision, including date of birth, home address and any distinguishing features (in case healthcare professionals need to identify an unconscious person, for example)
- • the name and address of the person's GP and whether they have a copy of the document
- • a statement that the document should be used if the person ever lacks capacity to make treatment decisions

- a clear statement of the decision, the treatment to be refused and the circumstances in which the decision will apply
- the date the document was written (or reviewed)
- the person's signature (or the signature of someone the person has asked to sign on their behalf and in their presence)
- the signature of the person witnessing the signature, if there is one (or a statement directing somebody to sign on the person's behalf)."

With regard to oral advance decisions made to a member of the patient's healthcare team, the Code suggests, at para.9.23, that the following information be included in the patient's medical notes:

"• a note that the decision should apply if the person lacks capacity to make treatment decisions in the future
- a clear note of the decision, the treatment to be refused and the circumstances in which the decision will apply
- details of someone who was present when the oral advance decision was recorded and the role in which they were present (for example, healthcare professional or family member), and
- whether they heard the decision, took part in it or are just aware that it exists."

If healthcare professionals are alerted to the possibility that a patient might have made an advance decision, reasonable efforts, such as contacting relatives of the patient and the patient's GP, should be made to establish whether this is the case. Treatment should not be delayed while attempts are made to establish whether an advance decision has been made if the delay would prejudice the patient's health.

Healthcare professionals who have a conscientious objection to respecting a patient's valid and applicable advance directive should ensure that the care of the patient is transferred to the care of another healthcare professional. The following extract from correspondence between the Parliamentary Under-Secretary of State for Health and the Opposition spokesperson on health was read into the record during the report stage of the Bill in the House of Lords at *Hansard*, H.L.Vol.670, col.1306:

"I promised to check GMC and BMA guidance on provisions for when a doctor does not want to carry out treatment. Doctors are entitled to have their personal beliefs respected and will not be pressured to act contrary to those beliefs. As I stated during the Committee, where a doctor has a conscientious objection they may withdraw from the care of the patient. In doing so however they must ensure, without delay, that arrangements have been made for another suitably qualified colleague to take over their role, so that the patient's care does not suffer. The individual doctor does not necessarily have to arrange personally for a transfer of care, provided there are alternative means of doing so. However, the doctor must not abandon the patient or otherwise cause their care to suffer."

Also of relevance in this context is the following guidance given by Butler-Sloss P. in *B (Consent to Treatment: Capacity), Re* [2002] EWHC 429 (Fam Div); [2002] 2 All E.R. 449 at para.100(viii) and (ix):

"If there is no disagreement about competence but the doctors are for any reason unable to carry out the wishes of the patient, their duty is to find other doctors who will do so."

Where a transfer to other healthcare professionals cannot be agreed, the court can issue a direction under s.17(1)(e).

Guidance on conscientious objection is given in the *Code of Practice* at paras 9.61–9.63. Freedom of thought, conscience and religion is provided for in Art.9 of the European Convention on Human Rights.

As an alternative to making an advance decision, the person could either leave decision making in the hands of healthcare professionals, make an advance statement (see below), or appoint someone to act as their donee under a lasting power of attorney (see s.9). A personal welfare LPA does not take effect until the donor loses capacity (s.11(7)(a)).

The provisions of the Bill relating to advance decisions caused considerable controversy, particularly because of evidence that suggested that well people tend not to make the same decisions as sick people; see further, the notes to s.25(4)(c). The Joint Committee set out some of the concerns that had been raised in paras 195–200 of its Report:

"A very considerable number of written submissions were received expressing grave concern about this aspect of the draft Bill. Many argued from a standpoint of moral conviction that it was wrong to introduce a statute that could enable decisions that would effectively shorten life. Others argued that it was wrong to require a doctor not to give treatment that the doctor believed was in the patient's best clinical interests.

A considerable body of written evidence claimed that the inclusion of advance decisions meant that the Bill was introducing 'euthanasia by the back door'. We took evidence on this matter and considered the issues at length. For several faith organisations and the Guild of Catholic Doctors the omission of treatment that might prolong life even if for a short period of time was considered unacceptable unless such treatment was likely itself to result in undue suffering. We noted that there was nothing in the Bill that allowed for an act that had the clear intent to end a person's life. This was confirmed in oral evidence by the Parliamentary Under-Secretary of the Department for Constitutional Affairs, Lord Filkin.

Allied to these concerns numerous witnesses objected to the fact that the draft Bill allows life sustaining treatment (e.g. artificial ventilation) to be refused. They drew attention to the Court ruling in the case of Bland that the provision of hydration and nutrition by artificial means amounted to 'treatment'. They argued that withdrawal of nutrition and hydration would result in undue suffering and an unpleasant and undignified death.The BMA in their evidence suggested that, while the use of artificial means of nutrition and hydration amounted to treatment and could therefore be refused, the Bill should stipulate that basic care could not be refused.

Witnesses from the medical profession also put to us that: (a) people when capable could not foresee how they might wish to act if they were to become incapable and therefore could not commit themselves to a course of action from which they could not withdraw having become incapable; (b) unforeseen circumstances, such as the development of a new treatment the use of which would be in their best interests, could arise after the advance decision had been made; and (c) the course of action specified in the advance decision might prolong suffering rather than relieving it. We heard evidence from Professor the Baroness Finlay of the difficulties she and her medical and nursing colleagues faced working in palliative care services. She told us that her personal choice would be that advance decisions should be advisory 'but case law seems to have taken us beyond that point already'.

Those who believed that advance decisions should be included argued that this was a logical and appropriate continuation of respect for a patient's individual autonomy in matters of medical treatment. The law already recognises that a capable person can refuse treatment even if that refusal might end their life. But for a doctor to proceed with treatment under such circumstances would be unlawful. Thus it was argued that the draft Bill only proposed to regularise the existing status quo and that it was a logical extension of the established principle of autonomy. For these reasons the making Decisions Alliance, for example, strongly supported the inclusion of advance decisions to refuse treatment in the Bill. Several witnesses regretted that the draft Bill did not require advance decisions to be made in writing, witnessed or made with the benefit of professional advice. Other feared that people might make advance decisions while in a state of despair or depression that they would not have made under more normal circumstances. The risk of advance decisions being made under coercion was also raised."

Advance statements

Unlike an advance decision, an advance statement is a non-legally binding document **1–185** which may identify a person's views and preferences on a large range of medical and other issues. Under s.4(6)(a), such a statement would need to be taken into account when decisions are made subsequent to the patient's mental incapacity. The Making Decisions Alliance briefing document on the second reading debate on the Bill states, at p.19, that "advance statements would enable an individual to express their views and preferences on a large range of issues, including:

- domestic arrangements
- treatment preferences
- financial arrangements
- childcare arrangements
- clarification of who to disclose information to, and the limits of what can be discussed
- dietary requirements."

The literature is replete with examples of a failure to appreciate the distinction between advance directives and advance statements: see the studies cited by T. Exworthy in "Psychiatric advance decisions—an opportunity missed" (September 2004) *Journal of Mental Health Law* 129 at p.132.

Subsection (1)

DECISION. A decision can only be made after full consideration of all relevant matters, **1–186** including the consequences for the patient if the treatment is not given (*W Healthcare NHS Trust v H* [2004] EWCA Civ 1324; [2005] 1 W.L.R. 834, para.17).

AGED 18. The 16 years of age cut off specified in s.2(4) is not used here as the refusal of a 16 or 17 year old to receive medical treatment may be overridden by a person with parental responsibility for the child, or by the court.

CAPACITY. The doctor should assume that the patient was capable in the absence of evidence to the contrary (s.1(2)).

Subsection (1) para.(a)

SUCH CIRCUMSTANCES AS HE MAY SPECIFY. For example, the treatment is not to be given if **1–187** there is no realistic prospect of P ever regaining mental capacity.

SPECIFIED TREATMENT. Care should be taken to ensure that there can be no doubt about the identity of the particular treatment that is being refused. In *W Healthcare NHS Trust v H*, above, para.21, the Court of Appeal found that a statement made by the patient that she would not wish "to be kept alive by machines" was not "an advance directive which was sufficiently clear to amount to a direction that she preferred to be deprived of food and drink for a period of time which would lead to her death in all circumstances". "Treatment" is widely defined in s.64(1). It can include the provision of nutrition and hydration to the patient by artificial means (*Airedale NHS Trust v Bland* [1993] 1 All E.R. 821, HL). The Joint Committee on Human Rights expressed its concern that the "classification of artificial nutrition and hydration as 'treatment' may not be well known to lay people" (23rd Report, para.2.46).

This Act distinguishes between "treatment"and "care": see, for example, s.5(1). The provision of "basic care" such as feeding and hydration which is not medically assisted, and care to maintain bodily cleanliness cannot be categorised as treatment and can therefore not be subject to an advance decision.

As an advance decision must relate to a specific treatment(s), a statement or a note which merely indicates a general desire not to be treated would not qualify.

AT THAT TIME HE LACKS CAPACITY. Section 2(2) states that "it does not matter" if the patient's incapacity is temporary or permanent. This provision will cause difficulty in cases where P has made an advance decision refusing treatment, P becomes incapacitated and P's capacity could be restored if P was treated. It is likely that s.25(4)(c) would apply in such a situation.

Situations can arise when it will only become apparent that a seemingly incapable person is, in fact, perfectly capable of making the decision in question if considerable time and trouble is taken in an attempt to communicate with that person. In a powerful and moving speech on the second reading of the Bill (*Hansard*, HC Vol.425, cols.64–67), Mrs Claire Curtis-Thomas MP recounted how her mother, who had been hospitalised after having suffered a massive stoke which had left her paralysed, was considered to be mentally incapable and was not being fed. Mrs Curtis-Thomas's mother had made an advance directive refusing treatment subsequent to her recovery from a previous stoke. Mrs Curtis-Thomas's attempts to communicate with her mother, which lasted a number of weeks, eventually succeeded and her mother was able to blink out "I want to live". This had the effect of revoking the advance directive. Mrs Curtis-Thomas said: "If my mother had not had me, all I believe would have happened is that she would have starved to death. I do not think that anybody would have taken the time or known her well enough to realise that she was actually present and capable of making decisions." The principle contained in s.1(3) is applicable to the situation described by Mrs Curtis-Thomas.

THE SPECIFIED TREATMENT IS NOT TO BE CARRIED OUT. An advance decision cannot be used to require that a patient be provided with any form of treatment that he might consider to be in his own best interests. However, s.4 requires an invalid advance decision of this nature to be taken into account when considering what is in the best interests of a patient if it is clear that the patient was attempting to refuse a particular treatment: see s.5(6)(a) and *R (on the application of Burke) v The General Medical Council* above, para.57.

Subsection (2)

1–188   Lay terms can be used as long as the use of such terms does not lead to any ambiguity about the identity of the treatment that is being refused. In *W Healthcare NHS Trust v H*, above, the Court of Appeal held that a purported advance directive was not valid partly on the ground that the patient, who has stated that she did not want to be kept alive by machines, had not specifically considered and refused artificial hydration and nutrition.

Subsection (3)

1–189   There is no procedure for withdrawing or altering an advance decision. A simple statement by a mentally capable person such as, "I no longer wish my advance decision to stand", would be sufficient to withdraw a decision. An alteration has to be in writing, and the formalities set out in s.25(6) complied with, if the decision relates to a life-sustaining treatment (subs.(5)).

Subsection (4)

1–190   It is therefore possible for a capable patient to withdraw a written advance decision immediately before an anaesthetic is administered.

Validity and applicability of advance decisions

1–191   **25.**—(1) An advance decision does not affect the liability which a person may incur for carrying out or continuing a treatment in relation to P unless the decision is at the material time—

(a) valid, and
(b) applicable to the treatment.

(2) An advance decision is not valid if P—

(a) has withdrawn the decision at a time when he had capacity to do so,

(b) has, under a lasting power of attorney created after the advance decision was made, conferred authority on the donee (or, if more than one, any of them) to give or refuse consent to the treatment to which the advance decision relates, or

(c) has done anything else clearly inconsistent with the advance decision remaining his fixed decision.

(3) An advance decision is not applicable to the treatment in question if at the material time P has capacity to give or refuse consent to it.

(4) An advance decision is not applicable to the treatment in question if—

(a) that treatment is not the treatment specified in the advance decision,

(b) any circumstances specified in the advance decision are absent, or

(c) there are reasonable grounds for believing that circumstances exist which P did not anticipate at the time of the advance decision and which would have affected his decision had he anticipated them.

(5) An advance decision is not applicable to life-sustaining treatment unless—

(a) the decision is verified by a statement by P to the effect that it is to apply to that treatment even if life is at risk, and

(b) the decision and statement comply with subsection (6).

(6) A decision or statement complies with this subsection only if—

(a) it is in writing,

(b) it is signed by P or by another person in P's presence and by P's direction,

(c) the signature is made or acknowledged by P in the presence of a witness, and

(d) the witness signs it, or acknowledges his signature, in P's presence.

(7) The existence of any lasting power of attorney other than one of a description mentioned in subsection (2)(b) does not prevent the advance decision from being regarded as valid and applicable.

DEFINITIONS

"advance decision": s.64(1)   **1–192**
"treatment": s.64(1)
"lasting power of attorney": s.64(1)
"life-sustaining treatment": s.64(1)

GENERAL NOTE

This section states that a person shall not be legally liable for providing treatment to a **1–193**
patient who has made an advance decision unless the decision is both valid and applicable.
It then proceeds to define both "valid' and "applicable'. In *HE v A Hospital NHS Trust*
[2003] EWHC 1017 (Fam Div); [2003] 2 F.L.R. 408, Munby J. said at para.24:

"Where life is at stake the evidence must be scrutinised with special care. Clear and convincing proof is required. The continuing validity and applicability of the advance directive must be clearly established by convincing and inherently reliable evidence."

Establishing whether an advance decision is both valid and applicable could lead to a significant increase in the workload of medical practitioners. As the Law Commission pointed out, the existence of a formal document is no guarantee of either validity of applicability, nor is the absence of such a document any guarantee that a valid and applicable advance decision has not been made (Law Com No.231, para.5.29).

An advance decision is not valid if P has withdrawn the decision while he or she had the mental capacity to do so, has made a subsequent lasting power of attorney (which has the effect of overriding the decision by enabling the donee to refuse consent to the treatment specified in the decision), or has acted in a manner which is clearly inconsistent with the terms of the decision (subs.(2)). In addition, an advance decision will not be valid if it was made either by a child or by an adult who lacked capacity (s.24(1)). Although an adult should be assumed to have been mentally capable at the time when the decision was made (s1(2)), the medical practitioner should investigate any factors that suggest that this assumption could be rebutted.

An advance decision will not be applicable if P is capable of making the treatment decision at the time the treatment is proposed (subs.(3)). It will also not be applicable to treatments not specified in the decision, if the circumstances specified in the decision are absent, or if there are reasonable grounds for believing that that the current circumstances were not anticipated by P and, if they had been anticipated they would have affected P's decision (subs.(4)). Finally, an advance decision is not applicable to life-sustaining treatment unless P has specified in writing that it should be, and the decision is signed and witnessed (subss.(5) and (6)).

A valid and applicable advance decision to refuse treatment will be as legally effective as a contemporaneous refusal of consent. It cannot be overridden by the Court of Protection, a deputy appointed by the court, the donee of a LPA made before the advance decision was made, or a person acting under s.5 (s.5(4)). Although the court may make declarations as to the existence, validity and applicability of an advance decision (s.15(1)(c)), it has no power to override a valid and applicable advance decision on the ground that it would not serve P's best interests. Life sustaining treatment or action to prevent a serious deterioration of the patient's condition may be provided while a decision is being sought from the court (s.26(5)).

In a survey of UK geriatricians, advice concerning the validity of "living wills" was sought by 44 per cent, most frequently from hospital lawyers (R. Schiff *et al.* "Living wills and the Mental Capacity Act: a postal questionnaire survey of UK geriatricians" (2006) 35 *Age and Ageing* 116).

Subsection (1)

1–194   The healthcare professional must be aware of the existence of the advance decision if he or she is to incur legal liability for providing the treatment (s.26(2)). If the healthcare professional has knowledge of the advance directive, the treatment can proceed if the professional considers that it is either invalid and/ or not applicable to the treatment.

Subsection (2) para. (a)

1–195   A written advance decision can be withdrawn orally. In the absence of evidence to the contrary, the healthcare professional should assume that the patient was capable of withdrawing the decision (s.1(2)).

Patients can change their minds about having treatment at a very late stage. The difficulties of relying on an advance decision that has not been revoked can be seen from the following clinical example given by Baroness Finlay to the Joint Committee concerning a patient who had taken a massive overdose of paracetamol:

> "He did not want to come to hospital but was persuaded to. He flatly refused any intervention or any treatment. Two psychiatrists spent a lot of time negotiating with him for several days and explained absolutely everything that might happen to him in graphic detail and he was adamant he wanted no treatment. They warned him of every scenario, including coughing up blood as he started to haemorrhage to death. When he started vomiting blood, he changed his mind and requested treatment. He ended up being transferred to King's [College Hospital] for a liver transplant" (Oral and Written Evidence, Ev 131).

If this patient had lost capacity at the point where he started to vomit blood, the doctors would have been bound by his advance decision (which, subsequent to the implementation of this Act, would have to comply with subss.(5),(6)) and the patient would have died. However, there must be a doubt as to whether a patient in this situation would have had the required capacity to make a valid advance decision. A high level of capacity would be required to make such a decision (*T (Adult: Refusal of Treatment), Re* [1992] 4 All E.R. 649, CA).

Subsection (2) para. (b)

It would be sensible for the advance decision to be withdrawn if a LPA of this nature is **1–196** created as there could be a danger of the healthcare professional being unaware of the LPA. Also see the note on s.11(7)(b).

Subsection (2) para. (c)

The inconsistent behaviour would indicate that P has had a change of mind. An example **1–197** of such behaviour is to be found in *HE v A Hospital NHS Trust*, noted under s.24 above, where the patient, when a Jehovah's Witness, had made an advance directive refusing blood. Subsequent to this she had become betrothed to a Muslim man upon condition that she would revert to being a Muslim, and had ceased attending Jehovah's Witness meetings. The judge held that the advance directive was founded entirely on the patient's faith and could not survive the abandonment of that faith.

Although the matter is not free from doubt, it is likely that the inconsistent behaviour of a mentally incapable patient would not qualify under this provision. This interpretation is consistent with s.24(3) which does not allow a mentally incapacitated patient to withdraw an advance decision. However, there is a counter argument. As by making a valid and applicable advance decision the patient has determined his or her own best interests (see the General Note to s.26), s.4 does not apply to such decisions. This means that the "present wishes and feelings" of an incompetent patient (see s.4(6)(a)) could not have the effect of invalidating the advance decision even if such wishes and feelings appeared to be inconsistent with the terms of the advance decision.

Subsection (4) para. (a)

As an advance decision is a refusal of a specific treatment, a suicide note written by a **1–198** capable person which does not specify a treatment that should not be given in the event of a suicide attempt that leads to mental incapacity is not an advance decision. Neither is a general statement such as: "If I become mentally incapacitated I do not wish my life to be sustained."

Subsection (4) para. (b)

The advance decision should be specific about the circumstances where it is to apply as a **1–199** generally written decision could give rise to a situation where the decision applies in unintended circumstances.

Subsection (4) para. (c)

It is anticipated that this paragraph will be frequently invoked as it is unlikely that **1–200** patients will have been able to precisely predict the circumstances that they will be in subsequent to the onset of their mental incapacity. In order to determine whether the unanticipated circumstances "would", rather than "may" have affected P's decision, the health care professional will need to step into P's shoes by effectively making a substituted judgment on behalf of P. An obvious and relevant change of circumstances could be the development of new treatments that radically change the prognosis for a particular condition. A significant change in P's family and/or personal circumstances could also be a relevant consideration.

Patients' views about the medical treatment that they would wish to receive are not fixed; they adapt to circumstances. In particular, healthy patients tend not make the same choices as sick ones as they may not fully comprehend what the future might hold for them should they become mentally incapacitated. It has been argued that patients need to experience a situation to know how they would feel about it and hence how they wish to be treated (Dr David Kingsley, Oral and written evidence, Ev 322). In *MB (Caesarean Section), Re* [1997] 2 F.L.R. 426, CA at 436 in a case concerning the mental capacity of a patient who was refusing to be anaesthetised in order to have a caesarean section, Butler-Sloss L.J. said that a "feature of some of the cases to which we have referred has been the favourable reaction of the patient who refused treatment to the subsequent medical intervention and successful outcome." A number of witnesses to the Joint Committee gave examples of patients who had made advance directives refusing life-prolonging treatment and had subsequently agreed to such treatment (see, for example, Dr Fiona Randall, Oral and written evidence, Ev 303). In her evidence to the Joint Committee, Baroness Finlay said:

> "It is a feature of people who are suddenly facing the reality that they are dying that they could not preconceive how they would feel at the time. That is also a situation that one sees in people who are very seriously ill" (Oral and written Evidence, Ev 127).

These issues should be considered by those who make advance decisions and by those who advise them. In particular, those who have made advance decisions should review them at regular intervals to ensure that they reflect their current view as evidence suggests that people may change their minds following experience of either an illness or its treatment: see J.R. Bach "Threats to 'informed' advance directives for the severely physically challenged?" (2003) 84 *Archives of Physical Medicine and Rehabilitation* 23 and L.L. Emanuel "Advance directives and advancing age" (2004) 52 *Journal of the American Geriatrics Society* 641.

Subsection (5)

1–201   This provision and subs.(6) were moved by the Government at the committee stage in the House of Lords to meet concerns that had been raised by Parliamentarians, outside bodies, and the Joint Committee on Human Rights. They are aimed at tipping "the balance of advance decisions even further in favour of preserving life", *per* the Parliamentary Under-Secretary of State (*Hansard*, HL Vol.668, col.1486).

If there is a dispute about the validity and/or applicability of an advance decision that relates to life sustaining treatment, P can be treated until the issue is determined by the court (s.26(5)). Any doubt as to the validity and/or applicability of an advance decision to refuse life-sustaining treatment should be resolved by the court in favour of preserving life (*HE v A Hospital NHS Trust*, above).

LIFE-SUSTAINING TREATMENT. The reference to "life" includes the life of an unborn child: see the note on s.4(10). A woman of child-bearing age should therefore consider whether she would want the advance decision to apply to her unborn child. If she did not wish it to apply to her unborn child, the terms of the decision should reflect this. It might be difficult to identify whether a treatment is a "life-sustaining treatment" in those cases where, for example, drugs do not have single, targeted effects. Treatments may be life-sustaining in some circumstances, and in others not. This concern has been addressed by the requirement that P must verify that the decision is to apply to the specified treatment "even if life is at risk". In other words, life-sustaining treatment is treatment that is needed to keep P alive.

With regard to artificial nutrition and hydration (ANH), "there can be no doubt that ANH constitutes life-sustaining treatment. Thus, if a person has not specified that the refusal is still to apply where ANH is necessary to sustain life then ANH (if in the person's best interests) will have to be given" (Letter from the Parliamentary-Under Secretary of State to the Chair of the Joint Committee on Human Rights, December 16, 2004, Annex, para.28).

Subsection (6)

1–202   Advance directives which relate to life-sustaining treatment and which were made under the common law prior to the implementation of this Act are invalid if they do not comply with this provision.

Given the difficulties that can arise when determining the validity and/or applicability of oral advance decisions, it is suggested that the approach set out in this provision be adopted for all advance decisions.

IN WRITING. There is no statutory form. "I want to make it clear what 'in writing' can mean. It means that an advance decision can be written by a family member or recorded in medical notes by a doctor or healthcare professional, and it can include electronic records', *per* the Parliamentary Under-Secretary of State (*Hansard*, HL Vol.668, col.1487).

IS SIGNED. The decision can be signed in P's presence and by his or her direction. This is to ensure that there is "no discrimination against people who, for whatever reason, are unable to write but have the capacity to make decisions", *ibid.*

Effect of advance decisions

26.—(1) If P has made an advance decision which is—   **1–203**

(a) valid, and

(b) applicable to a treatment,

the decision has effect as if he had made it, and had had capacity to make it, at the time when the question arises whether the treatment should be carried out or continued.

(2) A person does not incur liability for carrying out or continuing the treatment unless, at the time, he is satisfied that an advance decision exists which is valid and applicable to the treatment.

(3) A person does not incur liability for the consequences of withholding or withdrawing a treatment from P if, at the time, he reasonably believes that an advance decision exists which is valid and applicable to the treatment.

(4) The court may make a declaration as to whether an advance decision—

(a) exists;

(b) is valid;

(c) is applicable to a treatment.

(5) Nothing in an apparent advance decision stops a person—

(a) providing life-sustaining treatment, or

(b) doing any act he reasonably believes to be necessary to prevent a serious deterioration in P's condition,

while a decision as respects any relevant issue is sought from the court.

DEFINITIONS

"advance decision": s.64(1)   **1–204**

"treatment": s.64(1)

"the court": s.64(1)

"life-sustaining treatment": s.64(1)

GENERAL NOTE

If an advance decision is both valid and applicable as defined in s.25, it has the same **1–205** effect as a contemporaneous refusal of treatment by a person with capacity (subs.(1)). Subject to subs.(5), this means that the treatment specified in the decision cannot lawfully be given. If the treatment is given, the patient would be able to claim damages for the tort of battery and the person who provided the treatment could face criminal liability for assault. However, a treatment provider will be protected from legal liability unless satisfied that there is a valid and applicable advance decision (subs.(2)); and a treatment provider may safely withhold or withdraw treatment as long as he or she has reasonable grounds for believing that there is a valid and applicable advance decision (subs.(3)). The responsibility for determining whether an advance directive is both valid and applicable is that of the healthcare professional who would be responsible for providing the treatment specified in the decision.

A clinician who follows a valid and applicable advance decision is not acting "for or on behalf of a person who lacks capacity" for the purposes of s.1(5); he or she is acting on the instructions of a capacitated individual. Such a decision must therefore be complied with even if it conflicts with an objective evaluation of the patient's best interests. This is the case even if complying with the decision would lead to the patient's death. The principle of the sanctity of human life must yield to the principle of patient self-determination as long as the terms of s.25(5) and (6) are satisfied.

Any dispute about the existence, validity or applicability of an advance decision can be determined by the court (subs.(4)). However, action may be taken to prevent the death of the person concerned, or a serious deterioration to his or her condition, whilst a ruling is sought (subs.(5)).

The *Code of Practice* states at para.9.60:

"Some situations might be enough in themselves to raise concern about the existence, validity or applicability of an advance decision to refuse treatment. These could include situations when:

- a disagreement between relatives and healthcare professionals about whether verbal comments were really an advance decision
- evidence about the person's state of mind raises questions about their capacity at the time they made the decision
- evidence of important changes in the person's behaviour before they lost capacity that might suggest a change of mind.

In cases where serious doubt remains and cannot be resolved in any other way, it will be possible to seek a declaration from the court."

Subsection (2)

1–206   SATISFIED. In order to be satisfied that an advance decision is both valid and applicable, the clinician would need to make enquiries about (1) any doubts that might exist about the patient's mental capacity at the time when the purported advance decision was made; (2) the information that the patient received about the consequences of his or her decision; (3) the circumstances surrounding the making of the purported advance decision; (4) the possible effect of undue influence on the patient's decision; and (5) whether the purported advance decision is applicable to the proposed treatment and was intended to apply in the circumstances that have arisen. It is likely that few oral statements made by patients to lay people that are said to constitute advance decisions would survive such scrutiny, especially if the statements were made a considerable time ago. If the clinician has a real doubt about the existence of a valid and applicable advance decision, the treatment can be given. However, it would be advisable to ask the court to determine the issue in cases where the argument in favour of the existence of a valid and applicable advance decision is finely balanced or where there is a dispute between the clinician and the patient's family about whether such an advance decision has been made.

If the purported advance decision is invalid but it is clear that P was attempting to refuse a particular treatment, the decision should be treated as if it were an expression of the patient's wishes for the purpose of s.4(6)(a).

Subsection (3)

1–207   REASONABLY BELIEVES. This is an objective standard. The healthcare professional's belief must be supported by evidence.

Subsection (4)

1–208   The court has no power to determine that a valid and applicable advance decision is not in P's best interests.

Excluded decisions

Family relationships etc

27.—(1) Nothing in this Act permits a decision on any of the following matters **1–209** to be made on behalf of a person—

(a) consenting to marriage or a civil partnership,

(b) consenting to have sexual relations,

(c) consenting to a decree of divorce being granted on the basis of two years' separation,

(d) consenting to a dissolution order being made in relation to a civil partnership on the basis of two years' separation,

(e) consenting to a child's being placed for adoption by an adoption agency,

(f) consenting to the making of an adoption order,

(g) discharging parental responsibilities in matters not relating to a child's property,

(h) giving a consent under the Human Fertilisation and Embryology Act 1990 (c. 37).

(2) "Adoption order" means—

(a) an adoption order within the meaning of the Adoption and Children Act 2002 (c. 38) (including a future adoption order), and

(b) an order under section 84 of that Act (parental responsibility prior to adoption abroad).

GENERAL NOTE

This section lists decisions that can never be made by the Court of Protection, a deputy **1–210** appointed by the court, the donee of a LPA, or a person acting under s.5 on behalf of a person who lacks capacity.

Mental Health Act matters

28.—(1) Nothing in this Act authorises anyone— **1–211**

(a) to give a patient medical treatment for mental disorder, or

(b) to consent to a patient's being given medical treatment for mental disorder,

if, at the time when it is proposed to treat the patient, his treatment is regulated by Part 4 of the Mental Health Act.

(2) "Medical treatment", "mental disorder" and "patient" have the same meaning as in that Act.

DEFINITIONS

"Mental Health Act": s.64(1) **1–212**

GENERAL NOTE

If a mentally disordered patient who is also mentally incapacitated has been detained **1–213** under the long term provisions of the Mental Health Act 1983, the patient is subject to the regulatory regime for the treatment of his or her mental disorder which is set out in Pt IV of that Act. This section ensures that the provisions of this Act do not apply to any treatment given to a patient which is provided under the authority of Pt IV of the 1983 Act. In other words, the consent to treatment provisions contained in Pt IV will "trump" the provisions of this Act. This means that: (1) treatment for the patient's mental disorder cannot be given under the authority of this Act; (2) neither a donee of a LPA nor a deputy appointed by the court can either consent to or refuse treatment for mental disorder on the patient's behalf; and (3) an advance decision made by the patient that refuses treatment for mental disorder is not binding on the treating psychiatrist. Treatment decisions falling outside the scope of Pt IV, such as decisions about whether the patient should receive treatment for a physical disorder and treatments given to patients detained under the emergency provisions of the 1983 Act, are governed by this Act.

The 1983 Act should be invoked in respect of a mentally incapacitated patient who needs to be hospitalised for treatment for his or her mental disorder in the following circumstances if the criteria for admission under that Act can be satisfied:

1. Where the patient is subjected to a deprivation of his or her liberty (*HL v United Kingdom* (45508/99) (2005) 40 E.H.R.R. 32, ECHR). The provisions in ss.5 and 6 of this Act cannot be used to deprive a patient of his or her liberty (see s.6(5)). The Department of Health has issued *"Advice on the decision of the European Court of Human Rights in the case of HL v UK (the 'Bournewood' case)"* (December 10, 2004).
2. Where it is considered that the provisions of a valid and applicable advance decision refusing a particular treatment for the patient's mental disorder should be overridden in the patient's best interests.

In *HL v UK*, the patient, who was mentally incapacitated, alleged that he had been detained at the hospital as an informal patient in violation of Art.5(1) of the European Convention on Human Rights, and that the procedures available to him for a review of the legality of his detention did not satisfy the requirements of Art.5(4) which provides a person who has been deprived of his or her liberty with a right to a speedy independent legal review of the detention. The decision of the ECHR focussed on the finding of the House of Lords ([1998] 3 All E.R. 289) that the detention of a compliant mentally incapacitated patient could be justified under the doctrine of necessity. The ECHR held that:

1. In order to determine whether a person has been deprived of his or her liberty for the purposes of Art.5(1), the starting point must be the specific situation of the individual concerned and account must be taken of a whole range of factors arising in a particular case such as the type, duration, effects and manner of implementation of the measure in question. The distinction between a deprivation of, and a restriction upon, liberty is merely one of degree or intensity and not one of nature or substance (para.89).
2. The correspondence between HL's carers and his psychiatrist reflected boththe carer's wish to have HL immediately released to their care and, equally, the clear intention of the health care professionals to exercise strict control over his assessment, treatment, contacts and, notably, movement and residence: HL would only be released from the hospital to the care of his carers as and when the professionals considered it appropriate. It followed that HL was being deprived of his liberty because he "was under continuous supervision and control and was not free to leave" (para.91). The fact that HL might have been on award whichwas not "-locked" or "lockable" was not determinative (para.92). With regard to HL's compliance to his admission, the Court observed that "the right to liberty is too important in a democratic society for a person to lose the benefit of Convention protection for the single reason that he may have given himself up to be taken into detention, especially when it is not disputed that that person is legally incapable of consenting to, or disagreeing with, the proposed action" (para.90).
3. The ECHR found "striking the lack of any fixed procedural rules by which the admission and detention of compliant incapacitated patients is conducted" when contrasted with "the extensive network of safeguards applicable to psychiatric committals covered by the 1983 Act" (para.120). This absence of procedural safeguards in the doctrine of necessity failed to protect HL against arbitrary deprivations of his liberty. His detention therefore violated Art.5(1).
4. There had also been aviolation of Art.5(4) of the Convention as HL did not have the opportunity to have the lawfulness of his detention reviewed by a court as neither

judicial review nor other judicial remedies cited by the Government satisfied the requirements of Art.5(4) (para.141).

In *JE and DE v Surrey County Council* [2006] EWHC 3459 (Fam), para.77, Munby J. accepted counsel's (Mr Paul Bowen) approach to the identification of whether a person is "deprived of his liberty". Mr Bowen submitted that there are the following elements are relevant to the question of whether in the case of an adult there has been a "deprivation" of liberty engaging the State's obligations under Art.5(1):

(i)   an *objective* element of a person's confinement in a particular restricted space for a not negligible length of time. The key factor in a case where a relative wishes to take over the care of the person is whether the person is, or is not free to leave the place where he or she is being cared for. This may be tested by determining whether those treating and managing the person exercise complete and effective control over the person's care and movement (*HL v United Kingdom,* above, para.91);

(ii) a *subjective* element, namely that the person has not validly consented to the confinement in question. Where a person lacks the capacity to give a valid consent to their confinement, consent cannot be inferred from the fact that the person does not object (*ibid.,* para.90);

(iii) the deprivation of liberty must be imputable to the State (*Storck v Germany* (2006) 43 E.H.R.R. 6, para.89).

Judgments of the ECHR are binding on those who provide care and treatment for mentally incapacitated persons in institutional settings as s.6 of the Human Rights Act 1998 (c.42) requires public authorities to act in a way which is compatible with a Convention right, unless they are prevented from doing so by primary legislation. A Mental Health Act assessment should therefore be made in respect of a mentally incapacitated patient who is being deprived of his or her liberty as the absence of a "section" will result in a violation of that person's rights under Art.5. As the decision of the ECHR also applies to mentally incapacitated persons who are being deprived of their liberty in care homes, an application to authorise the deprivation should be made to the Court of Protection.

In *Guzzardi v Italy* (1980) 3 E.H.R.R. 33 the Court observed at para.93:

"The difference between deprivation of and restriction upon liberty is . . . merely one of degree or intensity, and not one of nature or substance. Although the process of classification into one or other of these categories sometimes proves to be no easy task in that in some borderline cases are a matter of pure opinion, the Court cannot avoid making the selection upon which the applicability of Art.5 depends."

This passage was cited by Collins J. in *R (on the application of G) v Mental Health Review Tribunal* [2004] EWHC 2193 (Admin), para.20, as authority for the proposition "that there will be borderline cases when a decision either way cannot be said to be wrong in law. The court must be careful not to interfere unless persuaded that the decision is wrong in law". His Lordship said that it is important to bear in mind that the purpose of any measure of restriction, while a relevant consideration, must not be given too much weight. This consideration was identified by Keene L.J in *Secretary of State for the Home Department v Mental Health Review Tribunal and PH* [2002] EWCA Civ 1868; [2003] M.H.L.R. 2002, where his lordship identified the following principles which are applicable to the interpretation of Art.5(1):

1. A basic distinction is to be drawn between mere restrictions on liberty of movement and the deprivation of liberty.
2. The distinction is one merely of degree or intensity of restrictions, not of nature and substance.
3. The court must start with the concrete or actual situation of the individual concerned and take account of a range of criteria, such as type, duration, effects and manner of implementation of the measure in question.
4. Account must be taken of the cumulative effect of the various restrictions.

5. The purpose of any measures of restriction is a relevant consideration.
6. If the measures are taken principally in the interests of the individual who is being restricted, they may well be regarded as not amounting to a deprivation of liberty. (NB: In *JE and DE v Surrey County Council*, above, para.70, Munby J., having reviewed recent Strasbourg caselaw, said that this proposition must be approached with an "appropriate degree of caution" because it receives "absolutely no support" from the subsequent decisions of the Court in *HL v United Kingdom* and *Storck v Germany*.)

Guzzardi was also cited in *Secretary of State for the Home Department v JJ* [2006] EWCA 1141, para.6, where it was common ground between the parties that the concept of "deprivation of liberty" is autonomous and in *R. (on the application of Gillan) v Metropolitan Police Commissioner* [2006] UKHL 12; [2006] 4 All E.R. 1041, where Lord Bingham said, at para.23, that the Strasbourg jurisprudence on what constitutes a deprivation of liberty "is closely focused on the facts of particular cases, and this makes it perilous to transpose the outcome of one case to another where the facts are different". In *Gillan,* it was held that a person who was detained for a short period by the police pursuant to a "stop and search" power was not deprived of his liberty for the purposes of Art.5.

Bearing in mind that there is no definitive legal test for what will amount to a deprivation of liberty, relevant European and domestic caselaw suggests that it is unlikely that a court would find that a mentally incapacitated patient who has been taken to hospital or a care home has been being deprived of his or her liberty for the purposes of Art.5(1) in the absence of one or more of the following factors:

1. Force or sedation being used to take a resisting patient to the hospital or care home.
2. The decision to admit the patient to the hospital or care home being opposed by relatives or carers who live with the patient.
3. Force being used to prevent the patient from leaving the hospital or care home in a situation where the patient is making a persistent and/or purposeful attempt to leave.
4. More than benign force being used in a non-emergency situation to ensure that a resisting patient receives necessary medical treatment.
5. The hospital or care home denying a request by relatives or carers for the patient to be discharged to their care. Given the judgment in *JE and DE v Surrey County Council*, above, the presence of this factor alone would suggest that the person is being deprived of his or her liberty. This would be the case even if the authorities had concerns about the quality of care that the patient would receive on being discharged.
6. A decision by the hospital or care home to deny or severely restrict access to the patient by relatives or carers.
7. The patient being denied freedom of association within the hospital or care home, or otherwise being subject to a care regime which severely restricts his or her autonomy.
8. The patient's access to the community being denied or severely restricted primarily due to concerns about public safety.

It is suggested that the following circumstances would not, by themselves, constitute a deprivation of liberty:

1. Benign force being used to take a confused patient to the hospital or care home.
2. The patient being treated or cared for in a locked environment.
3. The design of door handles or the use of key pads making it difficult for a confused patient to leave the hospital or care home.
4. Staff bringing the patient who has wandered back to the hospital or care home.
5. The use of benign force to feed, dress or provide medical treatment for the patient.
6. The use of restraint, medication or seclusion in an emergency situation in order to respond to the patient's disturbed, threatening or self-harming behaviour.

7. Dissuading a confused patient from attempting to leave the hospital or care home, using benign force if necessary. This would be the case even if the confused patient had attempted to leave the premises on more than one occasion.
8. Placing reasonable limitations on the visiting of the patient by relatives or carers.
9. A refusal to let the patient leave the hospital or care home in the absence of an escort whose role would be to support the patient rather than to protect the public.

The *Code of Practice* states at para.6.52:

"It is difficult to define the difference between actions that amount to a restriction of someone's liberty and those that result in a deprivation of liberty. In recent legal cases, the European Court of Human Rights said that the difference was 'one of degree or intensity, not one of nature or substance'. There must therefore be particular factors in the specific situation of the person concerned which provide the 'degree' or 'intensity' to result in a deprivation of liberty. In practice, this can relate to:

- the type of care being provided
- how long the situation lasts
- its effects, or
- the way in which a particular situation came about.

The European Court of Human Rights has identified the following as factors contributing to deprivation of liberty in its judgments on cases to date:

- restraint was used, including sedation, to admit a person who is resisting
- professionals exercised complete and effective control over care and movement for a significant period
- professionals exercised control over assessments, treatment, contacts and residence
- the person would be prevented from leaving if they made a meaningful attempt to do so
- a request by carers for the person to be discharged to their care was refused
- the person was unable to maintain social contacts because of restrictions placed on access to other people
- the person lost autonomy because they were under continuous supervision and control."

Phil Fennell argues that "if the person lacks capacity and the decision-maker is assuming complete control over treatment to the extent that they are making decisions about the administration of strong psychotropic medication or even ECT to a patient, then that is assuming complete control over treatment and would be a factor tipping the balance firmly towards there being a deprivation of liberty requiring the use of the Mental Health Act 1983 or at the very least use of the protective care provisions such as those proposed to fill the *Bournewood* Gap" ("The Mental Capacity Act 2005, the Mental Health Act, and the Common Law" (Nov 2005) *Journal of Mental Health Law* 167). As the provision of any medical treatment to an incapacitated patient involves a clinician assuming complete control over that patient's treatment, it is submitted that the provision of the treatments mentioned by Fennell in the absence of other factors confirming that "professionals treating and managing [the patient] exercised complete and effective control over his movements" (*Bournewood*, para.91) would not lead to a finding that there has been a deprivation of liberty. The caselaw of the European Court of Human Rights does not support the contention that a finding of a deprivation of liberty can be made solely on the basis that a particular treatment is being proposed for the patient: a "whole range of factors arising in a particular case" must be taken into account (*Bournewood*, para.89). In Peter Bartlett's opinion, "it would appear that electro-convulsive therapy can be given to an informal patient lacking capacity in his or her best interests, provided that the procedures in the [Mental Capacity Act 2005] are followed" (*Blackstone's Guide to the Mental Capacity Act 2005* (Oxford University Press, 2005) para.3.43).

The Royal College of Psychiatrists and Professor G. Richardson gave evidence to the Joint Committee expressing their concern that this provision, as it appeared in the draft Bill, could be interpreted to the effect that this Act "would not apply in any case in which treatment regulated under Pt IV may be required, i.e. when the Mental Health Act could potentially be applied". The Committee noted that the "effect of this would be to require the compulsory detention under the Mental Health Act of any person lacking capacity to consent to treatment for mental disorder, regardless of the circumstances" (para.218). As it is difficult to see how this provision could give rise to such an interpretation, the concern can be disregarded. This is also the view of the Government: see *"The Government Response to the Scrutiny Committee's Report on the draft Mental Incapacity Bill"* (Cm.6121).

Subsection (2)
1–214   Under s.145(1) of the 1983 Act, "medical treatment" is defined as including "nursing, and also includes care, habilitation and rehabilitation under medical supervision", and "patient" is defined as "a person suffering or appearing to be suffering from mental disorder". "Mental disorder" is defined in s.1 of that Act as meaning "mental illness, arrested or incomplete development of mind, psychopathic disorder and any other disorder or disability of mind".

Voting rights
1–215   **29.**—(1) Nothing in this Act permits a decision on voting at an election for any public office, or at a referendum, to be made on behalf of a person.

(2) "Referendum" has the same meaning as in section 101 of the Political Parties, Elections and Referendums Act 2000 (c. 41).

GENERAL NOTE
1–216   This section excludes decisions on voting at an election for public office, or at a referendum, from the remit of this Act.

Research

Research
1–217   **30.**—(1) Intrusive research carried out on, or in relation to, a person who lacks capacity to consent to it is unlawful unless it is carried out—
   (a) as part of a research project which is for the time being approved by the appropriate body for the purposes of this Act in accordance with section 31, and
   (b) in accordance with sections 32 and 33.
   (2) Research is intrusive if it is of a kind that would be unlawful if it was carried out—
   (a) on or in relation to a person who had capacity to consent to it, but
   (b) without his consent.
   (3) A clinical trial which is subject to the provisions of clinical trials regulations is not to be treated as research for the purposes of this section.
   (4) "Appropriate body", in relation to a research project, means the person, committee or other body specified in regulations made by the appropriate authority as the appropriate body in relation to a project of the kind in question.
   (5) "Clinical trials regulations" means—
   (a) the Medicines for Human Use (Clinical Trials) Regulations 2004 (S.I. 2004/1031) and any other regulations replacing those regulations or amending them, and

(b) any other regulations relating to clinical trials and designated by the Secretary of State as clinical trials regulations for the purposes of this section.

(6) In this section, section 32 and section 34, "appropriate authority" means—

(a) in relation to the carrying out of research in England, the Secretary of State, and

(b) in relation to the carrying out of research in Wales, the National Assembly for Wales.

GENERAL NOTE

The Draft Mental Incapacity Bill made no provision to enable incapacitated adults to take part in medical research.While recognising that "this is an ethically difficult area", the Joint Committee concluded that a clause should be included in the Bill "to enable strictly-controlled medical research to explore the causes and consequences of mental incapacity and to develop effective treatment for such conditions. This clause must include rigorous protocols to protect incapacitated adults from being exploited or harmed" (para.288). In its response to the Joint Committee's report (Cm.6121), the Government accepted that the Bill "should include provision for strictly-controlled research to fill the gap that exists in the current law and the uncertainty and inequality this creates." The provisions attempt to "balance the importance of properly conducted research into the treatment and care of people who lack capacity with the need to protect their interests and respect their current and previously expressed wishes and feelings", *per* Lord Hunt of Kings Heath, *Hansard*, HL Vol.689, col.GC107). **1–218**

The Joint Committee also recommended, at para.289, that the Bill "should set out the key principles governing research, such as those enshrined by the World Medical Association [in the Helsinki Declaration]. Those key principles should include the following:

- research involving people who may be incapacitated must be reviewed by a properly established and independent ethics committee and can only proceed if ethical permission is granted.
- where a person hasthe capacity to consent then his decisionwhether or not to partake in research must be respected.
- considerable care should be taken to ensure that under these circumstances consent to participate was freely given and not a consequence of coercion.
- the inclusion of people in research, who lacked the capacity to consent, must only occur when such research has the potential for direct benefit to those with that particular problem and could not have been done through the involvement of those with capacity.
- those undertaking research involving people lacking the capacity to consent must respect any indications that a person did not wish to participate (i.e. was dissenting). any discomfort or risk involved in the research must be, at the most, minimal."

The Government agreed that "key principles are important" and stated that it would "explore the extent to which these need be in statute, or whether they are already covered by existing Good Practice Guidance". Those carrying out research under this Act are required to act in accordance with the principles set out in s.1 and to have regard to the guidance contained in the *Code of Practice* (s.42(4)(c)). The Government has published a *Research Governance Framework for Health and Social Care* (Department of Health, 2nd ed., 2005) which outlines principles of good governance that applies to all research within the remit of the Secretary of State for Health.

This section, together with ss.31 to 34, make provision for "intrusive" research to be lawfully carried out on, or in relation to a person who lacks the capacity to consent to it, where the research is part of a research project which has been approved by the "appropriate body", as defined in subs.(4), and is carried out in accordance with the conditions set out in ss.32 and 33 (subs.(1)). Intrusive research is research that would require consent if it involved a person with capacity (subs.(2)). Intrusive research undertaken on people who lack capacity which does not satisfy the requirements of this Act is unlawful. In addition to the obligations placed on them by this Act, researchers must also comply with their wider legal obligations such as their duties under the data protection and health and safety legislation.

If a person with capacity has consented to his involvement in research, the fact that he subsequently loses capacity does not mean that he has to be withdrawn from the research, in so far as it relates to the matter that he has consented to, because the fact that he given his consent means that the research is not intrusive (see subs.(2)). Baroness Andrews said: "The Bill does not apply to research during temporary incapacity, such as general anaesthesia during surgery, providing that consent was obtained in advance. Consent endures the temporary loss of capacity" (*Hansard*, HL Vol.670, col.1521). However, if the research is a continuing project rather than a one-off event, any further research would be research undertaken without consent and would therefore be intrusive research that would trigger the procedures set out in ss.31–33. For example, if the person consents to a sample of blood being taken as part of a research project, the sample can be taken even if the person loses capacity before that point. The taking of any further samples would constitute intrusive research because of the absence of the person's consent. Transitional provisions are contained in s.34.

Clinical trials that are regulated by the clinical trials regulations, which are concerned with the conduct of clinical trials of medicines for human use, are excluded (subss.(3) and (5)) because the regulations already make provision for trials involving participants who lack capacity. The 2004 Regulations (as amended by SI 2005/2754, SI 2005/2759 and SI 2006/1928) were amended by the Medicines for Human Use (Clinical Trials) Amendment (No.2) Regulations 2006 (SI 2006/2984) which are aimed at making the regulations consistent with this Act in so far as they relate to emergency research conducted on mentally incapacitated patients. Paragraph 11.7 of the *Code of Practice* states:

"There are circumstances where no consent is needed to lawfully involve a person in research. These apply to all persons, whether they have capacity or not:

- Sometimes research only involves data that has been anonymised (it cannot be traced back to individuals). Confidentiality and data protection laws do not apply in this case.
- Under the Human Tissue Act 2004, research that deals only with human tissue that has been anonymised does not require consent . . . This applies to both those who have capacity and those who do not. But the research must have ethical approval, and the tissue must come from a living person.
- If researchers collected human tissue samples before 31 August 2006, they do not need a person's consent to work on them. But they will normally have to get ethical approval.
- Regulations made under section 251 of the NHS Act 2006 (formerly known as section 60 of the Health and Social Care Act 2001) allow people to use confidential patient information without breaking the law on confidentiality by applying to the Patient Information Advisory Group for approval on behalf of the Secretary of State."

The ethical and legal issues arising from medical research on mentally incompetent adults are considered by M.J. Gunn, J.G Wong, I.C.H. Clare and A.J. Holland in "Medical Research and Incompetent Adults" (2000) *Journal of Mental Health Law* 60. For the application of these Regulations to emergency medicine, see T.J. Coats, "Consent for emergency care research: the Mental Capacity Act 2005" (2006) 23 *Emergency Medical Journal* 893.

Research that began before October 1, 2007

Sections 30 to 34 come into force in England on October 1, 2008 in respect of any **1–219** research which (a) began before October 1, 2007; and (b) was approved before October 1, 2007 by a committee established to advise on, or on matters which include, the ethics of research in relation to people who lack capacity to consent to it (Mental Capacity Act 2005 (Commencement No.1) Order 2006 (SI 2006/2814), reg.4 (as amended by SI 2006/3473, art.2)).

The Human Tissue Act 2004

The Human Tissue Act 2004 sets up a framework to regulate the storage and use of **1–220** human organs and tissues from the living and the removal, storage and use of tissues and organs from the deceased, for specified health related purposes and public display. The Act establishes a regulatory authority, the Human Tissue Authority, to regulate these activities and transplantation. Although consent is a fundamental principle underpinning the operation of the Act, the Human Tissue Act 2004 (Persons who lack Capacity to Consent and Transplants) Regulations 2006 (SI 2006/1659) make provision as to the circumstances in which activities may be carried out in relation to material from the body of a person who lacks capacity to consent for the purposes of certain provisions of the Act, including DNA analysis. The regulations were drafted "to ensure that, given the Human Tissue Act 2004 will be brought into force before the Mental Capacity Act 2005, legitimate activities will not fall foul of one Act pending implementation of the other" (Explanatory Memorandum on SI 2006/1659, para.7.2).

Subsection (4)

By virtue of reg.2 of the Mental Capacity Act 2005 (Appropriate Body) (England) **1–221** Regulations 2006 (SI 2006/2810), the appropriate body in England for the purpose this section, s.31 and s.33 is a research ethics committee, i.e. "a committee—

(a) established to advise on, or on matters which include, the ethics of intrusive research in relation to people who lack capacity to consent to it; and
(b) recognised by that purpose by the Secretary of State".

SI 2006/2810 came into force on July 1, 2007 for the purposes of enabling applications for ethical approval of research to be made and determined under this Act, and on October 1, 2007 for all other purposes (*ibid.,* art.1, as amended by SI 2006/3474, art.2). A similar definition of appropriate body is made for Wales, with the same commencement dates, by the Mental Capacity Act 2005 (Appropriate Body) (Wales) Regulations 2007 (SI 2007/833 (W.71)) with the exception that the committee has to be recognised by the National Assembly for Wales (now the Welsh Ministers, see below).

The background to research ethics committees is set out in para.7.5 of the Explanatory Memorandum to the Mental Capacity Act 2005 (Appropriate Body) (England) Regulations 2006:

"NHS research ethics committees were established in England in 1991 following the publication of Department of Health guidance HSG (91)5. The appointing authorities for NHS research ethics committees are the Strategic Health Authorities in England. NHS research ethics committees are independent of the researcher and the organisation funding and hosting research. Training and accreditation for NHS committees is provided by the Central Office of Research Ethics Committees (COREC) to ensure national consistency. Before it can proceed, all research involving NHS patients requires approval from an NHS research ethics committee. Research governance is a core standard for health care and health care organisations have to take this standard into account in discharging their duty of quality under section 45 of the Health and Social Care (Community Health and Standards) Act 2003."

Subsection (5)

1–222   The 2004 Regulations, which came into force on May 1, 2004, implement European Clinical Trials Directive 2001/20/EC on "the approximation of the laws, regulations and administrative provisions of the Member States relating to the implementation of good clinical practice in the conduct of clinical trials on medicinal products for human use". The Regulations define "clinical trials" as meaning:

"any investigation in human subjects, other than a non-interventional trial, intended—

(a) to discover or verify the clinical, pharmacological or other pharmacodynamic effects of one or more medicinal products,
(b) to identify any adverse reactions to one or more such products, or
(c) to study absorption, distribution, metabolism and excretion of one or more such products

with the object of ascertaining the safety or efficacy of those products" (reg.2(1)).

Part 5 of Sch.1 to the regulations contains conditions and principles which apply to incapacitated adults.

Subsection (6) para.(b)

1–223   The functions of the National Assembly for Wales are performed by the Welsh Ministers (Government of Wales Act 2006, s.162, Sch.11, para.30).

Requirements for approval

1–224   **31.**—(1) The appropriate body may not approve a research project for the purposes of this Act unless satisfied that the following requirements will be met in relation to research carried out as part of the project on, or in relation to, a person who lacks capacity to consent to taking part in the project (P).

(2) The research must be connected with—

(a) an impairing condition affecting P, or
(b) its treatment.

(3) "Impairing condition" means a condition which is (or may be) attributable to, or which causes or contributes to (or may cause or contribute to), the impairment of, or disturbance in the functioning of, the mind or brain.

(4) There must be reasonable grounds for believing that research of comparable effectiveness cannot be carried out if the project has to be confined to, or relate only to, persons who have capacity to consent to taking part in it.

(5) The research must—

(a) have the potential to benefit P without imposing on P a burden that is disproportionate to the potential benefit to P, or
(b) be intended to provide knowledge of the causes or treatment of, or of the care of persons affected by, the same or a similar condition.

(6) If the research falls within paragraph (b) of subsection (5) but not within paragraph (a), there must be reasonable grounds for believing—

(a) that the risk to P from taking part in the project is likely to be negligible, and
(b) that anything done to, or in relation to, P will not—
(i) interfere with P's freedom of action or privacy in a significant way, or
(ii) be unduly invasive or restrictive.

(7) There must be reasonable arrangements in place for ensuring that the requirements of sections 32 and 33 will be met.

DEFINITIONS

1–225   "appropriate body": s.30(4)

GENERAL NOTE

This section sets out the requirements that must be satisfied before the Secretary of State **1–226** and the Welsh Ministers can approve a research project involving people who lack capacity. It does not preclude either observational or epidemiological research being undertaken. The research does not have to be undertaken in healthcare settings. Paragraph 11.2 of the *Code of Practice* states:

"The Act does not have a specific definition for 'research'. The Department of Health and National Assembly for Wales publications *Research governance framework for health and social care* both state:

'research can be defined as the attempt to derive generalisable new knowledge by addressing clearly defined questions with systematic and rigorous methods'.

Research may:

- provide information that can be applied generally to an illness, disorder or condition
- demonstrate how effective and safe a new treatment is
- add to evidence that one form of treatment works better than another
- add to evidence that one form of treatment is safer than another, or
- examine wider issues (for example, the factors that affect someone's capacity to make a decision)."

Research that can be undertaken under this provision includes "research on a person—involving direct contact with that person" and "research in relation to a person—indirect research on tissues, materials, data or information otherwise collected from the person" (Explanatory Memorandum to the Mental Capacity Act 2005 (Appropriate Body) (England) Regulations 2006, para.2).

There is a clear tension between the nature of some research contemplated by this section and the best interests principle established in s.1(5). This tension is illustrated by subss.(5) and (6) which contemplate research being undertaken which would be inconsistent with s.1(5). The Parliamentary Under-Secretary of State said that "the research procedures provide an alternative to a best interests determination" (*Hansard*, HL Vol.669, col.135). The Minister of State described the application of the best interests principle to research as being "difficult" (St. Comm. A, col.278), and that the principle is "interpreted slightly differently" when applied to research (*Hansard*, HC Vol.428, col.1604). At the third reading of the Bill, she said:

"[I]t is always difficult to prove that [research] can be in someone's best interests. We can only say that it is of potential benefit to that person, or might benefit him or her in the longer term, or might benefit him or her indirectly once more research has been done, or might benefit others with the same condition now or in the future" (*Hansard*, HC Vol.428, col.1603).

The Parliamentary Under-Secretary of State said:

"The purpose of [sections] 30 to 33 is to make provision for acts in connection with research that cannot necessarily be shown precisely to coincide with the person's best interests. It may be that the research procedure involves different or additional approaches to a person's care, which might not meet a narrow assessment of best interest" (*Hansard*, HL Vol.669, col.135).

Although the provisions of this Act relating to research are partly based on the Council of Europe Convention on Human Rights and Biomedicine (ETS No.164) (the Oviedo Convention), the UK Government has not ratified the Convention. The Convention was supplemented by an Additional Protocol concerning Biomedical Research, which was opened for signature by the signatories to the Convention on January 25, 2005. The Oviedo Convention and the Additional Protocol are reproduced in the first edition of this Manual.

The Joint Committee on Human Rights concluded that the "nature of the benefit from the research required in [subs.(5)] has the effect of lowering the threshold of when research will be permissible compared with the standards contained in the Convention" (23rd Report, para.2.60). The Government responded to this comment as follows:

"We have taken careful note of the Oviedo Convention, but are conscious that it does not appear to extend across the breadth of research activities that we wish to cover. For example, Arts.15–17 of the Oviedo Convention are concerned with research 'on a person', which is further clarified in the Explanatory memorandum as 'research on human beings' and in the Additional Protocol which refers to 'research activities in the health field involving interventions on human beings'. We wished to cover wider aspects of research that would not normally require consent from a person with incapacity, including research into medical records, or observation of P in a social care setting. We hope that this helps to explain why, in some cases, we have departed from the language used in the Oviedo Convention" ("Memorandum submitted to the Joint Committee on Human Rights in response to their letter of 18 November 2004 as published in their 23rd Report", paras 59 and 60).

Subsection (1)

1–227   APPROPRIATE BODY. See s.30(4).

Subsections (2) and (3)

1–228   These provisions identify the scope of the research that can be undertaken. Baroness Andrews explained:

"The emphasis is now more clearly on the requirement that the research must be connected to an impairing condition that the person has. It concedes that the relationship between the impairing condition and the impairment of, or disturbance in, the functioning of the mind or brain is sometimes not perfectly understood. It makes it clearer that it may be valid to conduct properly designed research to see whether the condition and the impairment or the disturbance are linked.

The amendment makes it clear that research, for example, to prevent kidney failure in a person in a coma following a car accident or heart attack would be permissible if the other safeguards are met. The impairing condition would be the trauma or shock following the sudden crash or heart attack. The research ethics committee would have to be satisfied that there was a good case for believing that the research into kidney failure was connected to the impairing condition, or its treatment" (*Hansard*, HL Vol.670, col.1500).

IMPAIRMENT OF, OR DISTURBANCE IN THE FUNCTIONING OF THE MIND OR BRAIN. See the note to s.2(1).

Subsection (4)

1–229   This provision was subject to a Government amendment to bring it closer to the wording of Art.17.1 iii of the Oviedo Convention which states that "research of comparable effectiveness cannot be carried out on individuals capable of giving consent".

Subsection (5) para. (a)

1–230   POTENTIAL TO BENEFIT P. If something is done which is intended to be of direct benefit to P, it would constitute treatment rather than research.

BURDEN THAT IS DISPROPORTIONATE. "By 'burden' we mean the risk or inconvenience of a trial. For example, researchers might submit a proposal to use an MRI scanner to understand the brain structures of people with dementia or schizophrenia. It might be of potential benefit to their treatment. But if the use of an MRI scanner required long confinement—we know that people with mental capacity or those suffering from cancer or claustrophobia can be very vulnerable to extreme worry in these situations—or perhaps regular and frequent scans, an ethics committee might decide that the research would simply not bring enough benefit to justify the extra scans or trauma that might be involved", *per* Baroness Andrews, (*Hansard*, HL Vol.669, col.154).

Subsection (5) para. (b)

The Explanatory Notes state, at para.98, that this category or research "might include **1–231** indirect research on medical notes, or on tissue already taken for other purposes. It may also include interviews or questionnaires with carers about health or social-care services received by the person or limited observation of the person. And it could include taking samples from the person, e.g. blood samples, specifiacally for the research project". It would also include research into how the incapacity, and the medical and other complications that are associated with it, might impact upon the care regime for the mentally incapacitated. Note that s.33(3) states that the "interests of the person must be assumed to outweigh those of science and society".

TREATMENT. This provision allows for research into diagnostic procedures (s.64(1)).

Subsection (6)

Paragraphs 11.18 and 11.19 of the *Code of Practice* state: **1–233**

"Any risk to people involved in this category of research must be 'negligible' (minimal). This means that a person should suffer no harm or distress by taking part. Researchers must consider risks to psychological wellbeing as well as physical wellbeing. This is particularly relevant for research related to observations or interviews.

Research in this category also must not affect a person's freedom of action or privacy in a significant way, and it should not be unduly invasive or restrictive. What will be considered as unduly invasive will be different for different people and different types of research. For example, in psychological research some people may think a specific question is intrusive, but others would not. Actions will not usually be classed as unduly invasive if they do not go beyond the experience of daily life, a routine medical examination or a psychological examination".

Consulting carers etc

32.—(1) This section applies if a person (R)— **1–234**
(a) is conducting an approved research project, and
(b) wishes to carry out research, as part of the project, on or in relation to a person (P) who lacks capacity to consent to taking part in the project.
(2) R must take reasonable steps to identify a person who—
(a) otherwise than in a professional capacity or for remuneration, is engaged in caring for P or is interested in P's welfare, and
(b) is prepared to be consulted by R under this section.
(3) If R is unable to identify such a person he must, in accordance with guidance issued by the appropriate authority, nominate a person who—
(a) is prepared to be consulted by R under this section, but
(b) has no connection with the project.
(4) R must provide the person identified under subsection (2), or nominated under subsection (3), with information about the proj ect and ask him—
(a) for advice as to whether P should take part in the project, and
(b) what, in his opinion, P's wishes and feelings about taking part in the project would be likely to be if P had capacity in relation to the matter.

(5) If, at any time, the person consulted advises R that in his opinion P's wishes and feelings would be likely to lead him to decline to take part in the project (or to wish to withdraw from it) if he had capacity in relation to the matter, R must ensure—

(a) if P is not already taking part in the project, that he does not take part in it;

(b) if P is taking part in the project, that he is withdrawn from it.

(6) But subsection (5)(b) does not require treatment that P has been receiving as part of the project to be discontinued if R has reasonable grounds for believing that there would be a significant risk to P's health if it were discontinued.

(7) The fact that a person is the donee of a lasting power of attorney given by P, or is P's deputy, does not prevent him from being the person consulted under this section.

(8) Subsection (9) applies if treatment is being, or is about to be, provided for P as a matter of urgency and R considers that, having regard to the nature of the research and of the particular circumstances of the case—

(a) it is also necessary to take action for the purposes of the research as a matter of urgency, but

(b) it is not reasonably practicable to consult under the previous provisions of this section.

(9) R may take the action if—

(a) he has the agreement of a registered medical practitioner who is not involved in the organisation or conduct of the research project, or

(b) where it is not reasonably practicable in the time available to obtain that agreement, he acts in accordance with a procedure approved by the appropriate body at the time when the research project was approved under section 31.

(10) But R may not continue to act in reliance on subsection (9) if he has reasonable grounds for believing that it is no longer necessary to take the action as a matter of urgency.

DEFINITIONS

1–235 "appropriate authority": s.30(6)
"lasting power of attorney": s.64(1)
"deputy": s.64(1)
"appropriate body": s.30(4)

GENERAL NOTE

1–236 This section provides that before any decision is taken to involve P in approved research, the researcher (R) must take reasonable steps to identify either an unpaid carer or a person who is interested in P's welfare in a non-professional capacity who is prepared to be consulted about P's involvement in the research (subss.(1), (2)). This person could be a deputy or a donee of a lasting power of attorney as long as that person is not acting in a paid or professional capacity (subs.(7)). If there is no such person, R must nominate (in accordance with guidance issued by the appropriate authority) a person who is willing to be consulted, but has no connection with the project (subs.(3)). The role of the consultee is to provide information to R; he or she does not provide consent for the research to proceed.

Subsection (4) identifies the purpose of the consultation. If the consultee advises R that, in his or her opinion, P would have been likely to decline to take part if he or she had capacity, P cannot be involved in the research, or if it is already underway P must be withdrawn from it (subs.(5)). However, if P has been receiving treatment as part of the research it should not be withdrawn if to do so would place P's health at significant risk (subs.(6)).

Subsections (8) and (9) allow for cases where P is being, or is about to be, provided with urgent treatment, research into that treatment must also be undertaken as a matter of urgency, and it is not reasonable practicable for R to consult. R may proceed to involve P in the research if he has the agreement of a doctor who is not concerned in the organisation or conduct of the research project, or, if there is no time to do this, he follows an approved procedure. R cannot continue to use these provisions if there is no longer an urgent need to act (subs.(10)). The Explanatory Notes, at para.104, state that examples of this type of research "may involve action by a paramedic or doctor to make measurements in the first few minutes following a serious head injury or stroke".

Subsection (2)
A PERSON. Such as a family member, advocate or friend.   **1–237**

ENGAGED IN CARING FOR. See the note on "anyone engaged in caring for the person" in s.4(7)(b).

Subsection (3)
APPROPRIATE AUTHORITY. See s.30(6).   **1–238**

CONNECTION WITH THE PROJECT. This phrase "would certainly include someone involved with, or connected to, either the study itself or a member of the research team. It would also cover wider connections, such as someone with a direct link to funding decisions for the study, for example, or who was involved with the research ethics committee" *per* Baroness Andrews (*Hansard*, HL Vol.670, col.1515).

Subsection (4)
Paragraph (b) requires R to ask the consultee to exercise a substituted judgment on behalf **1–239** of P. This will be an almost impossible task to perform if the consultee has had no previous contact with P. Professor Coats argues that in this situation the consultee "will simply reason that most people wish to improve medical treatment and for most trials, most of the patients approached agree to participate in research projects. Therefore, the incapacitated patient would probably agree to be included in the trial. Without any prior knowledge of the patient the 'consultee' will therefore always agree to patient entry. . ." (T.J. Coats, "Consent for emergency care research: the Mental Capacity Act 2005" (2006) 23 *Emergency Medical Journal* 893).

Subsection (5)
If P is withdrawn part way through the project, this provision does not provide that in- **1–240** formation collected with respect to P up to that point must be disregarded for the purposes of the project.

Subsection (7)
DEPUTY. "[W]e will amend the *Code of Practice* to make it clear that if a deputy has no **1–241** relationship to, or knowledge of, P before their appointment, they should not be consulted on the question of P's participation in research", *per* the Minister of State (*Hansard*, HC Vol.428, col.1605).

Subsection (9)
MAY TAKE THE ACTION. i.e. involve P in the research.   **1–242**

REGISTERED MEDICAL PRACTITIONER. The doctor to be consulted may be involved in the treatment of P. Baroness Andrews said:

"We want provide that a doctor who can be consulted may well be a consultant surgeon or even a GP whose patient suffers a sudden cardiac arrest or goes into septic shock, for example.

If the emergency happens in the community—outside the hospital—it is perfectly possible that a person's GP can be involved and give approval for research to be initiated by, for example, a paramedic attending the person at home. It is important to think that research in such a case may simply be the taking of a blood sample. As I hope is clear, those doctors are usually best placed to advise the researcher, as they are familiar with the patient's medical history" (*Hansard*, HL Vol.670, col.1501).

APPROPRIATE BODY. See s.30(4).

Additional safeguards

1–243 **33.**—(1) This section applies in relation to a person who is taking part in an approved research project even though he lacks capacity to consent to taking part.

(2) Nothing may be done to, or in relation to, him in the course of the research—

(a) to which he appears to object (whether by showing signs of resistance or otherwise) except where what is being done is intended to protect him from harm or to reduce or prevent pain or discomfort, or

(b) which would be contrary to—

(i) an advance decision of his which has effect, or

(ii) any other form of statement made by him and not subsequently withdrawn,

of which R is aware.

(3) The interests of the person must be assumed to outweigh those of science and society.

(4) If he indicates (in any way) that he wishes to be withdrawn from the project he must be withdrawn without delay.

(5) P must be withdrawn from the project, without delay, if at any time the person conducting the research has reasonable grounds for believing that one or more of the requirements set out in section 31(2) to (7) is no longer met in relation to research being carried out on, or in relation to, P.

(6) But neither subsection (4) nor subsection (5) requires treatment that P has been receiving as part of the project to be discontinued if R has reasonable grounds for believing that there would be a significant risk to P's health if it were discontinued.

DEFINITIONS

1–244 "advance decision': s.64(1)

GENERAL NOTE

1–245 This section provides that P's involvement in research must cease without delay if it appears that he objects to what is being done (this requirement is subject to the exceptions contained in subs.(2)(a)), if what is being done is contrary to either an advance decision made by P or to some other statement made by P, or if P indicates that he wishes to be withdrawn from the research (subss.(2),(4)). These provisions are subject to the principle that the interests of P must be assumed to outweigh those of science and society (subs.(3)). P must also be withdrawn from the research if the person conducting the research believes that one or more of requirements for approval is no longer met (subs.(5)). Subsection (6) makes it clear that any withdrawal from research does not require beneficial treatment to be halted.

Researchers have a duty to have regard to the guidance contained in the *Code of Practice* (s.42(4)(c)).

Subsection (3)
This principle is taken from section A.5 of the World Medical Association's Declaration of Helsinki on Ethical Principles for Medical Research Involving Human Subjects.

1–246

Loss of capacity during research project
34.—(1) This section applies where a person (P)—

1–243

  (a) has consented to take part in a research project begun before the commencement of section 30, but

  (b) before the conclusion of the project, loses capacity to consent to continue to take part in it.

(2) The appropriate authority may by regulations provide that, despite P's loss of capacity, research of a prescribed kind may be carried out on, or in relation to, P if—

  (a) the project satisfies prescribed requirements,

  (b) any information or material relating to P which is used in the research is of a prescribed description and was obtained before P's loss of capacity, and

  (c) the person conducting the project takes in relation to P such steps as may be prescribed for the purpose of protecting him.

(3) The regulations may, in particular,—

  (a) make provision about when, for the purposes of the regulations, a project is to be treated as having begun;

  (b) include provision similar to any made by section 31, 32 or 33.

DEFINITIONS
  "appropriate authority": s.30(6)
  "prescribed": s.64(1)

1–248

GENERAL NOTE
The purpose of this section was explained by the Baroness Andrews:

1–249

"[This section establishes] a transitional regulation-making power to cover ongoing research and provides for the necessary flexibility in the provisions for approval of research by a research ethics committee, with consultation of carers and additional safeguards. Why do we need transitional regulations? Primarily because it is necessary to smooth the transition for researchers from the current common law position to the new statutory safeguards for research involving those who lose capacity. We need them to avoid stopping ongoing and essential research

We already have the flexibility to cater for the majority of those in the ordinary powers for making transitional provisions in [s.65], but we need to provide for more comprehensive regulation-making powers to cover projects that enrol people with capacity who go on to lose capacity during the research projects

Our aim is to ensure that a research project can continue in relation to samples or data obtained from people before they lost capacity, subject to certain specified safeguards" (*Hansard*, HL Vol.670, cols 1520–1522).

The Mental Capacity Act 2005 (Loss of Capacity during Research Project) (England) Regulations 2007 (SI 2007/679), which are reproduced in Part 2, have been made under this section (for Wales, see SI 2007/837 (W.72)). They only apply where a person has consented to take part in a research project which started before October 1, 2007, but before the end of the project loses capacity. The person's consent to take part in the project must be given before March 31, 2008. The regulations allow the researcher to continue to use information or material obtained with consent *before* the loss of capacity. They do not apply to situations where the researchers wish to go back to a person who lacks capacity in order to obtain more information or material. Such projects will need to have approval under s.30. The regulations will have a long-term effect. The Minister gave the following example: "[A] person could join an existing study in October 2007 or January 2008 and lose capacity in the 2020s, and, if the study is continuing, the regulations would apply" (*Hansard*, HL Vol.689, col.GC108).

Subsection (2)

1–250   APPROPRIATE AUTHORITY. See s.30(6).

REGULATIONS. Regulations made under this power are subject to the affirmative resolution procedure (s.65(4)).

Independent mental capacity advocate service

Appointment of independent mental capacity advocates

1–251   **35.**—(1) The appropriate authority must make such arrangements as it considers reasonable to enable persons (independent mental capacity advocates) to be available to represent and support persons to whom acts or decisions proposed under sections 37, 38 and 39 relate.

(2) The appropriate authority may make regulations as to the appointment of independent mental capacity advocates.

(3) The regulations may, in particular, provide—

(a) that a person may act as an independent mental capacity advocate only in such circumstances, or only subject to such conditions, as may be prescribed;

(b) for the appointment of a person as an independent mental capacity advocate to be subject to approval in accordance with the regulations.

(4) In making arrangements under subsection (1), the appropriate authority must have regard to the principle that a person to whom a proposed act or decision relates should, so far as practicable, be represented and supported by a person who is independent of any person who will be responsible for the act or decision.

(5) The arrangements may include provision for payments to be made to, or in relation to, persons carrying out functions in accordance with the arrangements.

(6) For the purpose of enabling him to carry out his functions, an independent mental capacity advocate—

(a) may interview in private the person whom he has been instructed to represent, and

(b) may, at all reasonable times, examine and take copies of—

(i) any health record,

(ii) any record of, or held by, a local authority and compiled in connection with a social services function, and

(iii) any record held by a person registered under Part 2 of the Care Standards Act 2000 (c.14),

which the person holding the record considers may be relevant to the independent mental capacity advocate's investigation.

(7) In this section, section 36 and section 37, "the appropriate authority" means—

(a) in relation to the provision of the services of independent mental capacity advocates in England, the Secretary of State, and

(b) in relation to the provision of the services of independent mental capacity advocates in Wales, the National Assembly for Wales.

GENERAL NOTE

Sections 35–41 represent a partial attempt to address the concern expressed by the House **1–252** of Lords in *R. v Bournewood Community and Mental Health NHS Trust, Ex p. L* [1998] 3 All E.R. 289, that the common law doctrine of necessity (now see ss.5 and 6) does not provide any procedural safeguards for mentally incapacitated compliant patients who have been admitted to psychiatric hospitals informally. They create a scheme designed to provide the input of an independent mental capacity advocate ("IMCA") who will act as a representative and supporter of particularly vulnerable persons who lacks capacity where certain decisions need to be taken. Such people "may include older people with dementia who have lost contact with all friends and family, or people with severe learning disabilities or long term mental health problems who have been in residential institutions for long periods and lack outside contacts" (Explanatory Notes, para.109). The IMCA will become involved where there is no person, other than a professional or paid carer, to be consulted with about P's best interests. An IMCA will not become involved if one of the persons set out in s.40 can be consulted about P's best interests. The application of the IMCA scheme is far wider than the situation that obtained in the *Bournewood* case as it is not confined to situations where the mentally incapacitated person is hospitalised for psychiatric treatment. The Minister of State said:

"We estimate that about 20 per cent of people in England and Wales who lack capacity when major decisions are being taken about their living arrangements, care or treatment, have no friends or family to consult. The [IMCA] safeguard will provide the person with someone who is on their side so that there is never a closed relationship between the decision maker and the person lacking capacity.

. . . The [IMCA] will clearly have the right to talk to the person lacking capacity and a right of access to relevant records. They will find out as much as they possibly can about the likely wishes of the person and explore a range of possible outcomes that may be open to that individual. We want to give the person those powers so that they can take a broad view of what will eventually be in the best interests of the individual, which they can then recommend to the decision maker" (St. Comm. A, cols 314 and 315).

This section places a duty on the Secretary of State for Health and the Welsh Ministers to make arrangements for the provision of an IMCA service (subss.(1)–(4) and (7)) and provides the IMCA with the power to interview P in private and to examine relevant records (subs.(6)). The requirements set out in regulations made under subs.(2) must be satisfied before a person can be appointed to act as an IMCA. The IMCA, who could be remunerated for his or her services (subs.(5)), will act in P's best interests (ss.1(5)). However, as the role of the IMCA is to support and represent the person lacking capacity, he or she will not make the best interests judgment. The particular functions of IMCAs are set out in regulations (s.36). If the decision maker decides not to accept the advice proffered, the IMCA will need to consider whether take the matter further by, for example, using the NHS or local authority complaints procedure or, if the matter is particularly serious, seeking permission to refer the matter to the Court of Protection.

By virtue of reg.2 of the Mental Capacity Act 2005 (Independent Mental Capacity Advocates) (Expansion of Role) Regulations 2006 (SI 2006/2883), arrangements made by the Secretary of State under this section may include such provision as she considers reasonable for the purposes of enabling IMCAs to be available to represent and support persons in the circumstances specified in reg.3 or 4 of those regulations. SI 2006/2883 is reproduced in Part 2.

The Department of Health has estimated that the cost of the IMCA service in England will be £6.5m per annum and is making this resource available through the annual local authority settlement using a population based formula.

Guidance for commissioners on the IMCA service, produced by Turning Point, is available at *www.turning-point.co.uk/Information+Resources/Guidance+for+professionals/*. A guide to bidding for IMCA contracts, produced by Action for Advocacy, is available at *www.actionforadvocacy.org.uk*. Information from the Department of Health on aspects of implementing the IMCA service, together with IMCA training materials, can be found at *www.dh.gov.uk/imca*.

Subsection (1)

1–253   APPROPRIATE AUTHORITY. See subs.(7).

Subsection (2)

1–254   See reg.5 of the Mental Capacity Act 2005 (Independent Mental Capacity Advocates (General) Regulations 2006 (SI 2006/1832) which is reproduced in Part 2. Provision for the appointment of IMCAs in Wales is made by the Mental Capacity Act 2005 (Independent Mental Capacity Advocates) (Wales) Regulations 2007 (SI 2007/852 (W.77)), reg.5.

With regard to the training of IMCAs, the Government has said that at "this stage it is not possible to refer to a specific qualification. A notional advocacy qualification is being developed which could be accredited be the Qualifications and Curriculum Authority (QCA) and provided by an awarding body such as the Open College Network (OCN). However, this qualification will not be available before April 2007 when the Act comes into force. In the meantime, all those appointed to act as IMCAs will be provided with induction training" (Explanatory Memorandum to SI 2006/1832, para.7.6).

Under reg.5(3) of SI 2006/1832 and reg.5(8) of SI 2007/852 (W.77), criminal record certificates are required in determining whether a person meets the appointment requirements as to good character. The Police Act 1997 (Criminal Records) (Amendment No.2) Regulations 2006 (SI 2006/2181) amend the Police Act 1997 (Criminal Records) Regulations 2002 (SI 2002/233) to enable an enhanced criminal record certificate to be obtained in respect a person who is applying to act as an IMCA. An enhanced disclosure is not confined to checking the Police National Computer; it also includes a check of local police force records for information considered relevant to the position applied for. SI 2006/2181 also provides for applicants to be checked against the Protection of Vulnerable Adults (PoVA) list as part of the CRB disclosure application. The PoVA list system will be superseded in 2008 by the vetting and barring scheme established by the Safeguarding of Vulnerable Groups Act 2006. IMCAs have been named as a group that will be subject to mandatory checking under this scheme.

Subsection (6) para.(a)

1–255   The responsibility for determining the mental capacity of the person who is the subject of the decision is that of the decision-maker, not the IMCA.

Subsection (6) para.(b)

1–256   It is the responsibility of the record holder to determine whether a record is "relevant" to the IMCA's investigation. The record holder should therefore examine the record and ensure that the IMCA only has access to relevant material. The disclosure of irrelevant material to the IMCA would constitute a breach of P's right to respect for private life under Art.8 of the European Convention on Human Rights. If the IMCA is denied access to records that he or she considers are relevant to the investigation, a complaint should be made to the body that holds the record. Ultimately the IMCA could apply to the court for the record to be disclosed. The IMCA is subject to a duty of confidentiality in respect of information that is disclosed under this provision.

Subsection (7) para.(a)
SECRETARY OF STATE. In practice, the Secretary of State for Health.   **1–257**

Subsection (7) para.(b)
The functions of the National Assembly for Wales are performed by the Welsh Ministers **1–258**
(Government of Wales Act 2006, s.162, Sch.11, para.30).

Functions of independent mental capacity advocates

36.—(1) The appropriate authority may make regulations as to the functions of **1–259**
independent mental capacity advocates.

(2) The regulations may, in particular, make provision requiring an advocate to
take such steps as may be prescribed for the purpose of—
- (a) providing support to the person whom he has been instructed to represent
  (P) so that P may participate as fully as possible in any relevant decision;
- (b) obtaining and evaluating relevant information;
- (c) ascertaining what P's wishes and feelings would be likely to be, and the
  beliefs and values that would be likely to influence P, if he had capacity;
- (d) ascertaining what alternative courses of action are available in relation to P;
- (e) obtaining a further medical opinion where treatment is proposed and the
  advocate thinks that one should be obtained.

(3) The regulations may also make provision as to circumstances in which the
advocate may challenge, or provide assistance for the purpose of challenging, any
relevant decision.

DEFINITIONS
  "appropriate authority": s.35(7)   **1–260**
  "independent mental capacity advocate": s.64(1)
  "prescribed': s.64(1)

GENERAL NOTE
  This section enables the Secretary of State and the Welsh Ministers to make regulations **1–261**
as to the functions of IMCAs. The primary function of the IMCA is to advocate on behalf of
P in respect of decisions that require an IMCA involvement. The Mental Capacity Act 2005
(Independent Mental Capacity Advocates) (General) Regulations 2006 (SI 2006/1832)
have been made under this section. They apply not only where the IMCA is instructed
under ss.37 to 39 but also where he or she is instructed under regulations made under
s.41. Regulation 6 set out the steps an IMCA must take once he or she has been instructed
to act in a particular case. Note that the IMCA is only required to carry out the functions
identified in reg.6(4)(b) and (c) "to the extent that it is practicable and appropriate to do
so". The meaning of "practicable" is considered in the note to s.4(7). For Wales, see
the Mental Capacity Act 2005 (Independent Mental Capacity Advocates) (Wales)
Regulations 2007 (SI 2007/852 (W.77)), reg.6, which contains the same terminology.

Subsection (1)
REGULATIONS. See SI 2006/1832 and SI 2007/852 (W.77), above.   **1–262**

Subsection (2) para.(c)
WOULD BE LIKELY TO BE. As this provision would require the IMCA to make a substituted **1–263**
judgment on behalf of P, the IMCA should beware of the danger of expressing an opinion
which merely reflects his or her views about the matter in question.

Subsection (3)

1–264   Under reg.7 of SI 2006/1832, above, once a decision has been made about P in a matter where an IMCA has been instructed, the IMCA "has the same rights to challenge the decision as he would have if he were a person (other than an IMCA) engaged in caring for P or interested in his welfare" (for Wales, see SI 2007/852 (W.77), reg.7). Paragraph 7.8 of the Explanatory Memorandum, above, states that "it is intended that IMCAs will use existing complaints mechanisms to resolve disputes locally as far as possible, before making use of statutory procedures. In certain cases the IMCA may want to apply to the Court of Protection and he will be able to do this." Challenges can include a challenge to the decision that the person lacks capacity.

Provision of serious medical treatment by NHS body

1–265   **37.**—(1) This section applies if an NHS body—

(a) is proposing to provide, or secure the provision of, serious medical treatment for a person (P) who lacks capacity to consent to the treatment, and

(b) is satisfied that there is no person, other than one engaged in providing care or treatment for P in a professional capacity or for remuneration,

whom it would be appropriate to consult in determining what would be in P's best interests.

(2) But this section does not apply if P's treatment is regulated by Part 4 of the Mental Health Act.

(3) Before the treatment is provided, the NHS body must instruct an independent mental capacity advocate to represent P.

(4) If the treatment needs to be provided as a matter of urgency, it may be provided even though the NHS body has not been able to comply with subsection (3).

(5) The NHS body must, in providing or securing the provision of treatment for P, take into account any information given, or submissions made, by the independent mental capacity advocate.

(6) "Serious medical treatment" means treatment which involves providing, withholding or withdrawing treatment of a kind prescribed by regulations made by the appropriate authority.

(7) "NHS body" has such meaning as may be prescribed by regulations made for the purposes of this section by—

(a) the Secretary of State, in relation to bodies in England, or

(b) the National Assembly for Wales, in relation to bodies in Wales.

DEFINITIONS

1–266   "treatment": s.64(1)
"Mental Health Act": s.64(1)
"independent mental capacity advocate": s.64(1)

GENERAL NOTE

1–267   This section applies where "serious medical treatment" (apart from treatment regulated under Pt 4 of the Mental Health Act 1983 (subs.(2)) is to be provided by the NHS for a person who lacks capacity and there is no-one apart from a professional or paid carer for the treatment-provider to consult in determining what would be in P's best interests (subs.(1)). In this situation the treatment-provider must instruct an IMCA to represent P and any information given, or submissions made, by the IMCA must be taken into account when decisions are made about treating P (subs.(3),(5)). Such consultation is not required if the need for the treatment is urgent (subs.(4)). The particular types of treatment that will trigger the involvement of an IMCA have been prescribed by SI 2006/1832 and SI 2007/852 (W.77): see subs.(6).

Proper records should be taken by the treatment-provider of how the IMCA's representations has been taken into account and, where relevant, the reasons for disagreeing with or ignoring those representations. Where a disagreement arises, every effort must be made to resolve the disagreement at the earliest possible stage, where necessary using the authority's dispute resolution or complaint's procedure. If an unresolved disagreement relates to doubts over P's mental capacity or whether the proposed treatment is in P's best interests, consideration should be given to referring the matter to the court. Under reg.7 of SI 2006/1832 once a decision has been made about P in a matter where an IMCA has been instructed, the IMCA "has the same rights to challenge the decision as he would have if he were a person (other than an IMCA) engaged in caring for P or interested in his welfare".

Subsection (1)

NHS BODY. See subs.(7). Paragraph 10.9 of the *Code of Practice* states: **1–268**

"For decisions about serious medical treatment, the responsible body will be the NHS organisation providing the person's healthcare or treatment. But if the person is in an independent or voluntary sector hospital, the responsible body will be the NHS organisation arranging and funding the person's care, which should have arrangements in place with the independent or voluntary sector hospital to ensure that an IMCA is appointed promptly."

Subsection (1) para. (a)

SECURE THE PROVISION OF. The duty under this section will arise if the NHS is funding P's **1–269** treatment in the private sector.

PERSON. The obligation to appoint an IMCA applies if P is in prison.

Subsection (1) para. (b)

APPROPRIATE. It is for the responsible body to decide whether there is anyone, apart from **1–270** those listed in s.40, who comes within this category. It would not be appropriate to consult with a person who:

(a) has a history of abusing or ill-treating P;
(b) is likely to be the cause of distress to P if P was aware of the consultation;
(c) is not available to be consulted with because his or her whereabouts are unknown;
(d) could only be consulted with if a disproportionate amount of time was used in an attempt to contact that person;
(e) only has very limited knowledge of P; or
(f) is unwilling to be a consultee.

Subsection (2)

Treatments regulated by Part 4 of the Mental Health Act are excluded because Part 4 pro- **1–271** vides its own safeguards for patients.

Subsection (3)

This provision does not apply if a person listed in s.40 is available to be consulted.   **1–272**

Subsection (6)

By virtue of reg.4 of the Mental Capacity Act 2005 (Independent Mental Capacity **1–273** Advocates) (General) Regulations 2006 (SI 2006/1832), serious medical treatment "is treatment which involves providing, withdrawing or withholding treatment in circumstances where—

(a) in a case where a single treatment is being proposed, there is a fine balance between its benefits to the patient and the burdens and risks it is likely to entail for him,

(b) in a case where there is a choice of treatments, a decision as to which one to use is finely balanced, or

(c) what is proposed would be likely to involve serious consequences for the patient."

These criteria, which define serious medical treatment by reference to the characteristics of the treatment, allow for a significant amount of discretion to be exercised by the treating clinician. The wording of the criteria is such that electro-convulsive therapy, a treatment that would be regarded as being "serious" by most patients, might not be regarded by the clinician as coming within the terms of reg.4 if the treatment is being provided as a final treatment option in order to preserve life. It is also the case that relatively minor treatments could come within the scope of paras (a) and (b).

The term "likely" in para.(c) suggests a high degree of probability of serious consequences; a mere possibility would not be sufficient. Paragraph 10.44 of the *Code of Practice* states:

"'Serious consequences' are those which could have a serious impact on the patient, either from the effects of the treatment itself or its wider implications. This may include treatments which:

- cause serious and prolonged pain, distress or side effects
- have potentially major consequences for the patient (for example, stopping life-sustaining treatment or having major surgery), or
- have a serious impact on the patient's future life choices (for example, interventions for ovarian cancer)."

A similar definition of serious medical treatment has been established in relation to Wales by the Mental Capacity Act 2005 (Independent Mental Capacity Advocates) (Wales) Regulations 2007 (SI 2007/852 (W.77)), reg.4. The only difference between the two definitions is that the Welsh regulations refer to "a person (P)" rather than to "the patient".

Subsection (7)

1–274   For the purposes of this section and s.38, "NHS body" means a body in England which is—

(a) a Strategic Health Authority;
(b) an NHS foundation trust;
(c) a Primary Care Trust;
(d) an NHS Trust; or
(e) a Care Trust (SI 2006/1832, reg.3).

In Wales, "NHS body" means—

(a) a Local Health Board;
(b) an NHS trust all or most of whose hospitals, establishments and facilities are situated in Wales;
(c) a Special Health Authority performing functions only or mainly in respect of Wales (SI 2007/852 (W.77), reg.3).

Provision of accommodation by NHS body

1–275   **38.**—(1) This section applies if an NHS body proposes to make arrangements—

(a) for the provision of accommodation in a hospital or care home for a person (P) who lacks capacity to agree to the arrangements, or

(b) for a change in P's accommodation to another hospital or care home, and is satisfied that there is no person, other than one engaged in providing care or treatment for P in a professional capacity or for remuneration, whom it would be appropriate for it to consult in determining what would be in P's best interests.

(2) But this section does not apply if P is accommodated as a result of an obligation imposed on him under the Mental Health Act.

(3) Before making the arrangements, the NHS body must instruct an independent mental capacity advocate to represent P unless it is satisfied that—

(a) the accommodation is likely to be provided for a continuous period which is less than the applicable period, or

(b) the arrangements need to be made as a matter of urgency.

(4) If the NHS body—

(a) did not instruct an independent mental capacity advocate to represent P before making the arrangements because it was satisfied that subsection (3)(a) or (b) applied, but

(b) subsequently has reason to believe that the accommodation is likely to be provided for a continuous period—

(i) beginning with the day on which accommodation was first provided in accordance with the arrangements, and

(ii) ending on or after the expiry of the applicable period,

it must instruct an independent mental capacity advocate to represent P.

(5) The NHS body must, in deciding what arrangements to make for P, take into account any information given, or submissions made, by the independent mental capacity advocate.

(6) "Care home" has the meaning given in section 3 of the Care Standards Act 2000 (c.14).

(7) "Hospital" means—

(a) a health service hospital as defined by [section 275 of the National Health Service Act 2006 or section 206 of the National Health Service (Wales) Act 2006], or

(b) an independent hospital as defined by section 2 of the Care Standards Act 2000.

(8) "NHS body" has such meaning as may be prescribed by regulations made for the purposes of this section by—

(a) the Secretary of State, in relation to bodies in England, or

(b) the National Assembly for Wales, in relation to bodies in Wales.

(9) "Applicable period" means—

(a) in relation to accommodation in a hospital, 28 days, and

(b) in relation to accommodation in a care home, 8 weeks.

AMENDMENT

In subs.(7)(a), the words in square brackets were substituted by the National Health **1–276** Service (Consequential Provisions) Act 2006, s.2, Sch.1, para.278.

DEFINITIONS

"Mental Health Act": s.64(1) **1–277**

"independent mental capacity act advocate": s.64(1)

GENERAL NOTE

This section applies if a NHS body intends to arrange for P to be accommodated in a hos- **1–278** pital (either NHS or private) or a care home for a period likely to exceed 28 days (for a hospital) or eight weeks (for a care home), or for P to be moved between such accommodation, and there is no-one apart from a professional or paid carer for the NHS body to consult in determining what would be in P's best interests (subss.(1) and (9)). In this situation the NHS body must instruct an IMCA to represent P and must take into account any information given, or submissions made, by the IMCA when a decision is made about what arrangements to make for P (subss.(3) and (5)). Such consultation need not take place if the P is likely to stay in the accommodation for less than the applicable period or if the need for the move is urgent, for example, where P requires an emergency hospital admission, or where a care home place will be lost if P is not moved immediately (subs.(3)). However, the consultation must take place after the arrangements have been made if the NHS body subsequently believes that P will be accommodated at the hospital or care home for the applicable period (subs.(4)). The section does not apply if P is accommodated in the hospital or the care home as a result of an obligation imposed on him or her under the Mental Health Act 1983 (subs.(2)), as that Act contains its own safeguards. It will apply to decisions about providing accommodation for P if P is about to be discharged from detention under the 1983 Act.

Where an NHS body has made arrangements as to P's accommodation under this section and it is then proposed to review those arrangements, an IMCA may (not must) be instructed to represent P at the review: see the Mental Capacity Act 2005 (Independent Mental Capacity Advocates) (Expansion of Role) Regulations 2006 (SI 2006/2883), reg.3. The equivalent provision for Wales is the Mental Capacity Act 2005 (Independent Mental Capacity Advocates) (Wales) Regulations 2007 (SI 2007/852 (W.77)), reg.8.

Proper records should be taken by the responsible authority of how the IMCA's representations have been taken into account and, where relevant, the reasons for disagreeing with or ignoring the representations. Where a disagreement arises, every effort must be made to resolve the disagreement at the earliest possible stage, where necessary using the authority's dispute resolution or complaint's procedure. If the IMCA continues to believe that either the proposed or present placement is not in the best interests of P, he or she could seek advice from a solicitor to ascertain whether the decision could be subject to a legal challenge. Under reg.7 of the Mental Capacity Act 2005 (Independent Mental Capacity Advocates) (General) Regulations 2005 (SI 2006/1832), once a decision has been made about P in a matter where an IMCA has been instructed, the IMCA "has the same rights to challenge the decision as he would have if he were a person (other than an IMCA) engaged in caring for P or interested in his welfare". Challenges can include the decision that the person lacks capacity. For Wales, see SI 2007/852 (W.77), reg.7.

Subsection (1)

1–279   NHS BODY. See subs.(8). Paragraphs 10.10 to 10.12 of the *Code of Practice* state:

"For decisions about admission to accommodation in hospital for 28 days or more, the responsible body will be the NHS body that manages the hospital. For admission to an independent or voluntary sector hospital for 28 days or more, the responsible body will be the NHS organisation arranging and funding the person's care. The independent or voluntary hospital must have arrangements in place with the NHS organisation to ensure that an IMCA can be appointed without delay.

For decisions about moves into long term accommodation (for eight weeks or longer), or about a change of accommodation, the responsible body will be either:

- the NHS body that proposes the move or change of accommodation (e.g. a nursing home), or
- the local authority that has carried out an assessment of the person under the NHS and Community Care Act 1990 and decided the move may be necessary.

Sometimes NHS organisations and local authorities will make decisions together about moving a person into long-term care. In these cases, the organisation that must instruct the IMCA is the one that is ultimately responsible for the decision to move the person.

The IMCA to be instructed is the one who works wherever the person is at the time that the person needs support and representation."

HOSPITAL. See subs.(7).

CAREHOME. See subs.(6).

APPROPRIATE. See the note to s.37(1)(b).

Subsection (2)
OBLIGATION IMPOSED ON HIM UNDER THE MENTAL HEALTH ACT. Such as a condition imposed by **1–280** a Mental Health Review Tribunal under s.73 of the Act requiring the patient to reside at a particular place, a similar requirement imposed by the patient's guardian under s.8 of the Act, or a condition attached to the patient's leave of absence granted under s.17 of the Act requiring him to reside at a particular address. Such placements are excluded because the Mental Health Act provides its own safeguards for patients.

Subsection (3)
This provision does not apply if a person listed in s.40 is available to be consulted. **1–281**

APPLICABLE PERIOD. See subs.(9).

Subsection (4)
BEGINNING WITH. Including the day on which the accommodation was first provided (*Zoan* **1–282** *v Rouamba* [2000] 2 All E.R. 620, CA).

Subsection (8)
See the note on s.37(7). **1–283**

Provision of accommodation by local authority

39.—(1) This section applies if a local authority propose to make **1–284** arrangements—
  (a) for the provision of residential accommodation for a person (P) who lacks capacity to agree to the arrangements, or
  (b) for a change in P's residential accommodation,
and are satisfied that there is no person, other than one engaged in providing care or treatment for P in a professional capacity or for remuneration, whom it would be appropriate for them to consult in determining what would be in P's best interests.
  (2) But this section applies only if the accommodation is to be provided in accordance with—
  (a) section 21 or 29 of the National Assistance Act 1948 (c. 29), or
  (b) section 117 of the Mental Health Act,
as the result of a decision taken by the local authority under section 47 of the National Health Service and Community Care Act 1990 (c.19).
  (3) This section does not apply if P is accommodated as a result of an obligation imposed on him under the Mental Health Act.
  (4) Before making the arrangements, the local authority must instruct an independent mental capacity advocate to represent P unless they are satisfied that—
  (a) the accommodation is likely to be provided for a continuous period of less than 8 weeks, or

(b) the arrangements need to be made as a matter of urgency.

(5) If the local authority—

(a) did not instruct an independent mental capacity advocate to represent P before making the arrangements because they were satisfied that subsection (4)(a) or (b) applied, but

(b) subsequently have reason to believe that the accommodation is likely to be provided for a continuous period that will end 8 weeks or more after the day on which accommodation was first provided in accordance with the arrangements,

they must instruct an independent mental capacity advocate to represent P.

(6) The local authority must, in deciding what arrangements to make for P, take into account any information given, or submissions made, by the independent mental capacity advocate.

DEFINITIONS

1–285   "local authority": s.64(1)
"treatment": s.64(1)
"Mental Health Act": s.64(1)
"independent mental capacity act advocate": s.64(1)

GENERAL NOTE

1–286   This section applies if a local authority intends to arrange for P to be provided with long-stay residential accommodation provided under s.21 of the National Assistance Act 1948 (c.29) or s.117 of the Mental Health Act 1983 (c.20), or for the accommodation to be changed, and there is no-one apart from a professional or paid carer for the authority to consult in determining what would be in P's best interests (subss.(1) and (2)). In this situation the authority must instruct an IMCA to represent P and any information given, or submissions made, by the IMCA must be taken into account when a decision is made about what arrangements to make for P (subss.(4) and (6)). Such consultation need not take place if the P is likely to stay in the accommodation for less than eight weeks or if the need for the accommodation is urgent (subs.(4)). However, the consultation must take place after the placement has been effected if the authority subsequently believes that the accommodation will be provided for P for at least eight weeks (subs.(5)). This section does not apply if the accommodation is provided as a result of an obligation imposed on P under the 1983 Act (subs.(3)).

Where a local authority has made arrangements as to P's accommodation under this section and it is then proposed to review those arrangements, an IMCA may (not must) be instructed to represent P at the review: see the Mental Capacity Act 2005 (Independent Mental Capacity Advocates) (Expansion of Role) Regulations 2006 (SI 2006/2883), reg.3. The equivalent provision for Wales is the Mental Capacity Act 2005 (Independent Mental Capacity Advocates) (Wales) Regulations 2007 (SI 2007/852 (W.77)), reg.8.

Proper records should be taken by the responsible authority of how the IMCA's submissions have been taken into account and, where relevant, the reasons for disagreeing with or ignoring the submissions. Where a disagreement arises, every effort must be made to resolve the disagreement at the earliest possible stage, where necessary using the authority's dispute resolution or complaint's procedure. If the IMCA continue to believe that the proposed placement is not in the best interests of P, he or she could seek advice from a solicitor to ascertain whether the decision could be subject to a legal challenge. Under reg.7 of the Mental Capacity Act 2005 (Independent Mental Capacity Advocates) (General) Regulations 2005 (SI 2006/1832), once a decision has been made about P in a matter where an IMCA has been instructed, the IMCA "has the same rights to challenge the decision as he would have if he were a person (other than an IMCA) engaged in caring for P or interested in his welfare". Challenges can include the decision that the person lacks capacity. For Wales, see SI 2007/852 (W.77), reg.7.

Subsection (1)

LOCAL AUTHORITY. See the note on "NHS body" in s.37(1).   **1–287**

APPROPRIATE. See the note to s.37(1)(b).

Subsection (2)

A local authority may itself provide accommodation under s.21 or it can make arrange- **1–288** ments under s.29 of the 1948 Act for the accommodation to be provided by a third party. In *R. (on the application of Batantu) v Islington LBC* (2001) 4 C.C.L. Rep. 445, Henriques J. said that the meaning of accommodation under the 1948 Act is wide and flexible and embraces care homes, ordinary and sheltered housing, housing association and other registered social housing, and private sector housing which may have been purchased by the local authority. It would also include hostel accommodation. When making a placement decision under s.21, a local authority in England must comply with the National Assistance Act (Choice of Accommodation) Directions 1992 (reproduced at para.D4–001 of the *Encyclopedia of Social Services and Child Care Law*) which require the authority to provide the prospective resident with their preferred accommodation if certain conditions are satisfied. If prospective residents lack the mental capacity to express a preference for themselves, it "would be reasonable to expect councils to act on the preferences expressed by their advocate, carer or legal guardian in the same way that they would on the resident's own wishes, unless that would in the council's opinion be against the best interests of the resident" (Department of Health Circular LAC (2004) 20 *Guidance* para.5.1). An IMCA should be treated as an "advocate" for the purposes of this guidance.

Section 117 of the 1983 Act places a duty on the relevant NHS Trust and local authority to provide after-care services to patients who have been discharged from non-emergency detention under that Act. The after-care services can include accommodation that is required to meet the mental health needs of P. Accommodation provided under s.117 must be provided free of charge (*R. v Manchester City Council Ex p. Stennett* [2002] UKHL 34; [2002] 4 All E.R. 124).

Section 47 of the 1990 Act places a duty on local social services authorities to assess the care needs of any person who appears to be in need of community care services and decide in the light of the assessment whether services should be provided to that person.

Subsection (3)

See the note on s.38(2).   **1–289**

Subsection (4)

This provision does not apply if a person listed in s.40 is available to be consulted. **1–290**

Exceptions

40.—Sections 37(3), 38(3) and (4) and 39(4) and (5) do not apply if there is— **1–291**
(a) a person nominated by P(in whatever manner) as a person to be consulted in matters affecting his interests,
(b) a donee of a lasting power of attorney created by P,
(c) a deputy appointed by the court for P, or
(d) a donee of an enduring power of attorney (within the meaning of Schedule 4) created by P.

DEFINITIONS
"lasting power of attorney": s.64(1)   **1–292**
"deputy": s.64(1)

1–293   This section confirms that the independent mental advocacy scheme does not apply where there is a suitable person who can be consulted about P's best interests.

Paragraph (a)
1–294   The nomination may be written or oral. The decision-maker must be satisfied that the nomination was made when P was mentally capable and that the nominee is willing to be consulted.

Paragraph (b)
1–295   The donee is to be consulted about a personal welfare matter even though the LPA relates to P's financial affairs.

Paragraph (c)
1–296   The deputy is to be consulted about a personal welfare matter even though he or she has been appointed to manage P's financial affairs.

Paragraph (d)
1–297   The donee can be consulted about personal welfare matters even though an Enduring Power of Attorney only applies to financial matters.

Power to adjust role of independent mental capacity advocate
1–298   **41.**—(1) The appropriate authority may make regulations—
    (a) expanding the role of independent mental capacity advocates in relation to persons who lack capacity, and
    (b) adjusting the obligation to make arrangements imposed by section 35.
    (2) The regulations may, in particular—
    (a) prescribe circumstances (different to those set out in sections 37, 38 and 39) in which an independent mental capacity advocate must, or circumstances in which one may, be instructed by a person of a prescribed description to represent a person who lacks capacity, and
    (b) include provision similar to any made by section 37, 38, 39 or 40.
    (3) "Appropriate authority" has the same meaning as in section 35.

DEFINITIONS
1–299   "independent mental capacity advocate": s.64(1)

GENERAL NOTE
1–300   This section provides that scope of the independent mental advocacy scheme can be extended by regulations made by the Secretary of State or the Welsh Ministers. The Mental Capacity Act 2005 (Independent Mental Capacity Advocates) (Expansion of Role) Regulations 2006 (SI 2006/2883), which are reproduced in Part 2, have been made under this section. The equivalent provision for Wales is the Mental Capacity Act 2005 (Independent Mental Capacity Advocates) (Wales) Regulations 2007 (SI 2007/852 (W.77)), regs 8 and 9. These regulations do not prevent an NHS body or local authority from instructing an IMCA in other circumstances. However, the regulations only provide authority for the Secretary of State to make arrangements (i.e. provide funding) for IMCAs to be available in the circumstances set out in the regulations.
    The Mental Capacity Act 2005 (Independent Mental Capacity Advocates (General) Regulations 2006 (SI 2006/1832), which are considered in the notes to s.37, apply where an IMCA has been instructed under regulations made by virtue of this section (*ibid.*, reg.2(2)).

Subsection (1)

REGULATIONS. Regulations made under this power are subject to the affirmative resolution **1–301** procedure (s.65(4)).

Subsection (2) para. (a)

MUST, OR . . . MAY. This phrase was substituted for "must" at the report stage in the House **1–302** of Lords "for two reasons. First, concerns have been expressed about extending the [scheme] compulsorily to situations where there are family members. We agree that that it is not necessarily desirable or helpful. It is fair to say that family carers are at the heart of decision-making in many circumstances. We would not wish to get in the middle of that relationship, particularly when we know what a critical and crucial role family members play in supporting their loved ones. We will ensure that the *Code of Practice* refers to the central role at the heart that unpaid carers play, and makes it clear that they will often be the best people to speak up for the person lacking capacity. In addition, we believe that where people have successful, loving and supportive relationships, the obligatory use of an independent mental advocacy scheme would neither be helpful, nor an effective use of resources, frankly. Also, we want to ensure the maximum flexibility to enable us to accommodate all possible outcomes of the consultation on extending the service. Following the consultation, consensus may or may not favour the use of a discretionary power. By tabling the amendment, we are simply allowing for that possibility", *per* the Parliamentary Under-Secretary of State (*Hansard*, HL Vol.670, col.1528).

Miscellaneous and supplementary

Codes of practice

42.—(1) The Lord Chancellor must prepare and issue one or more codes of **1–303** practice—

(a) for the guidance of persons assessing whether a person has capacity in relation to any matter,

(b) for the guidance of persons acting in connection with the care or treatment of another person (see section 5),

(c) for the guidance of donees of lasting powers of attorney,

(d) for the guidance of deputies appointed by the court,

(e) for the guidance of persons carrying out research in reliance on any provision made by or under this Act (and otherwise with respect to sections 30 to 34),

(f) for the guidance of independent mental capacity advocates,

(g) with respect to the provisions of sections 24 to 26 (advance decisions and apparent advance decisions), and

(h) with respect to such other matters concerned with this Act as he thinks fit.

(2) The Lord Chancellor may from time to time revise a code.

(3) The Lord Chancellor may delegate the preparation or revision of the whole or any part of a code so far as he considers expedient.

(4) It is the duty of a person to have regard to any relevant code if he is acting in relation to a person who lacks capacity and is doing so in one or more of the following ways—

(a) as the donee of a lasting power of attorney,

(b) as a deputy appointed by the court,

(c) as a person carrying out research in reliance on any provision made by or under this Act (see sections 30 to 34),

(d) as an independent mental capacity advocate,

(e) in a professional capacity,

(f) for remuneration.

(5) If it appears to a court or tribunal conducting any criminal or civil proceedings that—

(a) a provision of a code, or

(b) a failure to comply with a code,

is relevant to a question arising in the proceedings, the provision or failure must be taken into account in deciding the question.

(6) A code under subsection (1)(d) may contain separate guidance for deputies appointed by virtue of paragraph 1(2) of Schedule 5(functions of deputy conferred on receiver appointed under the Mental Health Act).

(7) In this section and in section 43, "code" means a code prepared or revised under this section.

DEFINITIONS

1–304   "treatment": s.64(1)

"lasting power of attorney": s.64(1)

"deputy": s.64(1)

"the court": s.64(1)

"independent mental capacity advocate": s.64(1) "advance decision": s.64(1)

"Mental Health Act": s.64(1)

GENERAL NOTE

1–305   This section requires the Lord Chancellor to publish a *Code of Practice* (or *Codes of Practice*) to address the issues set out in subs.(1). The Code can be revised (subs.(2)). These responsibilities may be delegated (subs.(3)). The Code sets out how the legal rules contained in this Act and the associated regulations will work in practice. Donees, deputies, professionals, researchers, independent mental capacity advocates and paid workers acting on behalf of a person who lacks capacity must have regard to the Code (subs.(4)) The Code can be used as evidence in court or tribunal proceedings and, if relevant, will be taken into account in the determination (subs.(5)). However, no legal liability arises from a breach of the Code itself.

A *Code of Practice* was laid before Parliament in draft in February 2007, pursuant to this section and s.43 and was approved in April 2007. The Introduction to the Code states at p.1:

"The Act does not impose a legal duty on anyone to 'comply' with the Code – it should be viewed as guidance rather than instruction. But if they have not followed relevant guidance contained in the Code then they will be expected to give good reasons why they have departed from it."

Subsection (1)

1–306   GUIDANCE. In *R. v Secretary of State for the Environment Ex p. Lancashire* CC [1994] 4 All E.R. 165, 173, Jowitt J. said:

"The concept of guidance goes beyond simply providing a checklist of factors which should be taken into account. To guide someone is to lead, steer or point someone in a particular direction."

Subsection (1) para. (b)

1–307   Note the scope of this category, which includes informal and family carers. Such carers are not placed under an obligation to "have regard" to the Code (subs.(4)). The position of informal and family carers was examined by the Joint Committee:

"The position is different with regard to guidance issued to assist non-professional or informal decision makers, such as family members and unpaid carers acting under [s.5]. It is essential that family members and carers carrying out such responsibilities are provided with appropriate guidance and assistance, both to promote good practice and also to impress upon them the seriousness of their actions and the need to be accountable for them. We accept that it would be inappropriate to impose on them a strict requirement to act in accordance with the Code of Practice" (Vol.1, para.232).

While such an approach is understandable, this Act places unrealistic expectations on lay carers in that it does not recognise any distinction between lay and professional carers when it comes to adherence to the principles set out in s.1, the requirement to assess capacity under ss.2 and 3, and the determination of best interests under s.4. The Introduction to the Code states that lay carers "should follow the guidance in the Code as far as they are aware of it" (p.2).

Subsection (2)
The Code will "be revised fairly frequently", *per* the Parliamentary Under-Secretary of **1–308** State (*Hansard*, HL Vol.669, col.758).

Subsection (4)
HAVE REGARD TO. In *R. (on the application of Munjaz) v Mersey Care National Health* **1–309** *Service Trust* [2005] UKHL 58; [2006] 4 All E.R. 736, the House of Lords considered the legal status of the *Code of Practice* issued pursuant to s.118 of the Mental Health Act 1983. Although there are differences in the wording of s.118 and this section, the decision in *Munjaz* can be regarded as a clear indication of the approach that a court might adopt when interpreting the status of the Code issued under this Act. In *Munjaz* it was contended that the policy of Ashworth Hospital relating to the seclusion of patients was unlawful because it provided for less frequent medical reviews, particularly after the first week of seclusion, than that laid down in the Mental Health Act *Code of Practice*. Ashworth had also adopted a definition of seclusion that differed from that set out in the Code. It was held that:

1. The Code does not have the binding effect which a statutory provision or a statutory instrument would have. It is what it purports to be, guidance and not instruction.
2. The guidance in the Code should be given great weight. Although it is not instruction, the Code is much more than mere advice which an addressee is free to follow or not as it chooses.
3. The Code contains guidance which should be considered with great care, and should be followed unless there are cogent reasons for not doing so. The requirement that cogent reasons must be shown for any departure sets a high standard which is not easily satisfied. The reasons must be spelled out clearly, logically and convincingly.
4. In reviewing any departures from the Code, the court should scrutinise the reasons given for departure with the intensity which the importance and sensitivity of the subject matters requires.
5. For the purpose of determining whether Ashworth's policy was compatible with the European Convention on Human Rights, the Code is irrelevant: if the policy is incompatible, consistency with the Code will not save it; if it is compatible, it requires no support from the Code.

The following circumstances could provide cogent reasons for not following the guidance contained in the Code issued under this section:

1. The best interests of P (or a group of persons who share particular well-defined characteristics) would not be satisfied if the guidance was followed.
2. There has been a determination of the High Court that a particular aspect of the guidance is not legally accurate.
3. Legal advice has been received which casts a significant doubt on the legal correctness of an aspect of the guidance.
4. Following the guidance would involve breaching P's Convention rights.

5. A judgment is taken that a particular aspect of the guidance should not be followed for safety or other legitimate reason.

If a person fails to comply with the guidance contained in the Code, he or she must be prepared to give reasons to explain the non-compliance. It would be sensible for a contemporaneous record of such reasons to be made.

Subsection (4) para.(f)

1–310   FOR REMUNERATION. For example, a care assistant who works in a care home where the residents lack capacity.

Codes of practice: procedure

1–311   **43.**—(1) Before preparing or revising a code, the Lord Chancellor must consult—

(a) the National Assembly for Wales, and

(b) such other persons as he considers appropriate.

(2) The Lord Chancellor may not issue a code unless—

(a) a draft of the code has been laid by him before both Houses of Parliament, and

(b) the 40 day period has elapsed without either House resolving not to approve the draft.

(3) The Lord Chancellor must arrange for any code that he has issued to be published in such a way as he considers appropriate for bringing it to the attention of persons likely to be concerned with its provisions.

(4) "40 day period", in relation to the draft of a proposed code, means—

(a) if the draft is laid before one House on a day later than the day on which it is laid before the other House, the period of 40 days beginning with the later of the two days;

(b) in any other case, the period of 40 days beginning with the day on which it is laid before each House.

(5) In calculating the period of 40 days, no account is to be taken of any period during which Parliament is dissolved or prorogued or during which both Houses are adjourned for more than 4 days.

GENERAL NOTE

1–312   This section sets out the procedure for issuing and revising the *Code of Practice* and requires the Lord Chancellor to publish the Code in an appropriate format.

Subsection (1)(a)

1–313   The functions of the National Assembly for Wales are performed by the Welsh Ministers (Government of Wales Act 2006, s.162, Sch.11, para.30).

Subsection (2)

1–314   This procedure is known as the "negative resolution" procedure.

Ill-treatment or neglect

1–315   **44.**—(1) Subsection (2) applies if a person (D)—

(a) has the care of a person (P) who lacks, or whom D reasonably believes to lack, capacity,

(b) is the donee of a lasting power of attorney, or an enduring power of attorney (within the meaning of Schedule 4), created by P, or

(c) is a deputy appointed by the court for P.

(2) D is guilty of an offence if he ill-treats or wilfully neglects P.

(3) A person guilty of an offence under this section is liable—

(a) on summary conviction, to imprisonment for a term not exceeding 12 months or a fine not exceeding the statutory maximum or both;

(b) on conviction on indictment, to imprisonment for a term not exceeding 5 years or a fine or both.

DEFINITIONS

"lasting power of attorney": s.64(1) **1–316**

"deputy": s.64(1)

"the court": s.64(1)

GENERAL NOTE

This section creates the offence of ill-treatment or wilful neglect of a person who lacks **1–317** capacity or is believed to lack capacity. It is "aimed at capturing those individuals who are in a position of trust, care or power over people who are then ill-treated or neglected. That could be a donee of a lasting power of attorney, a deputy appointed by the court or a person who has the care of someone who lacks capacity, such as a member of staff in a hospital or care home or a family member", *per* the Parliamentary Under-Secretary of State, St. Comm. A, col.383.

In *R. v Newington (Susan)* (1990) 91 Cr. App. R. 247, a case under s.127 of the Mental Health Act 1983, the Court of Appeal said that "ill-treatment" could not be equated with "wilfully to neglect". The court therefore advised the Crown Prosecution Service that, when proceedings were brought, charges of "ill-treatment" and of "wilfully to neglect" should be put in separate counts in the indictment. This ruling applies to proceedings brought under this section.

The Government rejected recommendation 80 of the Joint Committee that this section be "extended to include the misappropriation of the person's property and financial assets"on the ground that a person who uses the funds of someone who lacks capacity for his own benefit may be prosecuted for the offence of theft and that a new offence of "misappropriation" would be very similar to that offence (*The Government Response to the Scrutiny Committee's Report on the Draft Mental Incapacity Bill*, Cm 6121).

The English "No Secrets" and the Welsh "In Safe Hands" guidance set out the multi-agency procedures to be followed when a vulnerable adult is believed to be suffering abuse. Abuse is defined as "a violation of an individual's human and civil rights by any other person or persons" (*No Secrets*, para.2.5). The Government rejected the Joint Committee's recommendation, at para.266, that the statutory authorities should be given additional powers of investigation and intervention in cases of alleged physical, sexual or financial abuse of people lacking the capacity to protect themselves from the risk of abuse:

"The Committee recommended that the draft Bill should go further in the protection it offers against abuse and exploitation of those lacking capacity. However, the Government is already taking action to protect vulnerable adults against abuse. In particular, the 'No Secrets' guidance requires Councils to liaise with other public authorities and other agencies in their area and to produce written and agreed local procedures for handling incidents of abuse concerning vulnerable adults. The new Public Guardian under the Bill would have a role working with Councils and other agencies. The new criminal offence of ill-treatment or wilful neglect would also be another valuable tool in tackling potential abuse" (Cm.6121).

This section is drafted in broader terms than s.127 of the Mental Health Act 1983. Section 127 creates three separate offences that could apply to incapacitated people who are also suffering from a mental disorder within the meaning of s.1 of that Act at the time when the offence was committed. Firstly, under subs.(1) it is an offence for an employee or manager of a hospital, independent hospital or care home to illtreat or wilfully to neglect an in-patient or out-patient of that hospital or home. Secondly, under subs.(2) it is an offence for a guardian appointed under the 1983 Act or some other person who has the custody or care of a mentally disordered person who is living in the community to ill-treat or wilfully to neglect that person. Thirdly, under subs.(2A) it is an offence for any person to ill-treat of wilfully to neglect a person who is subject to the supervised discharge provisions of the 1983 Act.

A donee of a lasting power of attorney, a deputy appointed by the court or a carer who abuses his or her position could be guilty of the offence of "fraud by abuse of position" under s.4 of the Fraud Act 2006. Section 4 reads:

"(1) A person is in breach of this section if he:
    (a) occupies a position in which he is expected to safeguard, or not act against, the financial interests of another person,
    (b) intends, by means of the abuse of that position—
        (i) to make a gain for himself or another, or
        (ii) to cause loss to another or to expose another to a risk of loss.

(2) A person may be regarded as having abused his position even though his conduct consisted of an omission rather than an act."

Sections 30 to 41 of the Sexual Offences Act 2003 create a number of offences "against persons with a mental disorder impeding choice."

Subsection (1) para.(a)

1–318   An offence under this section could be committed if either D is unaware of P's incapacity, or if D's belief that P lacks capacity is incorrect.

CARE. This is not defined. In *Minister of Health v Royal Midlands Counties Home for Incurables at Lemington Spa* [1954] Ch 530, Denning L.J. defined care as "the homely art of making people comfortable and providing for their well being so far as their condition allows".

PERSON. Of any age. Incapacity arising solely from the fact that P is not old enough to be considered capable would not qualify as incapacity for the purpose of this section.

CAPACITY. It is unclear what capacity means in this context as the functional test of capacity set out in s.3 is not obviously applicable to an offence. It is suggested that a person lacks capacity for the purposes of this provision if he or she is vulnerable due to a mentally disability arising from "an impairment of, or a disturbance in the functioning of, the mind or brain": see s.2(1).

Subsection (2)

1–319   ILL-TREATS. There is Crown Court authority to support the proposition that it is not necessary to establish a course of conduct as a single act, such as slapping a person's face on one occasion, could constitute ill-treatment (*R. v Holmes* [1979] Crim. L.R. 52, Crown Court (Bodmin)). As it is likely that there is no need for the prosecution to show that the treatment in question caused actual injury to the victim, "ill treatment" encompasses a wide range of conduct.

It is submitted that for the offence of ill-treatment to be proved, the prosecution would have to prove: (1) deliberate conduct by the accused which could properly be described as ill-treatment irrespective of whether it damaged or threatened to damage the victims health; (2) a guilty mind involving either an appreciation by the accused that he was inexcusably ill-treating a person or that he was reckless as to whether he was inexcusably acting in that way; and (3) that the victim was a person without capacity (*R. v Newington* (Susan), above). In *Newington* the court disapproved of a direction given by the trial judge "that violence would inevitably amount to ill-treatment" on the ground that violence necessarily used for the reasonable control of a patient would not amount to ill-treatment.

WILFULY NEGLECTS. The meaning to be attributed to the expression "wilful neglect" may vary according to the context but generally the expression should be taken to mean that there has been an intentional or purposive omission to do something that the person in question knows he or she has a duty to do (*De Maroussem v Commissioner of Income Tax* [2004] UKPC 43, para.41).

The leading case on the term "wilfully" is *R. v Sheppard (James Martin)* [1981] A.C. 394, HL, a case brought under s.1(1) of the Children and Young Persons Act 1933 (c.12). Lord Keith said at 418:

"It is used here to describe the mental element, which, in addition to the fact of neglect, must be proved The primary meaning of 'wilful' is 'deliberate'. So a parent who knows that his child needs medical care and deliberately, that is by conscious decision, refrains from calling a doctor, is guilty under the sub-section. As a matter of general principle, recklessness is to be equiparated with deliberation. A parent who fails to provide medical care which his child needs because he does not care whether it is needed or not is reckless of his child's welfare. He too is guilty of an offence. But a parent who has genuinely failed to appreciate that his child needs medical care, through personal inadequacy or stupidity or both, is not guilty."

A direction of the kind suggested by Lord Keith's reasoning, suitably tailored to the facts of the case, should be given by the trial judge hearing a case under this section (*R. v Morrell (Karen Victoria*) [2002] EWCA Crim 2547).

PART 2

THE COURT OF PROTECTION AND THE PUBLIC GUARDIAN

The Court of Protection

The Court of Protection

1–320   **45.**—(1) There is to be a superior court of record known as the Court of Protection.

(2) The court is to have an official seal.

(3) The court may sit at any place in England and Wales, on any day and at any time.

(4) The court is to have a central office and registry at a place appointed by the Lord Chancellor [, after consulting the Lord Chief Justice].

(5) The Lord Chancellor may [, after consulting the Lord Chief Justice] designate as additional registries of the court any district registry of the High Court and any county court office.

[(5A) The Lord Chief Justice may nominate any of the following to exercise his functions under this section—

(a) the President of the Court of Protection;

(b) a judicial office holder (as defined in section 109(4) of the Constitutional Reform Act 2005).]

(6) The office of the Supreme Court called the Court of Protection ceases to exist.

AMENDMENTS

1–321   The amendments to this section were made by SI 2006/1016, art.2, Sch.1, para.32.

GENERAL NOTE

1–322   This section establishes a new superior court of record called the Court of Protection which has a comprehensive jurisdiction over the health, welfare and financial affairs of people who lack capacity. Apart from having responsibility for applications under this Act, it also has responsibility for cases relating to adults that were previously dealt with under the inherent jurisdiction of the High Court. The court has the same powers, rights, privileges and authority as the High Court (s.47(1)). The former Court of Protection, which was an office of the Supreme Court dealing only with the patient's "property and affairs", is abolished (subs.(6)). The new court will be able to sit anywhere in England and Wales (subs.(3)). The Explanatory Notes state, at para.130, that it "is intended that the Court of Protection will have a regional presence but will have a central office and registry as designated by the Lord Chancellor. Additional registries (being High Court district registries or county courts) may also be designated". The Court will initially sit in the following locations:

• Birmingham
• Bristol
• Cardiff
• Manchester
• Newcastle
• Preston.

The court's central registry is located at Archway, North London.

In addition to the powers contained in s.16 to make an order and to appoint a deputy and the powers contained in ss.22 and 23 relating to lasting powers of attorney, the court also has the power under s.15 to make declarations on whether a person has capacity to make a particular decision, and whether an act done, or proposed to be done, in relation to a person who lacks capacity is lawful. When reaching a decision about a mentally incapacitated person the court must apply the principles set out in s.1. Provision for applications to be made to the court is made in s.50.

It is prima facie a contempt of court to publish information relating to proceedings which are brought under this Act and which are heard in private (Administration of Justice Act 1960, s.12).

Publicly Funded Legal Assistance

Paragraph 4.18 of "Draft Court Rules: Mental Capacity Act 2005 Court of Protection **1–323** Rules", Department of Constitutional Affairs Consultation Paper CP 10/06 states:

"When an application needs to be made to the Court of Protection, publicly funded legal assistance may be available. Publicly funded legal advice will be available to those who qualify under the 'Legal Help' scheme through Community Legal Service solicitors or advice agencies. Applications for full publicly funded legal representation before the Court of Protection may be made to the Legal Services Commission (LSC) by a solicitor, for cases where this is necessary."

Subsection (3)

The Law Commission anticipated a need for there to be at least one venue for each of the **1–324** six court circuits in England and Wales (Law Com No.231, para.10.16).

The judges of the Court of Protection

46.—(1) Subject to Court of Protection Rules under section 51(2)(d), the juris- **1–325** diction of the court is exercisable by a judge nominated for that purpose by—

  (a) the [Lord Chief Justice], or

 [(b) where nominated by the Lord Chief Justice to act on his behalf under this
        subsection –

      (a) the President of the Court of Protection;

      (b) a judicial office holder (as defined in section 109(4) of the
            Constitutional Reform Act 2005).]

  (2) To be nominated, a judge must be—

 (a) the President of the Family Division,

 (b) the Vice-Chancellor,

 (c) a puisne judge of the High Court,

 (d) a circuit judge, or

 (e) a district judge.

  (3) The [Lord Chief Justice, after consulting the Lord Chancellor,] must—

 (a) appoint one of the judges nominated by virtue of subsection (2)(a) to (c) to
        be President of the Court of Protection, and

 (b) appoint another of those judges to be Vice-President of the Court of
        Protection.

  (4) The [Lord Chief Justice, after consulting the Lord Chancellor,] must appoint one of the judges nominated by virtue of subsection (2)(d) or (e) to be Senior Judge of the Court of Protection, having such administrative functions in relation to the court as the Lord Chancellor[, after consulting the Lord Chief Justice,] may direct.

Mental Capacity Act 2005

AMENDMENTS
1–326 The amendments to this section were made by SI 2006/1016, art.2, Sch.1, para.33.

DEFINITIONS
1–327 "the court": s.64(1)

GENERAL NOTE
1–328 The jurisdiction of the Court of Protection will be exercised by judges nominated by the Lord Chancellor, or a person acting on his behalf, from the list set out in subs.(2). One of the nominated judges must be appointed as President of the Court of Protection and another to be Vice-President (subs.(3)). A judge must also be appointed to be Senior Judge of the Court of Protection (subs.(4)). He or she will have various administrative responsibilities.

Subsection (3)
1–329 Sir Mark Potter, the President of the Family Division, has been appointed President and Sir Andrew Morritt, the Vice-Chancellor, has been appointed Vice-President.

Subsection (4)
1–330 Master Denzil Lush has been appointed Senior Judge.

Supplementary powers

General powers and effect of orders etc
1–331 **47.**—(1) The court has in connection with its jurisdiction the same powers, rights, privileges and authority as the High Court.

(2) Section 204 of the Law of Property Act 1925 (c. 20) (orders of High Court conclusive in favour of purchasers) applies in relation to orders and directions of the court as it applies to orders of the High Court.

(3) Office copies of orders made, directions given or other instruments issued by the court and sealed with its official seal are admissible in all legal proceedings as evidence of the originals without any further proof.

DEFINITIONS
1–332 "the court": s.64(1)
"purchaser": s.64(1)

GENERAL NOTE

Subsection (1)
1–333 This gives the Court of Protection the same powers as the High Court, for example in relation to witnesses, injunctions, contempt, and enforcement.

Subsection (2)
1–334 Section 204 of the 1925 Act reads:

"(1) An order of the court under any statutory or other jurisdiction shall not, as against a purchaser, be invalidated on the ground of want of jurisdiction, or of want of any concurrence, consent, notice, or service, whether the purchaser has notice of any such want or not.

(2) This section has effect with respect to any lease, sale, or other act under the authority of the court, and purporting to be in pursuance of any statutory power notwithstanding any exception in such statute.

(3) This section applies to all orders made before or after the commencement of this Act."

134

Interim orders and directions

48.—The court may, pending the determination of an application to it in **1–335** relation to a person (P), make an order or give directions in respect of any matter if—

(a) there is reason to believe that P lacks capacity in relation to the matter,

(b) the matter is one to which its powers under this Act extend, and

(c) it is in P's best interests to make the order, or give the directions, without delay.

DEFINITIONS
"the court": s.64(1)   **1–336**

GENERAL NOTE
This section enables the court to make interim orders even if evidence of lack of capacity **1–337** is not yet available, where there is reason for the court to believe that the person lacks capacity in respect of a particular matter within the jurisdiction of the court and it is in the best interests of the person for the court to act without delay.

In *B Borough Council v Mrs S and Mr S (by the Official Solicitor)* [2006] EWHC 2584 (Fam), Charles J. said at para.44:

"When the Mental Capacity Act comes into force it will provide statutory jurisdiction for [granting interim declaratory and injunctive relief]. In my view the procedure relating to, and the evidence required for a without notice application will not alter materially when the applications are based on that statutory jurisdiction."

Guidance on the making of without notice applications to the court under the inherent jurisdiction was provided by his Lordship at paras 38–43 and 158.

Power to call for reports

49.—(1) This section applies where, in proceedings brought in respect of a per- **1–338** son (P) under Part 1, the court is considering a question relating to P.

(2) The court may require a report to be made to it by the Public Guardian or by a Court of Protection Visitor.

(3) The court may require a local authority, or an NHS body, to arrange for a report to be made—

(a) by one of its officers or employees, or

(b) by such other person (other than the Public Guardian or a Court of Protection Visitor) as the authority, or the NHS body, considers appropriate.

(4) The report must deal with such matters relating to P as the court may direct.

(5) Court of Protection Rules may specify matters which, unless the court directs otherwise, must also be dealt with in the report.

(6) The report may be made in writing or orally, as the court may direct.

(7) In complying with a requirement, the Public Guardian or a Court of Protection Visitor may, at all reasonable times, examine and take copies of—

(a) any health record,

(b) any record of, or held by, a local authority and compiled in connection with a social services function, and

(c) any record held by a person registered under Part 2 of the Care Standards Act 2000 (c.14),

so far as the record relates to P.

(8) If the Public Guardian or a Court of Protection Visitor is making a visit in the course of complying with a requirement, he may interview P in private.

(9) If a Court of Protection Visitor who is a Special Visitor is making a visit in the course of complying with a requirement, he may if the court so directs carry out in private a medical, psychiatric or psychological examination of P's capacity and condition.

(10) "NHS body" has the meaning given in section 148 of the Health and Social Care (Community Health and Standards) Act 2003 (c. 43).

(11) "Requirement" means a requirement imposed under subsection (2) or (3).

DEFINITIONS
1–339   "the court": s.64(1)
"Court of Protection Visitor": s.64(1)
"local authority": s.64(1)
"Court of Protection Rules": s.64(1)
"social services function": s.64(1)

GENERAL NOTE
1–340   This section makes provision for reports to be made to assist the Court of Protection in determining a case relating to P. The court can require either written or oral reports to be made by the Public Guardian, a Court of Protection Visitor, a local authority or a NHS body (subss.(2), (3) and (6)). The report, which could assist the court in determining whether an oral hearing of a case is needed, must deal with such matters as the court and/or the Court of Protection Rules direct (subss.(4) and (5)). The Public Guardian and a Court of Protection Visitor are given power to examine and take copies of relevant records and to interview P in private (subss.(7) and (8)). Where a Court of Protection Visitor is a Special Visitor (see s.61(2)), he or she may, on the directions of the court, carry out in private medical, psychiatric or psychological examinations of P's capacity and condition (subs.(9)).

Subsection (2)
1–341   A case heard under the Mental Health Act 1959 (c.2) suggests that in initial applications for the appointment of a deputy and in applications to determine proceedings, where the ultimate issue is whether an individual should either become or remain subject to the court's jurisdiction, the court should lean towards disclosing the Visitor's report, and the individual should be permitted to test the report by putting questions to the Visitor. The court should only withhold disclosure where this is deemed to be in the person's best interests. In all other cases, the judge should only direct disclosure if he sees a positive advantage in doing so, either in the interests of the person generally, or because he feels it would assist the judge in the exercise of his functions (*WLW, Re* [1972] Ch 456 at 457, *per* Goff J.).

It is a contempt of court to interfere with the discharge of a Visitor's duties (*Anon, Re* (1875–90) 18 Ch.D 26, *per* James L.J. at 27).

Subsection (3)
1–342   Paragraph (b) covers the situation where the local authority or NHS body has subcontracted its work to someone else.

NHS BODY. See subs.(10).

Subsection (6)
1–343   ORALLY. The power to receive oral reports will be particularly helpful in cases of urgency.

Subsections (7), (8) and (9)
1–344   REQUIREMENT. See subs.(11)

Under s.148 of the 2003 Act, an English NHS body means a Primary Care Trust, a **1–345**
Strategic Health Authority, an English NHS trust and a NHS foundation trust. A Welsh
NHS body means a Local Health Board, a Welsh NHS trust and a Special Health
Authority performing functions only or mainly in respect of Wales. A "NHS body" also
includes a cross-border Special Health Authority which means a SHA not performing func-
tions only or mainly in respect of England or only or mainly in respect of Wales.

Practice and procedure

Applications to the Court of Protection

50.—(1) No permission is required for an application to the court for the exer- **1–346**
cise of any of its powers under this Act—

(a) by a person who lacks, or is alleged to lack, capacity,

(b) if such a person has not reached 18, by anyone with parental responsibility
for him,

(c) by the donor or a donee of a lasting power of attorney to which the application relates,

(d) by a deputy appointed by the court for a person to whom the application
relates, or

(e) by a person named in an existing order of the court, if the application relates
to the order.

(2) But, subject to Court of Protection Rules and to paragraph 20(2) of
Schedule 3 (declarations relating to private international law), permission is
required for any other application to the court.

(3) In deciding whether to grant permission the court must, in particular, have
regard to—

(a) the applicant's connection with the person to whom the application relates,

(b) the reasons for the application,

(c) the benefit to the person to whom the application relates of a proposed order
or directions, and

(d) whether the benefit can be achieved in any other way.

(4) "Parental responsibility" has the same meaning as in the Children Act 1989
(c. 41).

DEFINITIONS
"the court": s.64(1)   **1–347**
"lasting power of attorney": s.64(1)
"deputy": s.64(1)
"Court of Protection Rules": s.64(1)

GENERAL NOTE
This section provides that persons listed in subs.(1) can make as application to the Court **1–348**
of Protection as of right. Other potential applicants will have to obtain the permission of the
court, although the Court of Protection Rules might provide that certain types of application
will not require permission. The factors that the court must have regard to when considering
whether to grant permission are set out in subs.(3). They "are designed to ensure that any
proposed application will promote the interests of the person concerned, rather than causing unnecessary distress or difficulty for him" (Explanatory Notes, para.136). It is
anticipated that the majority of applications to the court will be decided on the basis of
the judge's consideration of the papers without any of the parties attending.

The *Code of Practice* deals with the identity of the applicant at paras 8.7–8.10:

"The person making the application will vary, depending on the circumstances. For example, a person wishing to challenge a finding that they lack capacity may apply to the court, supported by others where necessary. Where there is a disagreement among family members, for example, a family member may wish to apply to the court to settle the disagreement – bearing in mind the need, in most cases, to get permission beforehand.

For cases about serious or major decisions concerning medical treatment . . . the NHS Trust or other organisation responsible for the patient's care will usually make the application. If social care staff are concerned about a decision that affects the welfare of a person who lacks capacity, the relevant local authority should make the application.

For decisions about the property and affairs of someone who lacks capacity to manage their own affairs, the applicant will usually be the person (for example, family carer) who needs specific authority from the court to deal with the individual's money or property.

If the applicant is the person who is alleged to lack capacity, they will always be a party to the court proceedings. In all other cases, the court will decide whether the person who lacks, or is alleged to lack, capacity should be involved as a party to the case. Where the person is a party to the case, the court may appoint the Official Solicitor to act for them."

As the European Court of Human Rights has identified that the State may have positive obligations designed to secure respect for private and family life under Art.8 of the European Convention on Human Rights (see, for example, *Glasser v United Kingdom* (2001) 33 E.H.R.R. 1), it is arguable that a local authority has an obligation to make an application to the court if a mentally incapacitated adult is assessed as being likely to suffer harm if he remained with his family. Also see *S (Adult Patient) (Inherent Jurisdiction; Family Life), Re* [2002] EWHC 2278; [2003] 1 F.L.R. 292, noted under s.16(2).

Subsection (1) (a)

1–349   The Court of Protection Rules will enable the court to appoint someone to act for this person (s.51(2)(e)).

Court of Protection Rules

1–350   **51.**—[(1) Rules of court with respect to the practice and procedure of the court (to be called "Court of Protection Rules") may be made in accordance with Part 1 of Schedule 1 to the Constitutional Reform Act 2003.]

(2) Court of Protection Rules may, in particular, make provision—

(a) as to the manner and form in which proceedings are to be commenced;

(b) as to the persons entitled to be notified of, and be made parties to, the proceedings;

(c) for the allocation, in such circumstances as may be specified, of any specified description of proceedings to a specified judge or to specified descriptions of judges;

(d) for the exercise of the jurisdiction of the court, in such circumstances as may be specified, by its officers or other staff;

(e) for enabling the court to appoint a suitable person (who may, with his consent, be the Official Solicitor) to act in the name of, or on behalf of, or to represent the person to whom the proceedings relate;

(f) for enabling an application to the court to be disposed of without a hearing;

(g) for enabling the court to proceed with, or with any part of, a hearing in the absence of the person to whom the proceedings relate;

(h) for enabling or requiring the proceedings or any part of them to be conducted in private and for enabling the court to determine who is to be admitted when the court sits in private and to exclude specified persons when it sits in public;

(i) as to what may be received as evidence (whether or not admissible apart from the rules) and the manner in which it is to be presented;

(j) for the enforcement of orders made and directions given in the proceedings.

(3) Court of Protection Rules may, instead of providing for any matter, refer to provision made or to be made about that matter by directions.

(4) Court of Protection Rules may make different provision for different areas.

AMENDMENT
Subs.(1) was substituted by SI 2006/1016, art.2, Sch.1, para.34.   **1–351**

DEFINITIONS
"the court": s.64(1)   **1–352**

[Practice directions
52.—(1) Directions as to the practice and procedure of the court may be given **1–353** in accordance with Part 1 of Schedule 2 to the Constitutional Reform Act 2005.

(2) Practice directions given otherwise than under subsection (1) may not be given without the approval of—

(a) the Lord Chancellor, and

(b) the Lord Chief Justice.

(3) The Lord Chief Justice may nominate any of the following to exercise his functions under this section—

(a) the President of the Court of Protection;

(b) a judicial office holder (as defined in section 109(4) of the Constitutional Reform Act 2005).]

AMENDMENT
This section was substituted by SI 2006/1016, art.2, Sch.1, para.35.   **1–354**

DEFINITIONS
"the court": s.64(1)   **1–355**

GENERAL NOTE
This section provides for practice directions to be made regarding the court's practice **1–356** and procedure. Section 51(3) enables the Court of Protection Rules, instead of providing for any matter, to refer to provision made by a practice direction. The "intention is to make rules accompanied by practice directions, on the model of the Civil Procedure Rules 1998" (Explanatory Notes, para.138).

Rights of appeal
53.—(1) Subject to the provisions of this section, an appeal lies to the Court of **1–357** Appeal from any decision of the court.

(2) Court of Protection Rules may provide that where a decision of the court is made by—

(a) a person exercising the jurisdiction of the court by virtue of rules made under section 51(2)(d),

(b) a district judge, or

(c) a circuit judge,

an appeal from that decision lies to a prescribed higher judge of the court and not to the Court of Appeal.

(3) For the purposes of this section the higher judges of the court are—

(a) in relation to a person mentioned in subsection (2)(a), a circuit judge or a district judge;

(b) in relation to a person mentioned in subsection (2)(b), a circuit judge;

(c) in relation to any person mentioned in subsection (2), one of the judges nominated by virtue of section 46(2)(a) to (c).

(4) Court of Protection Rules may make provision—

(a) that, in such cases as may be specified, an appeal from a decision of the court may not be made without permission;

(b) as to the person or persons entitled to grant permission to appeal;

(c) as to any requirements to be satisfied before permission is granted;

(d) that where a higher judge of the court makes a decision on an appeal, no appeal may be made to the Court of Appeal from that decision unless the Court of Appeal considers that—

(i) the appeal would raise an important point of principle or practice, or

(ii) there is some other compelling reason for the Court of Appeal to hear it;

(e) as to any considerations to be taken into account in relation to granting or refusing permission to appeal.

DEFINITIONS
1–358   "the court": s.64(1)

GENERAL NOTE
1–359   This section, which will be supplemented by the Court of Protection Rules, is concerned with appeals from decisions of the Court of Protection. The appeal will either be to the Court of Appeal or, if the decision was made by a judge at a lower level in the judicial hierarchy of the court, to a higher judge within the court (subss.(1) and (2)). The Department of Constitutional Affairs has stated that it "is proposed that an appeal from a decision of a District Judge is heard by a Circuit Judge, and that an appeal from the decision of a Circuit Judge is heard by a High Court Judge. Appeals from decisions of a High Court Judge would be heard by the Court of Appeal" ("Draft Court Rules: Mental Capacity Act 2005 Court of Protection Rules", Consultation Paper CP 10/06, para.4.14).

Fees and costs

Fees
1–360   **54.**—(1) The Lord Chancellor may with the consent of the Treasury by order prescribe fees payable in respect of anything dealt with by the court.

(2) An order under this section may in particular contain provision as to—

(a) scales or rates of fees;

(b) exemptions from and reductions in fees;

(c) remission of fees in whole or in part.

(3) Before making an order under this section, the Lord Chancellor must consult—

(a) the President of the Court of Protection,

(b) the Vice-President of the Court of Protection, and

(c) the Senior Judge of the Court of Protection.

(4) The Lord Chancellor must take such steps as are reasonably practicable to bring information about fees to the attention of persons likely to have to pay them.

(5) Fees payable under this section are recoverable summarily as a civil debt.

DEFINITIONS
"the court": s.64(1)   **1–361**

GENERAL NOTE
The "Court of Protection and Office of the Public Guardian Fees", Department of **1–362** Constitutional Affairs Consultation Paper CP 23/06 states at p.11:

> "In Her Majesty's Courts Service (HMCS), fees are set in line with the general principles of the Government's policy on charging fees for services. These are set out in the *Fee and Charges Guide* produced by HM Treasury. They require that fees should reflect a financial objective agreed by ministers, which should reflect (and not exceed) the cost to the organisation of providing the service. The new Court of Protection and Office of the Public Guardian will not be part of HMCS but will operate under the same principles. For the first year of their operation, the Court of Protection and the Office of Public Guardian's fees will be set at a level to recover approximately 80% of the costs of the two organisations, rather than pass on the full costs of operating the services to those applying to the new organisations. Fee exemptions and remissions will ensure that access to justice is protected for those who are unable to pay."

Subsection (1)
BY ORDER. See s.65(2).   **1–363**

Subsection (2)
The principle underpinning this provision was explained by the Parliamentary Under- **1–364** Secretary of State: "[W]e believe that it is right that people should pay a fair price for the court's work on their behalf, but it is also right that fee reduction and remission arrangements exist so that no one is prevented from going to court if paying the fees would cause them financial hardship, or if there are other exceptional circumstances" (*Hansard*, HL Vol. 669, col.754).

Paper CP 23/06, above, states at p.34:

> "Where clients are not entitled to an automatic exemption they may apply for remission of the fee. Remissions are undertaken on [a] discretionary basis."

Costs

55.—(1) Subject to Court of Protection Rules, the costs of and incidental to all **1–365** proceedings in the court are in its discretion.

(2) The rules may in particular make provision for regulating matters relating to the costs of those proceedings, including prescribing scales of costs to be paid to legal or other representatives.

(3) The court has full power to determine by whom and to what extent the costs are to be paid.

(4) The court may, in any proceedings—

(a) disallow, or

(b) order the legal or other representatives concerned to meet,

the whole of any wasted costs or such part of them as may be determined in accordance with the rules.

(5) "Legal or other representative", in relation to a party to proceedings, means any person exercising a right of audience or right to conduct litigation on his behalf.

(6) "Wasted costs" means any costs incurred by a party—
(a) as a result of any improper, unreasonable or negligent act or omission on the part of any legal or other representative or any employee of such a representative, or
(b) which, in the light of any such act or omission occurring after they were incurred, the court considers it is unreasonable to expect that party to pay.

DEFINITIONS
1–366 "Court of Protection Rules": s.64(1)
"the court": s.64(1)

Fees and costs: supplementary
1–367 **56.**—(1) Court of Protection Rules may make provision—
(a) as to the way in which, and funds from which, fees and costs are to be paid;
(b) for charging fees and costs upon the estate of the person to whom the proceedings relate;
(c) for the payment of fees and costs within a specified time of the death of the person to whom the proceedings relate or the conclusion of the proceedings.
(2) A charge on the estate of a person created by virtue of subsection (1)(b) does not cause any interest of the person in any property to fail or determine or to be prevented from recommencing.

DEFINITIONS
1–367a "Court of Protection Rules": s.64(1)

The Public Guardian

The Public Guardian
1–368 **57.**—(1) For the purposes of this Act, there is to be an officer, to be known as the Public Guardian.
(2) The Public Guardian is to be appointed by the Lord Chancellor.
(3) There is to be paid to the Public Guardian out of money provided by Parliament such salary as the Lord Chancellor may determine.
(4) The Lord Chancellor may, after consulting the Public Guardian—
(a) provide him with such officers and staff, or
(b) enter into such contracts with other persons for the provision (by them or their sub-contractors) of officers, staff or services,
as the Lord Chancellor thinks necessary for the proper discharge of the Public Guardian's functions.
(5) Any functions of the Public Guardian may, to the extent authorised by him, be performed by any of his officers.

GENERAL NOTE
1–368a This section provides for a new public official, the Public Guardian, to be appointed by the Lord Chancellor, and for the Lord Chancellor either to provide the Public Guardian with officers and staff and/or to enter into contacts with other persons for the provision of officers, staff or services for the discharge of the Public Guardian's functions. The Public Guardian, who will be supported by the Office of the Public Guardian, an executive agency of the Department of Constitutional Affairs, has both administrative and supervisory functions. These are set out in s.58. The Public Guardian, who will be subject to the scrutiny of the Public Guardian Board (s.59), is required to produce annual reports (s.60).

The first Public Guardian is Richard Brook, a former Chief Executive of MIND. His address is:

Archway Tower
Junction Road
London
N19 5SZ

tel: 0845 330 2900
fax: 0870 739 580

website: *www.guardianship.gov.uk*. This will change to *www.publicguardian.gov.uk* from October 2007.

Functions of the Public Guardian

58.—(1) The Public Guardian has the following functions—   **1–369**
  (a) establishing and maintaining a register of lasting powers of attorney,
  (b) establishing and maintaining a register of orders appointing deputies,
  (c) supervising deputies appointed by the court,
  (d) directing a Court of Protection Visitor to visit—
    (i) a donee of a lasting power of attorney,
    (ii) a deputy appointed by the court, or
    (iii) the person granting the power of attorney or for whom the deputy is appointed (P),

and to make a report to the Public Guardian on such matters as he may direct,
  (e) receiving security which the court requires a person to give for the discharge of his functions,
  (f) receiving reports from donees of lasting powers of attorney and deputies appointed by the court,
  (g) reporting to the court on such matters relating to proceedings under this Act as the court requires,
  (h) dealing with representations (including complaints) about the way in which a donee of a lasting power of attorney or a deputy appointed by the court is exercising his powers,
  (i) publishing, in any manner the Public Guardian thinks appropriate, any information he thinks appropriate about the discharge of his functions.

(2) The functions conferred by subsection (1)(c) and (h) may be discharged in co-operation with any other person who has functions in relation to the care or treatment of P.

(3) The Lord Chancellor may by regulations make provision—
  (a) conferring on the Public Guardian other functions in connection with this Act;
  (b) in connection with the discharge by the Public Guardian of his functions.

(4) Regulations made under subsection (3)(b) may in particular make provision as to—
  (a) the giving of security by deputies appointed by the court and the enforcement and discharge of security so given;
  (b) the fees which may be charged by the Public Guardian;
  (c) the way in which, and funds from which, such fees are to be paid;
  (d) exemptions from and reductions in such fees;

    (e) remission of such fees in whole or in part;

    (f) the making of reports to the Public Guardian by deputies appointed by the court and others who are directed by the court to carry out any transaction for a person who lacks capacity.

(5) For the purpose of enabling him to carry out his functions, the Public Guardian may, at all reasonable times, examine and take copies of—

    (a) any health record,

    (b) any record of, or held by, a local authority and compiled in connection with a social services function, and

    (c) any record held by a person registered under Part 2 of the Care Standards Act 2000 (c.14),

so far as the record relates to P.

(6) The Public Guardian may also for that purpose interview P in private.

DEFINITIONS

1–370   "lasting power of attorney": s.64(1)
"deputy": s.64(1)
"the court": s.64(1)
"Court of ProtectionVisitor": s.64(1)
"health record": s.64(1)
"local authority": s.64(1)
"social services function": s.64(1)

GENERAL NOTE

1–371   The functions of the Public Guardian listed in subs.(1) may be supplemented by regulations made by the Lord Chancellor (subs.(3)). His functions include establishing and maintaining registers of LPAs and orders appointing deputies, supervising deputies to ensure that they exercise their responsibilities in line with the authority given to them, dealing with representations about the way both donees of LPAs and deputies are exercising their powers, and making enquiries or referring matters to the court where there are concerns that donees or deputies are not acting appropriately. The Public Guardian is given power to examine and take copies of relevant health or social services records, and also interview P in private (subss.(5) and (6)). Similar rights are provided for when the Public Guardian is reporting to the Court of Protection (s.49(7)–(8)).

The Public Guardian has no power of enforcement or sanction. An application to the court would have to be made if such power needs to be exercised.

Subsection (1)(h)

1–372   The Public Guardian might wish to refer a complaint concerning the personal welfare of P to the relevant health or social care agency. If the complaint suggests that a criminal offence has been committed, this will be referred to the police.

Subsection (2)

1–373   It "is intended that the Public Guardian will work closely with organisations such as local authorities and NHS bodies" (Explanatory Notes, para.146). Although the Public Guardian's supervisory function will be mainly focused on financial affairs, he "would have a role in identifying and tackling possible abuse with other agencies by providing a focus for concerns and fielding them to the appropriate agency" (Department of Constitutional Affairs, Oral and written evidence, Ev 265).

Public Guardian Board

1–374   **59.**—(1) There is to be a body, to be known as the Public Guardian Board.

(2) The Board's duty is to scrutinise and review the way in which the Public Guardian discharges his functions and to make such recommendations to the Lord Chancellor about that matter as it thinks appropriate.

(3) The Lord Chancellor must, in discharging his functions under sections 57 and 58, give due consideration to recommendations made by the Board.

(4) [*Repealed by SI 2006/1016, art.2, Sch.1, para.36.*]

(5) The Board must have—

(a) at least one member who is a judge of the court, and

(b) at least four members who are persons appearing to the Lord Chancellor to have appropriate knowledge or experience of the work of the Public Guardian.

[(5A) Where a person to be appointed as a member of the Board is a judge of the court, the appointment is to be made by the Lord Chief Justice after consulting the Lord Chancellor.

(5B) In any other case, the appointment of a person as a member of the Board is to be made by the Lord Chancellor.]

(6) The Lord Chancellor may by regulations make provision as to—

(a) the appointment of members of the Board (and, in particular, the procedures to be followed in connection with appointments);

(b) the selection of one of the members to be the chairman;

(c) the term of office of the chairman and members;

(d) their resignation, suspension or removal;

(e) the procedure of the Board (including quorum);

(f) the validation of proceedings in the event of a vacancy among the members or a defect in the appointment of a member.

(7) Subject to any provision made in reliance on subsection (6)(c) or (d), a person is to hold and vacate office as a member of the Board in accordance with the terms of the instrument appointing him.

(8) The Lord Chancellor may make such payments to or in respect of members of the Board by way of reimbursement of expenses, allowances and remuneration as he may determine.

(9) The Board must make an annual report to the Lord Chancellor about the discharge of its functions.

[(10) The Lord Chief Justice may nominate any of the following to exercise his functions under this section—

(a) the President of the Court of Protection;

(b) a judicial office holder (as defined in section 109(4) of the Constitutional Reform Act 2005).]

AMENDMENTS

The amendments to this section were made by SI 2006/1016, art.2, Sch.1.   **1–375**

GENERAL NOTE

This section provides for the establishment of the Public Guardian Board which is **1–376** charged with the duty of scrutinising and reviewing the manner in which the Public Guardian discharges his or her functions. The Board may make recommendations to the Lord Chancellor who must, in discharging his or her functions under ss.57 and 58, give them due consideration.

Annual report

1–377   **60.**—(1) The Public Guardian must make an annual report to the Lord Chancellor about the discharge of his functions.

(2) The Lord Chancellor must, within one month of receiving the report, lay a copy of it before Parliament.

DEFINITIONS

1–378   "Public Guardian": s.64(1)

Court of Protection Visitors

1–379   **61.**—(1) A Court of Protection Visitor is a person who is appointed by the Lord Chancellor to—

(a) a panel of Special Visitors, or

(b) a panel of General Visitors.

(2) A person is not qualified to be a Special Visitor unless he—

(a) is a registered medical practitioner or appears to the Lord Chancellor to have other suitable qualifications or training, and

(b) appears to the Lord Chancellor to have special knowledge of and experience in cases of impairment of or disturbance in the functioning of the mind or brain.

(3) A General Visitor need not have a medical qualification.

(4) A Court of Protection Visitor—

(a) may be appointed for such term and subject to such conditions, and

(b) may be paid such remuneration and allowances,

as the Lord Chancellor may determine.

(5) For the purpose of carrying out his functions under this Act in relation to a person who lacks capacity (P), a Court of Protection Visitor may, at all reasonable times, examine and take copies of—

(a) any health record,

(b) any record of, or held by, a local authority and compiled in connection with a social services function, and

(c) any record held by a person registered under Part 2 of the Care Standards Act 2000 (c.14),

so far as the record relates to P.

(6) A Court of Protection Visitor may also for that purpose interview P in private.

DEFINITIONS

1–380   "health record": s.64(1)
         "local authority": s.64(1)
         "social services function": s.64(1)

GENERAL NOTE

1–381   This section provides for the Lord Chancellor to appoint Special Visitors, who will be medical practitioners, and General Visitors. Their role is to carry out visits and produce independent reports on matters relating to the exercise of powers under this Act as directed by the Court of Protection (s.49(2)) or the Public Guardian (s.58(1)(d)). The Visitors have the power to examine and take copies of relevant records, and to interview P in private.

GENERAL VISITORS. Under the equivalent provision in the Mental Health Act 1983 a **1–382** "patient" would receive a visit from a General Visitor if they "are a minor, if they are living in their own home or with a relative, if they are in a nursing home, other than a NHS hospital and are not being regularly visited by relatives or friends, or if their receiver is a local authority" (35th report of the Public Accounts Committee for Session 1998–1999, p.15, n.13).

PART 3

MISCELLANEOUS AND GENERAL

Declaratory provision

Scope of the Act

1–383   **62.**—For the avoidance of doubt, it is hereby declared that nothing in this Act is to be taken to affect the law relating to murder or manslaughter or the operation of section 2 of the Suicide Act 1961 (c. 60) (assisting suicide).

GENERAL NOTE

1–383a   This section, which was inserted following representations from the Catholic Bishops' Conference of England and Wales, seeks to address the concerns that were expressed to the Joint Committee that this legislation might pave the way for "euthanasia by the back-door" (see para.196). Euthanasia, which is "a deliberate intervention with the express aim of ending life", is illegal (*Who Decides: Making Decisions on Behalf of Mentally Incapacitated Adults*, Cm.3803, para.1.8). Notwithstanding the declaration made in this section, it is the case that both a valid and applicable written advance decision to refuse life-sustaining treatment (see ss.24–26) and a refusal of such treatment by a donee under a lasting power of attorney, if such power is granted to the donee (see s.11(8)), are lawful and must be obeyed by healthcare professionals. A mentally capable patient can therefore use either of these mechanisms to bring about his or her death during a subsequent mental incapacity by refusing either the provision of nutrition and hydration by artificial means or other potentially life saving medical interventions in specified circumstances. In such an eventuality there can be no question of the person having committed suicide, nor therefore of the doctor having aided and abetted him or her in doing so (*Airedale NHS Trust v Bland* [1993] 1 All E.R. 821, HL, *per* Lord Goff at 866). However, if a donee "wanted to refuse consent to treatment and the doctors thought that this was with the intention of murder or manslaughter then the doctor could continue to treat", *per* the Parliamentary Under-Secretary of State in correspondence quoted at (*Hansard*, HL Vol.688, col.1150.

Whether a decision to discontinue treatment that would inevitably lead to the patient's death constitutes euthanasia was considered by Lord Goff in *Bland* at 867:

"[T]he law draws a crucial distinction between cases in which a doctor decides not to provide, or continue to provide, for his patient treatment or care which could or might prolong his life and those in which he decides, for example by administering a lethal drug, actively to bring his patient's life to an end. As I have already indicated, the former may be lawful, either because the doctor is giving effect to his patient's wishes by with-holding the treatment or care, even in certain circumstances in which the patient is incapacitated from stating whether or not he gives his consent. But it is not lawful for a doctor to administer a drug to his patient to bring about his death, even though that course is prompted by a humanitarian desire to end his suffering, however great that suffering may be: see *R v Cox* (September 18,1992, unreported) *per* Ognall J in the Crown Court at Winchester. So to act is to cross the Rubicon which runs between on the one hand the care of the living patient and on the other hand euthanasia—actively causing his death to avoid or to end his suffering. Euthanasia is not lawful at common law. It is, of course well known that there are many responsible members of our society who believe that euthanasia should be made lawful; but that result could I believe, only be achieved by legislation which expresses the democratic will that so fundamental a change should be made in our law, and can, if enacted, ensure that such legalised killing can only be carried out subject to appropriate supervision and control. It is true that the drawing of this distinction may lead to a charge of hypocrisy, because it can be asked why, if the doctor, by discontinuing treatment, is entitled in consequence to let his patient die, it should not be lawful to put him out of his misery straight away, in a more humane manner, by a lethal injection, rather than to let him linger on in pain until he dies. But the law does not feel able to authorise euthanasia, even in circumstances such as these, for, once euthanasia is recognised as lawful in these circumstances, it is difficult to see any logical basis for excluding it in others."

In *Bland* the House of Lords held that treatment, including the provision of nutrition and hydration to the patient by artificial means, could be withheld from a mentally incapacitated patient who had no hope of recovery when it was known that the patient would shortly thereafter die, provided that responsible and competent medical opinion was of the view that it would be in the patient's best interests not to prolong his life by continuing the treatment because such treatment would be futile and would not confer any benefit on him.

Private international law

International protection of adults

63.—Schedule 3—   **1–384**

(a) gives effect in England and Wales to the Convention on the International Protection of Adults signed at the Hague on 13th January 2000 (Cm. 5881) (in so far as this Act does not otherwise do so), and

(b) makes related provision as to the private international law of England and Wales.

GENERAL NOTE

Schedule 3 makes provision as to the private international law of England and Wales in **1–385** relation to persons who cannot protect their interests. In particular, it gives effect in England and Wales to the Convention on the International Protection of Adults (Cm.5881) which was signed at the Hague on January 13, 2000. For the purposes of the Convention, England and Wales, Scotland and Northern Ireland are treated separately because they constitute separate jurisdictions. The provisions of Sch.3 are intended to be compatible with the provisions of Sch.3 to the Adults with Incapacity (Scotland) Act 2000 (asp 4) which provides for the private international law of Scotland in this field, and implemented the Convention in Scotland. The Explanatory Memorandum states at para.170:

"Scotland is as yet, the only country to have ratified the Convention, which will enter into force only once it has been ratified by three states. However, Sch.3 provides private international law rules to govern jurisdictional issues between Scotland and England/ Wales, irrespective of whether the Convention is in force."

The aims of the Convention are set out in Art.1. They are to:

- provide for the protection in international situations of adults who, by reason of impairment or insufficiency in their personal faculties, are not in a position to defend their interests
- establish rules on jurisdiction, applicable law, international recognition and enforcement of protective measures which are to be respected by all Contracting States, and co-operation between Contracting States.

Interpretation

1–386   **64.**—(1) In this Act—

"the 1985 Act" means the Enduring Powers of AttorneyAct 1985 (c. 29),
"advance decision" has the meaning given in section 24(1),
"the court" means the Court of Protection established by section 45, "Court of Protection Rules" has the meaning given in section 51(1), "Court of Protection Visitor" has the meaning given in section 61, "deputy" has the meaning given in section 16(2)(b),
"enactment" includes a provision of subordinate legislation (within the meaning of the Interpretation Act 1978 (c. 30)),
"health record" has the meaning given in section 68 of the Data Protection Act 1998 (c. 29) (as read with section 69 of that Act),
"the Human Rights Convention" has the same meaning as "the Convention" in the Human Rights Act 1998 (c. 42),
"independent mental capacity advocate" has the meaning given in section 35(1),
"lasting power of attorney" has the meaning given in section 9,
"life-sustaining treatment" has the meaning given in section 4(10),
"local authority" means—
   (a) the council of a county in England in which there are no district councils,
   (b) the council of a district in England,
   (c) the council of a county or county borough in Wales,
   (d) the council of a London borough,
   (e) the Common Council of the City of London, or
   (f) the Council of the Isles of Scilly,
"Mental Health Act" means the Mental Health Act 1983 (c. 20),
"prescribed", in relation to regulations made under this Act, means prescribed by those regulations,
"property" includes any thing in action and any interest in real or personal property,
"public authority" has the same meaning as in the Human Rights Act 1998, "Public Guardian" has the meaning given in section 57,
"purchaser" and "purchase" have the meaning given in section 205(1) of the Law of PropertyAct 1925 (c. 20),
"social services function" has the meaning given in section 1A of the Local Authority Social Services Act 1970 (c. 42),
"treatment" includes a diagnostic or other procedure,
"trust corporation" has the meaning given in section 68(1) of the Trustee Act 1925 (c.19), and
"will" includes codicil.

(2) In this Act, references to making decisions, in relation to a donee of a lasting power of attorney or a deputy appointed by the court, include, where appropriate, acting on decisions made.

(3) In this Act, references to the bankruptcy of an individual include a case where a bankruptcy restrictions order under the Insolvency Act 1986 (c. 45) has effect in respect of him.

(4)"Bankruptcy restrictions order" includes an interim bankruptcy restrictions order.

GENERAL NOTE

Subsection (1)

TREATMENT. The provision of nutrition and hydration to a patient which involves the **1–387** application of a medical technique is "medical treatment" (*Airedale NHS Trust v Bland* [1993] 1 All E.R. 821, HL).

Rules, regulations and orders

65.—(1) Any power to make rules, regulations or orders under this Act [, other **1–388** than the powers in section 21]—

(a) is exercisable by statutory instrument;
(b) includes power to make supplementary, incidental, consequential, transitional or saving provision;
(c) includes power to make different provision for different cases.

(2) Any statutory instrument containing rules, regulations or orders made by the Lord Chancellor or the Secretary of State under this Act, other than—

(a) regulations under section 34 (loss of capacity during research project),
(b) regulations under section 41 (adjusting role of independent mental capacity advocacy service),
(c) regulations under paragraph 32(1)(b) of Schedule 3 (private international law relating to the protection of adults),
(d) an order of the kind mentioned in section 67(6) (consequential amendments of primary legislation), or
(e) an order under section 68 (commencement),

is subject to annulment in pursuance of a resolution of either House of Parliament.

(3) A statutory instrument containing an Order in Council under paragraph 31 of Schedule 3 (provision to give further effect to Hague Convention) is subject to annulment in pursuance of a resolution of either House of Parliament.

(4) A statutory instrument containing regulations made by the Secretary of State under section 34 or 41 or by the Lord Chancellor under paragraph 32(1)(b) of Schedule 3 may not be made unless a draft has been laid before and approved by resolution of each House of Parliament.

[(5) An order under section 21—

(a) may include supplementary, incidental, consequential, transitional or saving provision;
(b) may make different provision for different cases;
(c) is to be made in the form of a statutory instrument to which the Statutory Instruments Act 1946 applies as if the order were made by a Minister of the Crown; and
(d) is subject to annulment in pursuance of a resolution of either House of Parliament.]

AMENDMENTS

The amendments to this section were made by SI 2006/1016, art.2, Sch.1. **1–389**

Existing receivers and enduring powers of attorney etc

66.—(1) The following provisions cease to have effect— **1–390**

(a) Part 7 of the Mental Health Act,
(b) the Enduring Powers of AttorneyAct 1985 (c. 29).

(2) No enduring power of attorney within the meaning of the 1985 Act is to be created after the commencement of subsection (1)(b).

(3) Schedule 4 has effect in place of the 1985 Act in relation to any enduring power of attorney created before the commencement of subsection (1)(b).

(4) Schedule 5 contains transitional provisions and savings in relation to Part 7 of the Mental Health Act and the 1985 Act.

GENERAL NOTE

1–391   This section repeals Pt VII of the Mental Health Act 1983 and the whole of the Enduring Powers of Attorney Act 1985, but provides through transitional provisions contained in Schs 4 and 5 that those with valid powers as attorneys under the 1985 Act or receivers appointed under the 1983 Act do not lose their powers on the implementation of the repeals. It will no longer be possible to create an enduring power of attorney once the repeal of the 1985 Act has taken effect.

Subsection (3)

1–392   Schedule 4 has effect in relation to enduring powers of attorney created before the implementation of this Act. It ensures that such instruments will continue to have the same legal effect as they had at the time they were made. They will also continue to be governed by the same legal rules and procedures which were in place at the time they were made. The Schedule therefore reproduces, with amendments, the relevant provisions of the 1985 Act and provides that the principles set out in s.1 shall not retrospectively apply to EPAs. The amendments are directed to the way in which tasks performed by the replaced Court of Protection will, on implementation of this Act, be divided between the Court of Protection and the Office of Public Guardian.

The 1985 Act is considered by S.M. Cretney and D. Lush in *Enduring Powers of Attorney* (5th edn, Jordans, London, 2001).

Subsection (4)

1–393   Schedule 5 contains transitional provisions that apply to circumstances where a receiver was appointed under the Mental Health Act 1983 before this Act came into force. The "Court of Protection and Office of the Public Guardian Fees" Consultation Paper CP 23/06 (DCA September, 2006) states at p.20:

"The Public Guardianship Office will communicate with all receivers in advance of April 2007, explaining how they will be affected by [the] transitional provisions and the steps that the court and the Public Guardianship Office propose to take to ensure that [the] provisions can take effect.

All receiverships will be reviewed within the first year of operation of the new Act During this time, receiverships will be individually reviewed (which may involve Nominated Officers) and any changes to the court order needed to set up the case to operate as a deputyship under the new Act would be made."

Minor and consequential amendments and repeals

1–394   **67.**—(1) Schedule 6 contains minor and consequential amendments.

(2) Schedule 7 contains repeals.

(3) The Lord Chancellor may by order make supplementary, incidental, consequential, transitional or saving provision for the purposes of, in consequence of, or for giving full effect to a provision of this Act.

(4) An order under subsection (3) may, in particular—

(a)   provide for a provision of this Act which comes into force before another provision of this Act has come into force to have effect, until the other provision has come into force, with specified modifications;

(b) amend, repeal or revoke an enactment, other than one contained in an Act or Measure passed in a Session after the one in which this Act is passed.

(5) The amendments that may be made under subsection (4)(b) are in addition to those made by or under any other provision of this Act.

(6) An order under subsection (3) which amends or repeals a provision of an Act or Measure may not be made unless a draft has been laid before and approved by resolution of each House of Parliament.

Commencement and extent

68.—(1) This Act, other than sections 30 to 41, comes into force in accordance **1–395** with provision made by order by the Lord Chancellor.

(2) Sections 30 to 41 come into force in accordance with provision made by order by—

(a) the Secretary of State, in relation to England, and

(b) the National Assembly for Wales, in relation to Wales.

(3) An order under this section may appoint different days for different provisions and different purposes.

(4) Subject to subsections (5) and (6), this Act extends to England and Wales only.

(5) The following provisions extend to the United Kingdom—

(a) paragraph 16(1) of Schedule 1(evidence of instruments and of registration of lasting powers of attorney),

(b) paragraph 15(3) of Schedule 4(evidence of instruments and of registration of enduring powers of attorney).

(6) Subject to any provision made in Schedule 6, the amendments and repeals made by Schedules 6 and 7 have the same extent as the enactments to which they relate.

GENERAL NOTE

The following commencement orders has been made under this section: the Mental **1–396** Capacity Act 2005 (Commencement No.1) Order 2006 (SI 2006/2814) (as amended by SI 2006/3473) and the Mental Capacity Act 2005 (Commencement No.1) (England and Wales) Order 2007 (SI 2007/563). The Explanatory Note to SI 2007/563 explains the effect of the two orders:

"The Mental Capacity Act 2005 (Commencement No. 1) Order (2006/2814) (as amended by SI 2006/3473) brought or brings the following provisions of the Act into force in England as follows—

Provision	Date of commencement
Sections 30 to 34 (in respect of any research carried out as part of a project begun on or after 1 October 2007).	01.10.2007
Sections 30 to 34 (for the purpose of enabling research applications to be made to, and determined by, an appropriate body).	01.07.2007
Sections 30 to 34 (where a research project has begun before 1 October 2007 and was approved before that date).	01.10.2008
Sections 35 to 41 (to enable the Secretary of State for Health to make arrangements to make independent mental capacity advocates available and to enable local authorities to approve independent mental capacity advocates).	01.11.2006
Sections 35 to 41 (fully into force).	01.04.2007

Article 2(1) of this Order brings sections 42(1), (2), (3), (6) and (7) (codes of practice), 43 (codes of practice: procedure) and 44 (ill-treatment or neglect) of the Act into force in relation to England and Wales on 1 April 2007.

Article 2(2) of this Order brings sections 1 (principles), 2 (people who lack capacity), 3 (inability to make decisions), 4 (best interests), 42(4) (duty to have regard to codes of practice) and 42(5) (relevance of codes of practice to criminal or civil proceedings) of the Act into force on 1 April 2007 for purposes relating to the independent mental capacity advocate service (sections 35 to 41). Article 2(2) applies to England only.

Article 2(3) of this Order brings sections 1 (principles), 2 (people who lack capacity), 3 (inability to make decisions), 4 (best interests), 42(4) (duty to have regard to codes of practice) and 42(5) (relevance of codes of practice to criminal or civil proceedings) of the Act into force on 1 April 2007 for the purposes of section 44 (ill-treatment or neglect). Article 2(3) applies to England and Wales.

Article 2(4) brings section 64 (interpretation) into force on 1 April 2007 for the purposes of Articles 2(1), 2(2) and 2(3). Articles 2(1) and 2(3) apply to England and Wales and Article 2(2) applies to England."

Similar commencement provisions relating to ss.30 to 34 were made in respect of Wales by the Mental Capacity Act 2005 (Commencement) (Wales) Order 2007 (SI 2007/856 (W.79)), arts 2 to 4. Unlike the position in England, art.5 of this Order commences ss.35 to 41 in Wales on October 1, 2007.

Subsection (2)(b)

1–397 The functions of the National Assembly for Wales are performed by the Welsh Ministers (Government of Wales Act 2006, s.162, Sch.11, para.30).

Short title

1–398 **69.** This Act may be cited as the Mental Capacity Act 2005.

SCHEDULES

SCHEDULE 1   **Section 9**

LASTING POWERS OF ATTORNEY: FORMALITIES

PART 1

MAKING INSTRUMENTS

General requirements as to making instruments

1–399 **1.**—(1) An instrument is not made in accordance with this Schedule unless—
  (a) it is in the prescribed form,
  (b) it complies with paragraph 2, and
  (c) any prescribed requirements in connection with its execution are satisfied.
(2) Regulations may make different provision according to whether—
  (a) the instrument relates to personal welfare or to property and affairs (or to both);
  (b) only one or more than one donee is to be appointed (and if more than one, whether jointly or jointly and severally).
(3) In this Schedule—
  (a) "prescribed" means prescribed by regulations, and
  (b) "regulations" means regulations made for the purposes of this Schedule by the Lord Chancellor.

Requirements as to content of instruments

1–400

2.—(1) The instrument must include—
  (a) the prescribed information about the purpose of the instrument and the effect of a lasting power of attorney,
  (b) a statement by the donor to the effect that he—
    (i) has read the prescribed information or a prescribed part of it (or has had it read to him), and
    (ii) intends the authority conferred under the instrument to include authority to make decisions on his behalf in circumstances where he no longer has capacity,
  (c) a statement by the donor—
    (i) naming a person or persons whom the donor wishes to be notified of any application for the registration of the instrument, or
    (ii) stating that there are no persons whom he wishes to be notified of any such application,
  (d) a statement by the donee (or, if more than one, each of them) to the effect that he—
    (i) has read the prescribed information or a prescribed part of it (or has had it read to him), and
    (ii) understands the duties imposed on a donee of a lasting power of attorney under sections 1(the principles) and 4 (best interests), and
  (e) a certificate by a person of a prescribed description that, in his opinion, at the time when the donor executes the instrument—
    (i) the donor understands the purpose of the instrument and the scope of the authority conferred under it,
    (ii) no fraud or undue pressure is being used to induce the donor to create a lasting power of attorney, and
    (iii) there is nothing else which would prevent a lasting power of attorney from being created by the instrument.
  (2) Regulations may—
  (a) prescribe a maximum number of named persons;
  (b) provide that, where the instrument includes a statement under sub-paragraph (1)(c)(ii), two persons of a prescribed description must each give a certificate under sub-paragraph (1)(e).
  (3) The persons who may be named persons do not include a person who is appointed as donee under the instrument.
  (4) In this Schedule, "named person" means a person named under sub-paragraph (1)(c).
  (5) A certificate under sub-paragraph (1)(e)—
  (a) must be made in the prescribed form, and
  (b) must include any prescribed information.
  (6) The certificate may not be given by a person appointed as donee under the instrument.

Failure to comply with prescribed form

3.—(1) If an instrument differs in an immaterial respect in form or mode of expression from the **1–401** prescribed form, it is to be treated by the Public Guardian as sufficient in point of form and expression.
  (2) The court may declare that an instrument which is not in the prescribed form is to be treated as if it were, if it is satisfied that the persons executing the instrument intended it to create a lasting power of attorney.

PART 2

REGISTRATION

4.—(1) An application to the Public Guardian for the registration of an instrument intended to **1–402** create a lasting power of attorney—
  (a) must be made in the prescribed form, and
  (b) must include any prescribed information.
  (2) The application may be made—
  (a) by the donor,
  (b) by the donee or donees, or
  (c) if the instrument appoints two or more donees to act jointly and severally in respect of any matter, by any of the donees.
  (3) The application must be accompanied by—
  (a) the instrument, and
  (b) any fee provided for under section 58(4)(b).

(4) A person who, in an application for registration, makes a statement which he knows to be false in a material particular is guilty of an offence and is liable—

    (a) on summary conviction, to imprisonment for a term not exceeding 12 months or a fine not exceeding the statutory maximum or both;

    (b) on conviction on indictment, to imprisonment for a term not exceeding 2 years or a fine or both.

1–403   5. Subject to paragraphs 11 to 14, the Public Guardian must register the instrument as a lasting power of attorney at the end of the prescribed period.

1–404   6.—(1) A donor about to make an application under paragraph 4(2)(a) must notify any named persons that he is about to do so.

(2) The donee (or donees) about to make an application under paragraph 4(2)(b) or (c) must notify any named persons that he is (or they are) about to do so.

1–405   7. As soon as is practicable after receiving an application by the donor under paragraph 4(2)(a), the Public Guardian must notify the donee (or donees) that the application has been received.

1–406   8.—(1) As soon as is practicable after receiving an application by a donee (or donees) under paragraph 4(2)(b), the Public Guardian must notify the donor that the application has been received.

(2) As soon as is practicable after receiving an application by a donee under paragraph 4(2)(c), the Public Guardian must notify—

    (a) the donor, and

    (b) the donee or donees who did not join in making the application,

that the application has been received.

1–407   9.—(1) A notice under paragraph 6 must be made in the prescribed form.

(2) A notice under paragraph 6, 7 or 8 must include such information, if any, as may be prescribed.

1–408   10. The court may—

    (a) on the application of the donor, dispense with the requirement to notify under paragraph 6(1), or

    (b) on the application of the donee or donees concerned, dispense with the requirement to notify under paragraph 6(2),

if satisfied that no useful purpose would be served by giving the notice.

1–409   11.—(1) If it appears to the Public Guardian that an instrument accompanying an application under paragraph 4 is not made in accordance with this Schedule, he must not register the instrument unless the court directs him to do so.

(2) Sub-paragraph (3) applies if it appears to the Public Guardian that the instrument contains a provision which—

    (a) would be ineffective as part of a lasting power of attorney, or

    (b) would prevent the instrument from operating as a valid lasting power of attorney.

(3) The Public Guardian—

    (a) must apply to the court for it to determine the matter under section 23(1), and

    (b) pending the determination by the court, must not register the instrument.

(4) Sub-paragraph (5) applies if the court determines under section 23(1) (whether or not on an application by the Public Guardian) that the instrument contains a provision which—

    (a) would be ineffective as part of a lasting power of attorney, or

    (b) would prevent the instrument from operating as a valid lasting power of attorney.

(5) The court must—

    (a) notify the Public Guardian that it has severed the provision, or

    (b) direct him not to register the instrument.

(6) Where the court notifies the Public Guardian that it has severed a provision, he must register the instrument with a note to that effect attached to it.

1–410   12.—(1) Sub-paragraph (2) applies if it appears to the Public Guardian that—

    (a) there is a deputy appointed by the court for the donor, and

    (b) the powers conferred on the deputy would, if the instrument were registered, to any extent conflict with the powers conferred on the attorney.

(2) The Public Guardian must not register the instrument unless the court directs him to do so.

1–411   13.—(1) Sub-paragraph (2) applies if a donee or a named person—

    (a) receives a notice under paragraph 6, 7 or 8 of an application for the registration of an instrument, and

    (b) before the end of the prescribed period, gives notice to the Public Guardian of an objection to the registration on the ground that an event mentioned in section 13(3) or (6)(a) to (d) has occurred which has revoked the instrument.

(2) If the Public Guardian is satisfied that the ground for making the objection is established, he must not register the instrument unless the court, on the application of the person applying for the registration—

    (a) is satisfied that the ground is not established, and

(b) directs the Public Guardian to register the instrument.

(3) Sub-paragraph (4) applies if a donee or a named person—

(a) receives a notice under paragraph 6, 7 or 8 of an application for the registration of an instrument, and

(b) before the end of the prescribed period—

(i) makes an application to the court objecting to the registration on a prescribed ground, and

(ii) notifies the Public Guardian of the application.

(4) The Public Guardian must not register the instrument unless the court directs him to do so.

14.—(1) This paragraph applies if the donor— **1–412**

(a) receives a notice under paragraph 8 of an application for the registration of an instrument, and

(b) before the end of the prescribed period, gives notice to the Public Guardian of an objection to the registration.

(2) The Public Guardian must not register the instrument unless the court, on the application of the donee or, if more than one, any of them—

(a) is satisfied that the donor lacks capacity to object to the registration, and

(b) directs the Public Guardian to register the instrument.

15. Where an instrument is registered under this Schedule, the Public Guardian must give notice of **1–413** the fact in the prescribed form to—

(a) the donor, and

(b) the donee or, if more than one, each of them.

16.—(1) A document purporting to be an office copy of an instrument registered under this **1–414** Schedule is, in any part of the United Kingdom, evidence of—

(a) the contents of the instrument, and

(b) the fact that it has been registered.

(2) Sub-paragraph (1) is without prejudice to—

(a) section 3 of the Powers of Attorney Act 1971 (c. 27) (proof by certified copy), and

(b) any other method of proof authorised by law.

PART 3

CANCELLATION OF REGISTRATION AND NOTIFICATION OF SEVERANCE

17.—(1) The Public Guardian must cancel the registration of an instrument as a lasting power of **1–415** attorney on being satisfied that the power has been revoked—

(a) as a result of the donor's bankruptcy, or

(b) on the occurrence of an event mentioned in section 13(6)(a) to (d).

(2) If the Public Guardian cancels the registration of an instrument he must notify—

(a) the donor, and

(b) the donee or, if more than one, each of them.

18. The court must direct the Public Guardian to cancel the registration of an instrument as a lasting **1–416** power of attorney if it—

(a) determines under section 22(2)(a) that a requirement for creating the power was not met,

(b) determines under section 22(2)(b) that the power has been revoked or has otherwise come to an end, or

(c) revokes the power under section 22(4)(b) (fraud etc.).

19.—(1) Sub-paragraph (2) applies if the court determines under section 23(1) that a lasting power **1–417** of attorney contains a provision which—

(a) is ineffective as part of a lasting power of attorney, or

(b) prevents the instrument from operating as a valid lasting power of attorney.

(2) The court must—

(a) notify the Public Guardian that it has severed the provision, or

(b) direct him to cancel the registration of the instrument as a lasting power of attorney.

20. On the cancellation of the registration of an instrument, the instrument and any office copies of **1–418** it must be delivered up to the Public Guardian to be cancelled.

Partial revocation or suspension of power as a result of bankruptcy

1–419   **21.** If in the case of a registered instrument it appears to the Public Guardian that under section 13 a lasting power of attorney is revoked, or suspended, in relation to the donor's property and affairs (but not in relation to other matters), the Public Guardian must attach to the instrument a note to that effect.

Termination of appointment of donee which does not revoke power

1–420   **22.** If in the case of a registered instrument it appears to the Public Guardian that an event has occurred—

    (a) which has terminated the appointment of the donee, but

    (b) which has not revoked the instrument,

the Public Guardian must attach to the instrument a note to that effect.

Replacement of donee

1–421   **23.** If in the case of a registered instrument it appears to the Public Guardian that the donee has been replaced under the terms of the instrument the Public Guardian must attach to the instrument a note to that effect.

Severance of ineffective provisions

1–422   **24.** If in the case of a registered instrument the court notifies the Public Guardian under paragraph 19(2)(a) that it has severed a provision of the instrument, the Public Guardian must attach to it a note to that effect.

Notification of alterations

1–423   **25.** If the Public Guardian attaches a note to an instrument under paragraph 21, 22, 23 or 24 he must give notice of the note to the donee or donees of the power (or, as the case may be, to the other donee or donees of the power).

DEFINITIONS

1–424   "lasting power of attorney": s.64(1)

    "Public Guardian": s.64(1)

    "the court": s.64(1)

    "deputy": s.64(1)

    "bankruptcy": s.64(3)

GENERAL NOTE

1–425   This Schedule sets out the requirements with regard to the formalities of a LPA. A LPA is not created unless it is made and registered in accordance with the provisions s.9(2).

In summary, the requirements are:

Making instruments

1–426
- The LPA must be in the prescribed form.
- The form must contain statements by both the donor and donee to the effect that they have read (or in the case of the donor, had read to them) prescribed information.
- The LPA must include the names of any persons (a "named person"), not being a donee, whom the donor wishes to be notified of any application to register the LPA or a statement that there are no such persons.
- The form must include a certificate by a person of a prescribed description that, in his or her opinion, at the time when the donor executes the instrument the donor understands the purpose of the instrument and the scope of the authority conferred, that no fraud or undue pressure is being used to induce the donor to create a LPA, and that there is nothing else that would prevent a LPA being created.
- The Public Guardian may treat a LPA differing in an immaterial respect from the prescribed form as sufficient to create a LPA.

- The Court of Protection has the power to declare that an instrument not in the prescribed form is to be treated as if it were.

Registration

- The powers given in a LPA to the donee cannot be exercised until the document has been regis- **1–427** tered with the Public Guardian.
- The application, which must be in the prescribed form, can be made by the donor or donee.
- The named person must be notified of the pending registration by the donor or donee.
- The Public Guardian must notify the applicant that the application has been received unless the court has dispensed with this requirement.
- The donee or the named person may object to the LPA within a prescribed period.
- The objection is made to the either the Public Guardianor the court, depending upon the nature of the objection.
- If the LPA is registered, the Public Guardian must notify the donor and donee.

Cancellation of registration

- The Public Guardian will cancel the LPA if satisfied that the power has been revoked on the **1–428** basis of the donor's bankruptcy, the donee disclaiming the appointment, the death or bankruptcy of the donee, the dissolution or annulment of a marriage or civil partnership between the donor and donee, and the lack of capacity of the donee.
- The court must direct the Public Guardian to cancel the registration of a LPA if the court decides that a requirement for creating the LPA was not met, decides that the LPA has been revoked or otherwise come to an end, or it revokes the power on fraud or undue pressure grounds.
- On cancellation the Public Guardian will notify both the donor and donee.

Records of alterations in registered powers

- The Public Guardian must attach a note to the LPA in the circumstances set out in paras 21–24. **1–429**
- The Public Guardian must give the donor and donee notice of any notes attached.

Paragraph 2(1)(e)

"The relevant person would interview the donor without the presence of the proposed [donee] and **1–430** immediately before the signing of the LPA", *per* the Parliamentary Under-Secretary of State, St.Comm.A, para.142.

SCHEDULE 2   **Section 18(4)**

PROPERTY AND AFFAIRS: SUPPLEMENTARY PROVISIONS

1. Paragraphs 2 to 4 apply in relation to the execution of a will, by virtue of section 18, on behalf of **1–431** P.

2. The will may make any provision (whether by disposing of property or exercising a power or **1–432** otherwise) which could be made by a will executed by P if he had capacity to make it.

3.—(1) Sub-paragraph (2) applies if under section 16 the court makes an order or gives directions **1–433** requiring or authorising a person (the authorised person) to execute a will on behalf of P.

(2) Any will executed in pursuance of the order or direction—

(a) must state that it is signed by P acting by the authorised person,

(b) must be signed by the authorised person with the name of P and his own name, in the presence of two or more witnesses present at the same time,

(c) must be attested and subscribed by those witnesses in the presence of the authorised person, and

(d) must be sealed with the official seal of the court.

4.—(1) This paragraph applies where a will is executed in accordance with paragraph 3. **1–434**

(2) The Wills Act 1837 (c. 26) has effect in relation to the will as if it were signed by P by his own hand, except that—

(a) section 9 of the 1837 Act (requirements as to signing and attestation) does not apply, and

(b) in the subsequent provisions of the 1837 Act any reference to execution in the manner required by the previous provisions is to be read as a reference to execution in accordance with paragraph 3.

(3) The will has the same effect for all purposes as if—

(a) P had had the capacity to make a valid will, and

(b) the will had been executed by him in the manner required by the 1837 Act.

(4) But sub-paragraph (3) does not have effect in relation to the will—

(a) in so far as it disposes of immovable property outside England and Wales, or

(b) in so far as it relates to any other property or matter if, when the will is executed—

    (i) P is domiciled outside England and Wales, and

    (ii) the condition in sub-paragraph (5) is met.

(5) The condition is that, under the law of P's domicile, any question of his testamentary capacity would fall to be determined in accordance with the law of a place outside England and Wales.

1–435   **5.**—(1) If provision is made by virtue of section 18 for—

(a) the settlement of any property of P, or

(b) the exercise of a power vested in him of appointing trustees or retiring from a trust,

the court may also make as respects the property settled or the trust property such consequential vesting or other orders as the case may require.

(2) The power under sub-paragraph (1) includes, in the case of the exercise of such a power, any order which could have been made in such a case under Part 4 of theTrustee Act 1925 (c.19).

1–436   **6.**—(1) If a settlement has been made by virtue of section 18, the court may by order vary or revoke the settlement if—

(a) the settlement makes provision for its variation or revocation,

(b) the court is satisfied that a material fact was not disclosed when the settlement was made, or

(c) the court is satisfied that there has been a substantial change of circumstances.

(2) Any such order may give such consequential directions as the court thinks fit.

1–437   **7.**—(1) Sub-paragraph (2) applies if the court is satisfied—

(a) that under the law prevailing in a place outside England and Wales a person (M) has been appointed to exercise powers in respect of the property or affairs of P on the ground (however formulated) that P lacks capacity to make decisions with respect to the management and administration of his property and affairs, and

(b) that, having regard to the nature of the appointment and to the circumstances of the case, it is expedient that the court should exercise its powers under this paragraph.

(2) The court may direct—

(a) any stocks standing in the name of P, or

(b) the right to receive dividends from the stocks,

to be transferred into M's name or otherwise dealt with as required by M, and may give such directions as the court thinks fit for dealing with accrued dividends from the stocks.

(3) "Stocks" includes—

(a) shares, and

(b) any funds, annuity or security transferable in the books kept by any body corporate or unincorporated company or society or by an instrument of transfer either alone or accompanied by other formalities,

and "dividends" is to be construed accordingly.

1–438   **8.**—(1) Sub-paragraphs (2) and (3) apply if—

(a) P's property has been disposed of by virtue of section 18,

(b) under P's will or intestacy, or by a gift perfected or nomination taking effect on his death, any other person would have taken an interest in the property but for the disposal, and

(c) on P's death, any property belonging to P's estate represents the property disposed of.

(2) The person takes the same interest, if and so far as circumstances allow, in the property representing the property disposed of.

(3) If the property disposed of was real property, any property representing it is to be treated, so long as it remains part of P's estate, as if it were real property.

(4) The court may direct that, on a disposal of P's property—

(a) which is made by virtue of section 18, and

(b) which would apart from this paragraph result in the conversion of personal property into real property,

property representing the property disposed of is to be treated, so long as it remains P's property or forms part of P's estate, as if it were personal property.

(5) References in sub-paragraphs (1) to (4) to the disposal of property are to—

(a) the sale, exchange, charging of or other dealing (otherwise than by will) with property other than money;

(b) the removal of property from one place to another;

(c) the application of money in acquiring property;

(d) the transfer of money from one account to another;

and references to property representing property disposed of are to be construed accordingly and as including the result of successive disposals.

(6) The court may give such directions as appear to it necessary or expedient for the purpose of facilitating the operation of sub-paragraphs (1) to (3), including the carrying of money to a separate account and the transfer of property other than money.

9.—(1) Sub-paragraph (2) applies if the court has ordered or directed the expenditure of money— **1–439**
(a) for carrying out permanent improvements on any of P's property, or
(b) otherwise for the permanent benefit of any of P's property.
(2) The court may order that—
(a) the whole of the money expended or to be expended, or
(b) any part of it,
is to be a charge on the property either without interest or with interest at a specified rate.

(3) An order under sub-paragraph (2) may provide for excluding or restricting the operation of paragraph 8(1) to (3).

(4) A charge under sub-paragraph (2) may be made in favour of such person as may be just and, in particular, where the money charged is paid out of P's general estate, may be made in favour of a person as trustee for P.

(5) No charge under sub-paragraph (2) may confer any right of sale or foreclosure during P's lifetime.

10.—(1) Any functions which P has as patron of a benefice may be discharged only by a person (R) **1–440** appointed by the court.

(2) R must be an individual capable of appointment under section 8(1)(b) of the 1986 Measure (which provides for an individual able to make a declaration of communicant status, a clerk in Holy Orders, etc. to be appointed to discharge a registered patron's functions).

(3) The 1986 Measure applies to R as it applies to an individual appointed by the registered patron of the benefice under section 8(1)(b) or (3) of that Measure to discharge his functions as patron.

(4) "The 1986 Measure" means the Patronage (Benefices) Measure 1986 (No.3).

DEFINITIONS
  "will": s.64(1) **1–441**
  "property": s.64(1)
  "the court": s.64(1)

GENERAL NOTE
  This Schedule contains detailed provisions relating to the court's powers in relation to property and **1–442** affairs, in particular the making of wills and settlements.

Paragraph 3(2)(b)
  As the authorised person is not a witness, he or she would not be precluded from benefiting under **1–443** s.15 of the Wills Act 1837 (c.26).

Paragraph 3(2)(d)
  "The benefit of a court seal is that it provides authentication as to the originality of a document. It **1–444** helps prevent fraud, and it reassures the financial institutions that they are dealing with the right person", *per* the Parliamentary Under-Secretary of State, St.Comm.A, para.188.

Paragraph 4(3)
  A statutory will has the same effect as a will made by a competent testator. **1–445**

Paragraph 7
  The purpose of this provision is to enable the court to recognise judicially the operation of foreign **1–446** law, whereby some form of curatorship has been constituted for a patient, without itself having to go into questions of mental status and capacity.

Paragraph 8
  This ensures that those who have an interest in property that has been disposed of by virtue this Act **1–447** should preserve that interest.

Paragraph 10

1–448   A "benefice" is a freehold office of the Church of England, such as the vicar of a parish. The patron of a benefice has the right to appoint a cleric to that office. The representative of P "will have to be an individual who is a communicant of the Church of England or a church in communion with it or a clerk in holy orders. The representative will fulfil the patron's role not only in presenting a priest to a vacant benefice under the Patronage Benefices Measure 1986 (m.3) but also in performing the other functions of a patron such as acting as a consultee when there is a proposal to suspend presentation under s.67 of the Pastoral Measure 1983 (m.1). In discharging his or her functions the representative will be subject to the provisions of the 1986 Measure in the same way that a registered patron would be", *per* the Under-Secretary of State (*Hansard*, HL Vol.670, col.1496).

SCHEDULE 3   **Section 63**

INTERNATIONAL PROTECTION OF ADULTS

PART 1

PRELIMINARY

Introduction

1–449   1. This Part applies for the purposes of this Schedule.

The Convention

1–450   2.—(1) "Convention" means the Convention referred to in section 63.

(2) "Convention country" means a country in which the Convention is in force.

(3) A reference to an Article or Chapter is to an Article or Chapter of the Convention.

(4) An expression which appears in this Schedule and in the Convention is to be construed in accordance with the Convention.

Countries, territories and nationals

1–451   3.—(1) "Country" includes a territory which has its own system of law.

(2) Where a country has more than one territory with its own system of law, a reference to the country, in relation to one of its nationals, is to the territory with which the national has the closer, or the closest, connection.

Adults with incapacity

1–452   4. "Adult" means a person who—

(a) as a result of an impairment or insufficiency of his personal faculties, cannot protect his interests, and

(b) has reached 16.

Protective measures

1–453   5.—(1) "Protective measure" means a measure directed to the protection of the person or property of an adult; and it may deal in particular with any of the following—

(a) the determination of incapacity and the institution of a protective regime,

(b) placing the adult under the protection of an appropriate authority,

(c) guardianship, curatorship or any corresponding system,

(d) the designation and functions of a person having charge of the adult's person or property, or representing or otherwise helping him,

(e) placing the adult in a place where protection can be provided,

(f) administering, conserving or disposing of the adult's property,

(g) authorising a specific intervention for the protection of the person or property of the adult.

(2) Where a measure of like effect to a protective measure has been taken in relation to a person before he reaches 16, this Schedule applies to the measure in so far as it has effect in relation to him once he has reached 16.

Central Authority

6.—(1) Any function under the Convention of a Central Authority is exercisable in England and **1–454** Wales by the Lord Chancellor.

(2) A communication may be sent to the Central Authority in relation to England and Wales by sending it to the Lord Chancellor.

PART 2

JURISDICTION OF COMPETENT AUTHORITY

7.—(1) The court may exercise its functions under this Act (in so far as it cannot otherwise do so) in **1–455** relation to—

(a)   an adult habitually resident in England and Wales,

(b)   an adult's property in England and Wales,

(c)   an adult present in England and Wales or who has property there, if the matter is urgent, or

(d)   an adult present in England and Wales, if a protective measure which is temporary and limited in its effect to England and Wales is proposed in relation to him.

(2) An adult present in England and Wales is to be treated for the purposes of this paragraph as habitually resident there if—

(a)   his habitual residence cannot be ascertained,

(b)   he is a refugee, or

(c)   he has been displaced as a result of disturbance in the country of his habitual residence.

8.—(1) The court may also exercise its functions under this Act (in so far as it cannot otherwise do **1–456** so) in relation to an adult if sub-paragraph (2) or (3) applies in relation to him.

(2) This sub-paragraph applies in relation to an adult if—

(a)   he is a British citizen,

(b)   he has a closer connection with England and Wales than with Scotland or Northern Ireland, and

(c)   Article 7 has, in relation to the matter concerned, been complied with.

(3) This sub-paragraph applies in relation to an adult if the Lord Chancellor, having consulted such persons as he considers appropriate, agrees to a request under Article 8 in relation to the adult.

9.—(1) This paragraph applies where jurisdiction is exercisable under this Schedule in connection **1–457** with a matter which involves a Convention country other than England and Wales.

(2) Any Article on which the jurisdiction is based applies in relation to the matter in so far as it involves the other country (and the court must, accordingly, comply with any duty conferred on it as a result).

(3) Article 12 also applies, so far as its provisions allow, in relation to the matter in so far as it involves the other country.

10. A reference in this Schedule to the exercise of jurisdiction under this Schedule is to the exercise **1–458** of functions under this Act as a result of this Part of this Schedule.

PART 3

APPLICABLE LAW

11. In exercising jurisdiction under this Schedule, the court may, if it thinks that the matter has a **1–459** substantial connection with a country other than England and Wales, apply the law of that other country.

12. Where a protective measure is taken in one country but implemented in another, the conditions **1–460** of implementation are governed by the law of the other country.

13.—(1) If the donor of a lasting power is habitually resident in England and Wales at the time of **1–461** granting the power, the law applicable to the existence, extent, modification or extinction of the power is—

(a)   the law of England and Wales, or

(b)   if he specifies in writing the law of a connected country for the purpose, that law.

(2) If he is habitually resident in another country at that time, but England and Wales is a connected country, the law applicable in that respect is—

(a)   the law of the other country, or

(b)   if he specifies in writing the law of England and Wales for the purpose, that law.

(3) A country is connected, in relation to the donor, if it is a country—

(a)   of which he is a national,

(b) in which he was habitually resident, or

(c) in which he has property.

(4) Where this paragraph applies as a result of sub-paragraph (3)(c), it applies only in relation to the property which the donor has in the connected country.

(5) The law applicable to the manner of the exercise of a lasting power is the law of the country where it is exercised.

(6) In this Part of this Schedule, "lasting power" means—

(a) a lasting power of attorney (see section 9),

(b) an enduring power of attorney within the meaning of Schedule 4, or

(c) any other power of like effect.

1–462 **14.**—(1) Where a lasting power is not exercised in a manner sufficient to guarantee the protection of the person or property of the donor, the court, in exercising jurisdiction under this Schedule, may disapply or modify the power.

(2) Where, in accordance with this Part of this Schedule, the law applicable to the power is, in one or more respects, that of a country other than England and Wales, the court must, so far as possible, have regard to the law of the other country in that respect (or those respects).

1–463 **15.** Regulations may provide for Schedule 1(lasting powers of attorney: formalities) to apply with modifications in relation to a lasting power which comes within paragraph 13(6)(c) above.

1–464 **16.**—(1) This paragraph applies where a person (a representative) in purported exercise of an authority to act on behalf of an adult enters into a transaction with a third party.

(2) The validity of the transaction may not be questioned in proceedings, nor may the third party be held liable, merely because—

(a) where the representative and third party are in England and Wales when entering into the transaction, sub-paragraph (3) applies;

(b) where they are in another country at that time, sub-paragraph (4) applies.

(3) This sub-paragraph applies if—

(a) the law applicable to the authority in one or more respects is, as a result of this Schedule, the law of a country other than England and Wales, and

(b) the representative is not entitled to exercise the authority in that respect (or those respects) under the law of that other country.

(4) This sub-paragraph applies if—

(a) the law applicable to the authority in one or more respects is, as a result of this Part of this Schedule, the law of England and Wales, and

(b) the representative is not entitled to exercise the authority in that respect (or those respects) under that law.

(5) This paragraph does not apply if the third party knew or ought to have known that the applicable law was—

(a) in a case within sub-paragraph (3), the law of the other country;

(b) in a case within sub-paragraph (4), the law of England and Wales.

1–465 **17.** Where the court is entitled to exercise jurisdiction under this Schedule, the mandatory provisions of the law of England and Wales apply, regardless of any system of law which would otherwise apply in relation to the matter.

1–466 **18.** Nothing in this Part of this Schedule requires or enables the application in England and Wales of a provision of the law of another country if its application would be manifestly contrary to public policy.

PART 4

RECOGNITION AND ENFORCEMENT

1–467 **19.**—(1) A protective measure taken in relation to an adult under the law of a country other than England and Wales is to be recognised in England and Wales if it was taken on the ground that the adult is habitually resident in the other country.

(2) A protective measure taken in relation to an adult under the law of a Convention country other than England and Wales is to be recognised in England and Wales if it was taken on a ground mentioned in Chapter 2 (jurisdiction).

(3) But the court may disapply this paragraph in relation to a measure if it thinks that—

(a) the case in which the measure was taken was not urgent,

(b) the adult was not given an opportunity to be heard, and

(c) that omission amounted to a breach of natural justice.

(4) It may also disapply this paragraph in relation to a measure if it thinks that—

(a) recognition of the measure would be manifestly contrary to public policy,

(b) the measure would be inconsistent with a mandatory provision of the law of England and Wales, or

(c) the measure is inconsistent with one subsequently taken, or recognised, in England and Wales in relation to the adult.

(5) And the court may disapply this paragraph in relation to a measure taken under the law of a Convention country in a matter to which Article 33 applies, if the court thinks that that Article has not been complied with in connection with that matter.

20.—(1) An interested person may apply to the court for a declaration as to whether a protective **1–468** measure taken under the law of a country other than England and Wales is to be recognised in England and Wales.

(2) No permission is required for an application to the court under this paragraph.

21. For the purposes of paragraphs 19 and 20, any finding of fact relied on when the measure was **1–469** taken is conclusive.

22.—(1) An interested person may apply to the court for a declaration as to whether a protective **1–470** measure taken under the law of, and enforceable in, a country other than England and Wales is enforceable, or to be registered, in England and Wales in accordance with Court of Protection Rules.

(2) The court must make the declaration if—

(a) the measure comes within sub-paragraph (1) or (2) of paragraph 19, and

(b) the paragraph is not disapplied in relation to it as a result of sub-paragraph (3), (4) or (5).

(3) A measure to which a declaration under this paragraph relates is enforceable in England and Wales as if it were a measure of like effect taken by the court.

23.—(1) This paragraph applies where— **1–471**

(a) provision giving effect to, or otherwise deriving from, the Convention in a country other than England and Wales applies in relation to a person who has not reached 16, and

(b) a measure is taken in relation to that person in reliance on that provision.

(2) This Part of this Schedule applies in relation to that measure as it applies in relation to a protective measure taken in relation to an adult under the law of a Convention country other than England and Wales.

24. The court may not review the merits of a measure taken outside England and Wales except to **1–472** establish whether the measure complies with this Schedule in so far as it is, as a result of this Schedule, required to do so.

25. Court of Protection Rules may make provision about an application under paragraph 20 or 22. **1–473**

PART 5

CO-OPERATION

26.—(1) This paragraph applies where a public authority proposes to place an adult in an establish- **1–474** ment in a Convention country other than England and Wales.

(2) The public authority must consult an appropriate authority in that other country about the proposed placement and, for that purpose, must send it—

(a) a report on the adult, and

(b) a statement of its reasons for the proposed placement.

(3) If the appropriate authority in the other country opposes the proposed placement within a reasonable time, the public authority may not proceed with it.

27. A proposal received by a public authority under Article 33 in relation to an adult is to proceed **1–475** unless the authority opposes it within a reasonable time.

28.—(1) This paragraph applies if a public authority is told that an adult— **1–476**

(a) who is in serious danger, and

(b) in relation to whom the public authority has taken, or is considering taking, protective measures,

is, or has become resident, in a Convention country other than England and Wales.

(2) The public authority must tell an appropriate authority in that other country about—

(a) the danger, and

(b) the measures taken or under consideration.

29. A public authority may not request from, or send to, an appropriate authority in a Convention **1–477** country information in accordance with Chapter 5(co-operation) in relation to an adult if it thinks that doing so—

(a) would be likely to endanger the adult or his property, or

(b) would amount to a serious threat to the liberty or life of a member of the adult's family.

1–478   **30.** A certificate given under Article 38 by an authority in a Convention country other than England and Wales is, unless the contrary is shown, proof of the matters contained in it.

1–479   **31.** Her Majesty may by Order in Council confer on the Lord Chancellor, the court or another public authority functions for enabling the Convention to be given effect in England and Wales.

1–480   **32.**—(1) Regulations may make provision—

(a) giving further effect to the Convention, or

(b) otherwise about the private international law of England and Wales in relation to the protection of adults.

(2) The regulations may—

(a) confer functions on the court or another public authority;

(b) amend this Schedule;

(c) provide for this Schedule to apply with specified modifications;

(d) make provision about countries other than Convention countries.

1–481   **33.** Nothing in this Schedule applies, and no provision made under paragraph 32 is to apply, to any matter to which the Convention, as a result of Article 4, does not apply.

1–481a   **34.** A reference in this Schedule to regulations or an order (other than an Order in Council) is to regulations or an order made for the purposes of this Schedule by the Lord Chancellor.

1–481b   **35.** The following provisions of this Schedule have effect only if the Convention is in force in accordance with Article 57—

(a) paragraph 8,

(b) paragraph 9,

(c) paragraph 19(2) and (5),

(d) Part 5,

(e) paragraph 30.

DEFINITIONS

1–482   "property": s.64(1)

"the court": s.64(1)

"Court of Protection Rules": s.64(1)

GENERAL NOTE

1–483   See the notes to s.63. This Schedule is divided into six parts. Part 1 contains definitions and introductory provisions. Part 2 provides the grounds, based on Arts 5-11 of the Hague Convention on the International Protection of Adults, on which the Court of Protection will exercise its jurisdiction under this Act when dealing with cases with an international element. Part 3 makes provision as to the law of which country is to apply in various situations. It also provides protection for a third party who enters into a transaction with a representative on behalf of a person, where that representative was actually not entitled so to act under the law of a country other than England and Wales applicable by virtue of Pt 3. Part 4 provides for the recognition and enforcement of protective measures taken in other countries. Part 5 provides for co-operation between authorities in England and Wales and authorities in other Convention countries. Part 6 includes powers to make further provision as to private international by Order in Council and regulations and provisions on commencement.

SCHEDULE 4   **Section 66(3)**

PROVISIONS APPLYING TO EXISTING ENDURING POWERS OF ATTORNEY

PART 1

ENDURING POWERS OF ATTORNEY

Enduring power of attorney to survive mental incapacity of donor

1–484   **1.**—(1) Where an individual has created a power of attorney which is an enduring power within the meaning of this Schedule—

(a) the power is not revoked by any subsequent mental incapacity of his,

(b) upon such incapacity supervening, the donee of the power may not do anything under the authority of the power except as provided by sub-paragraph (2) unless or until the instrument creating the power is registered under paragraph 13, and

(c) if and so long as paragraph (b) operates to suspend the donee's authority to act under the power, section 5 of the Powers of Attorney Act 1971 (c. 27) (protection of donee and third persons), so far as applicable, applies as if the power had been revoked by the donor's mental incapacity,

and, accordingly, section 1 of this Act does not apply.

(2) Despite sub-paragraph (1)(b), where the attorney has made an application for registration of the instrument then, until it is registered, the attorney may take action under the power—

(a) to maintain the donor or prevent loss to his estate, or

(b) to maintain himself or other persons in so far as paragraph 3(2) permits him to do so.

(3) Where the attorney purports to act as provided by sub-paragraph (2) then, in favour of a person who deals with him without knowledge that the attorney is acting otherwise than in accordance with sub-paragraph (2)(a) or (b), the transaction between them is as valid as if the attorney were acting in accordance with sub-paragraph (2)(a) or (b).

Characteristics of an enduring power of attorney

2.—(1) Subject to sub-paragraphs (5) and (6) and paragraph 20, a power of attorney is an enduring **1–485** power within the meaning of this Schedule if the instrument which creates the power—

(a) is in the prescribed form,

(b) was executed in the prescribed manner by the donor and the attorney, and

(c) incorporated at the time of execution by the donor the prescribed explanatory information.

(2) In this paragraph, "prescribed" means prescribed by such of the following regulations as applied when the instrument was executed—

(a) the Enduring Powers of Attorney (Prescribed Form) Regulations 1986 (S.I.1986/ 126),

(b) the Enduring Powers of Attorney (Prescribed Form) Regulations 1987 (S.I.1987/ 1612),

(c) the Enduring Powers of Attorney (Prescribed Form) Regulations 1990 (S.I.1990/ 1376),

(d) the Enduring Powers of Attorney (Welsh Language Prescribed Form) Regulations 2000 (S.I. 2000/289).

(3) An instrument in the prescribed form purporting to have been executed in the prescribed manner is to be taken, in the absence of evidence to the contrary, to be a document which incorporated at the time of execution by the donor the prescribed explanatory information.

(4) If an instrument differs in an immaterial respect in form or mode of expression from the prescribed form it is to be treated as sufficient in point of form and expression.

(5) A power of attorney cannot be an enduring power unless, when he executes the instrument creating it, the attorney is—

(a) an individual who has reached 18 and is not bankrupt, or

(b) a trust corporation.

(6) A power of attorney which gives the attorney a right to appoint a substitute or successor cannot be an enduring power.

(7) An enduring power is revoked by the bankruptcy of the donor or attorney.

(8) But where the donor or attorney is bankrupt merely because an interim bankruptcy restrictions order has effect in respect of him, the power is suspended for so long as the order has effect.

(9) An enduring power is revoked if the court—

(a) exercises a power under sections 16 to 20 in relation to the donor, and

(b) directs that the enduring power is to be revoked.

(10) No disclaimer of an enduring power, whether by deed or otherwise, is valid unless and until the attorney gives notice of it to the donor or, where paragraph 4(6) or 15(1) applies, to the Public Guardian.

Scope of authority etc. of attorney under enduring power

3.—(1) If the instrument which creates an enduring power of attorney is expressed to confer general **1–486** authority on the attorney, the instrument operates to confer, subject to—

(a) the restriction imposed by sub-paragraph (3), and

(b) any conditions or restrictions contained in the instrument,

authority to do on behalf of the donor anything which the donor could lawfully do by an attorney at the time when the donor executed the instrument.

(2) Subject to any conditions or restrictions contained in the instrument, an attorney under an enduring power, whether general or limited, may (without obtaining any consent) act under the power so as to benefit himself or other persons than the donor to the following extent but no further—

(a) he may so act in relation to himself or in relation to any other person if the donor might be expected to provide for his or that person's needs respectively, and

(b) he may do whatever the donor might be expected to do to meet those needs.

(3) Without prejudice to sub-paragraph (2) but subject to any conditions or restrictions contained in the instrument, an attorney under an enduring power, whether general or limited, may (without obtaining any consent) dispose of the property of the donor by way of gift to the following extent but no further—

(a) he may make gifts of a seasonal nature or at a time, or on an anniversary, of a birth, a marriage or the formation of a civil partnership, to persons (including himself) who are related to or connected withthe donor, and

(b) he may make gifts to any charity to whom the donor made or might be expected to make gifts, provided that the value of each such gift is not unreasonable having regard to all the circumstances and in particular the size of the donor's estate.

PART 2

ACTION ON ACTUAL OR IMPENDING INCAPACITY OF DONOR

Duties of attorney in event of actual or impending incapacity of donor

1–487   **4.**—(1) Sub-paragraphs (2) to (6) apply if the attorney under an enduring power has reason to believe that the donor is or is becoming mentally incapable.

(2) The attorney must, as soon as practicable, make an application to the Public Guardian for the registration of the instrument creating the power.

(3) Before making an application for registration the attorney must comply with the provisions as to notice set out in Part 3 of this Schedule.

(4) An application for registration—

(a) must be made in the prescribed form, and

(b) must contain such statements as may be prescribed.

(5) The attorney—

(a) may, before making an application for the registration of the instrument, refer to the court for its determination any question as to the validity of the power, and

(b) must comply with any direction given to him by the court on that determination.

(6) No disclaimer of the power is valid unless and until the attorney gives notice of it to the Public Guardian; and the Public Guardian must notify the donor if he receives a notice under this subparagraph.

(7) A person who, in an application for registration, makes a statement which he knows to be false in a material particular is guilty of an offence and is liable—

(a) on summary conviction, to imprisonment for a term not exceeding 12 months or a fine not exceeding the statutory maximum or both;

(b) on conviction on indictment, to imprisonment for a term not exceeding 2 years or a fine or both.

(8) In this paragraph, "prescribed" means prescribed by regulations made for the purposes of this Schedule by the Lord Chancellor.

PART 3

NOTIFICATION PRIOR TO REGISTRATION

1–488   **5.** Subject to paragraph 7, before making an application for registration the attorney must give notice of his intention to do so to all those persons (if any) who are entitled to receive notice by virtue of paragraph 6.

1–489   **6.**—(1) Subject to sub-paragraphs (2) to (4), persons of the following classes (relatives) are entitled to receive notice under paragraph 5—

(a) the donor's spouse or civil partner,

(b) the donor's children,

(c) the donor's parents,

(d) the donor's brothers and sisters, whether of the whole or half blood,

(e) the widow, widower or surviving civil partner of a child of the donor,

(f) the donor's grandchildren,

(g) the children of the donor's brothers and sisters of the whole blood,

(h) the children of the donor's brothers and sisters of the half blood,

(i)   the donor's uncles and aunts of the whole blood,

(j)   the children of the donor's uncles and aunts of the whole blood.

(2) A person is not entitled to receive notice under paragraph 5 if—

(a)   his name or address is not known to the attorney and cannot be reasonably ascertained by him, or

(b)   the attorney has reason to believe that he has not reached 18 or is mentally incapable.

(3) Except where sub-paragraph (4) applies—

(a)   no more than 3 persons are entitled to receive notice under paragraph 5, and

(b)   in determining the persons who are so entitled, persons falling within the class in subparagraph (1)(a) are to be preferred to persons falling within the class in sub-paragraph (1)(b), those falling within the class in sub-paragraph (1)(b) are to be preferred to those falling within the class in sub-paragraph (1)(c), and so on.

(4) Despite the limit of 3 specified in sub-paragraph (3), where—

(a)   there is more than one person falling within any of classes (a) to (j) of sub-paragraph (1), and

(b)   at least one of those persons would be entitled to receive notice under paragraph 5, then, subject to sub-paragraph (2), all the persons falling within that class are entitled to receive notice under paragraph 5.

7.—(1) An attorney is not required to give notice under paragraph 5—   **1–490**

(a)   to himself, or

(b)   to any other attorney under the power who is joining in making the application, even though he or, as the case may be, the other attorney is entitled to receive notice by virtue of paragraph 6.

(2) In the case of any person who is entitled to receive notice by virtue of paragraph 6, the attorney, before applying for registration, may make an application to the court to be dispensed from the requirement to give him notice; and the court must grant the application if it is satisfied—

(a)   that it would be undesirable or impracticable for the attorney to give him notice, or

(b)   that no useful purpose is likely to be served by giving him notice.

8.—(1) Subject to sub-paragraph (2), before making an application for registration the attorney   **1–491** must give notice of his intention to do so to the donor.

(2) Paragraph 7(2) applies in relation to the donor as it applies in relation to a person who is entitled to receive notice under paragraph 5.

9. A notice to relatives under this Part of this Schedule must—   **1–492**

(a)   be in the prescribed form,

(b)   state that the attorney proposes to make an application to the Public Guardian for the registration of the instrument creating the enduring power in question,

(c)   inform the person to whom it is given of his right to object to the registration under paragraph 13(4), and

(d)   specify, as the grounds on which an objection to registration may be made, the grounds set out in paragraph 13(9).

10. A notice to the donor under this Part of this Schedule—   **1–493**

(a)   must be in the prescribed form,

(b)   must contain the statement mentioned in paragraph 9(b), and

(c)   must inform the donor that, while the instrument remains registered, any revocation of the power by him will be ineffective unless and until the revocation is confirmed by the court.

11.—(1) Subject to sub-paragraph (2), before making an application for registration an attorney   **1–494** under a joint and several power must give notice of his intention to do so to any other attorney under the power who is not joining in making the application; and paragraphs 7(2) and 9 apply in relation to attorneys entitled to receive notice by virtue of this paragraph as they apply in relation to persons entitled to receive notice by virtue of paragraph 6.

(2) An attorney is not entitled to receive notice by virtue of this paragraph if—

(a)   his address is not known to the applying attorney and cannot reasonably be ascertained by him, or

(b)   the applying attorney has reason to believe that he has not reached 18 or is mentally incapable.

12. Despite section 7 of the Interpretation Act 1978 (c. 30) (construction of references to service by   **1–495** post), for the purposes of this Part of this Schedule a notice given by post is to be regarded as given on the date on which it was posted.

Registration of instrument creating power

1–496   **13.**—(1) If an application is made in accordance with paragraph 4(3) and (4) the Public Guardian must, subject to the provisions of this paragraph, register the instrument to which the application relates.

(2) If it appears to the Public Guardian that—

(a) there is a deputy appointed for the donor of the power created by the instrument, and

(b) the powers conferred on the deputy would, if the instrument were registered, to any extent conflict with the powers conferred on the attorney,

the Public Guardian must not register the instrument except in accordance with the court's directions.

(3) The court may, on the application of the attorney, direct the Public Guardian to register an instrument even though notice has not been given as required by paragraph 4(3) and Part 3 of this Schedule to a person entitled to receive it, if the court is satisfied—

(a) that it was undesirable or impracticable for the attorney to give notice to that person, or

(b) that no useful purpose is likely to be served by giving him notice.

(4) Sub-paragraph (5) applies if, before the end of the period of 5 weeks beginning with the date (or the latest date) on which the attorney gave notice under paragraph 5 of an application for registration, the Public Guardian receives a valid notice of objection to the registration from a person entitled to notice of the application.

(5) The Public Guardian must not register the instrument except in accordance with the court's directions.

(6) Sub-paragraph (7) applies if, in the case of an application for registration—

(a) it appears from the application that there is no one to whom notice has been given under paragraph 5, or

(b) the Public Guardian has reason to believe that appropriate inquiries might bring to light evidence on which he could be satisfied that one of the grounds of objection set out in subparagraph (9) was established.

(7) The Public Guardian—

(a) must not register the instrument, and

(b) must undertake such inquiries as he thinks appropriate in all the circumstances.

(8) If, having complied with sub-paragraph (7)(b), the Public Guardian is satisfied that one of the grounds of objection set out in sub-paragraph (9) is established—

(a) the attorney may apply to the court for directions, and

(b) the Public Guardian must not register the instrument except in accordance with the court's directions.

(9) A notice of objection under this paragraph is valid if made on one or more of the following grounds—

(a) that the power purported to have been created by the instrument was not valid as an enduring power of attorney,

(b) that the power created by the instrument no longer subsists,

(c) that the application is premature because the donor is not yet becoming mentally incapable,

(d) that fraud or undue pressure was used to induce the donor to create the power,

(e) that, having regard to all the circumstances and in particular the attorney's relationship to or connection with the donor, the attorney is unsuitable to be the donor's attorney.

(10) If any of those grounds is established to the satisfaction of the court it must direct the Public Guardian not to register the instrument, but if not so satisfied it must direct its registration.

(11) If the court directs the Public Guardian not to register an instrument because it is satisfied that the ground in sub-paragraph (9)(d) or (e) is established, it must by order revoke the power created by the instrument.

(12) If the court directs the Public Guardian not to register an instrument because it is satisfied that any ground in sub-paragraph (9) except that in paragraph (c) is established, the instrument must be delivered up to be cancelled unless the court otherwise directs.

Register of enduring powers

1–497   **14.** The Public Guardian has the function of establishing and maintaining a register of enduring powers for the purposes of this Schedule.

Effect and proof of registration

15.—(1) The effect of the registration of an instrument under paragraph 13 is that— **1–498**

(a) no revocation of the power by the donor is valid unless and until the court confirms the revocation under paragraph 16(3);

(b) no disclaimer of the power is valid unless and until the attorney gives notice of it to the Public Guardian;

(c) the donor may not extend or restrict the scope of the authority conferred by the instrument and no instruction or consent given by him after registration, in the case of a consent, confers any right and, in the case of an instruction, imposes or confers any obligation or right on or creates any liability of the attorney or other persons having notice of the instruction or consent.

(2) Sub-paragraph (1) applies for so long as the instrument is registered under paragraph 13 whether or not the donor is for the time being mentally incapable.

(3) A document purporting to be an office copy of an instrument registered under this Schedule is, in any part of the United Kingdom, evidence of—

(a) the contents of the instrument, and

(b) the fact that it has been so registered.

(4) Sub-paragraph (3) is without prejudice to section 3 of the Powers of Attorney Act 1971 (c. 27) (proof by certified copies) and to any other method of proof authorised by law.

Functions of court with regard to registered power

16.—(1) Where an instrument has been registered under paragraph 13, the court has the following **1–499** functions with respect to the power and the donor of and the attorney appointed to act under the power.

(2) The court may—

(a) determine any question as to the meaning or effect of the instrument;

(b) give directions with respect to—

   (i) the management or disposal by the attorney of the property and affairs of the donor;

   (ii) the rendering of accounts by the attorney and the production of the records kept by him for the purpose;

   (iii) the remuneration or expenses of the attorney whether or not in default of or in accordance with any provision made by the instrument, including directions for the repayment of excessive or the payment of additional remuneration;

(c) require the attorney to supply information or produce documents or things in his possession as attorney;

(d) give any consent or authorisation to act which the attorney would have to obtain from a mentally capable donor;

(e) authorise the attorney to act so as to benefit himself or other persons than the donor otherwise than in accordance with paragraph 3(2) and (3) (but subject to any conditions or restrictions contained in the instrument);

(f) relieve the attorney wholly or partly from any liability which he has or may have incurred on account of a breach of his duties as attorney.

(3) On application made for the purpose by or on behalf of the donor, the court must confirm the revocation of the power if satisfied that the donor—

(a) has done whatever is necessary in law to effect an express revocation of the power, and

(b) was mentally capable of revoking a power of attorney when he did so (whether or not he is so when the court considers the application).

(4) The court must direct the Public Guardian to cancel the registration of an instrument registered under paragraph 13 in any of the following circumstances—

(a) on confirming the revocation of the power under sub-paragraph (3),

(b) on directing under paragraph 2(9)(b) that the power is to be revoked,

(c) on being satisfied that the donor is and is likely to remain mentally capable,

(d) on being satisfied that the power has expired or has been revoked by the mental incapacity of the attorney,

(e) on being satisfied that the power was not a valid and subsisting enduring power when registration was effected,

(f) on being satisfied that fraud or undue pressure was used to induce the donor to create the power,

(g) on being satisfied that, having regard to all the circumstances and in particular the attorney's relationship to or connection with the donor, the attorney is unsuitable to be the donor's attorney.

(5) If the court directs the Public Guardian to cancel the registration of an instrument on being satisfied of the matters specified in sub-paragraph (4)(f) or (g) it must by order revoke the power created by the instrument.

(6) If the court directs the cancellation of the registration of an instrument under sub-paragraph (4) except paragraph (c) the instrument must be delivered up to the Public Guardian to be cancelled, unless the court otherwise directs.

Cancellation of registration by Public Guardian

1–500   **17.** The Public Guardian must cancel the registration of an instrument creating an enduring power of attorney—

(a) on receipt of a disclaimer signed by the attorney;
(b) if satisfied that the power has been revoked by the death or bankruptcy of the donor or attorney or, if the attorney is a body corporate, by its winding up or dissolution;
(c) on receipt of notification from the court that the court has revoked the power;
(d) on confirmation from the court that the donor has revoked the power.

PART 6

PROTECTION OF ATTORNEY AND THIRD PARTIES

Protection of attorney and third persons where power is invalid or revoked

1–501   **18.**—(1) Sub-paragraphs (2) and (3) apply where an instrument which did not create a valid power of attorney has been registered under paragraph 13 (whether or not the registration has been cancelled at the time of the act or transaction in question).

(2) An attorney who acts in pursuance of the power does not incur any liability (either to the donor or to any other person) because of the non-existence of the power unless at the time of acting he knows—

(a) that the instrument did not create a valid enduring power,
(b) that an event has occurred which, if the instrument had created a valid enduring power, would have had the effect of revoking the power, or
(c) that, if the instrument had created a valid enduring power, the power would have expired before that time.

(3) Any transaction between the attorney and another person is, in favour of that person, as valid as if the power had then been in existence, unless at the time of the transaction that person has knowledge of any of the matters mentioned in sub-paragraph (2).

(4) If the interest of a purchaser depends on whether a transaction between the attorney and another person was valid by virtue of sub-paragraph (3), it is conclusively presumed in favour of the purchaser that the transaction was valid if—

(a) the transaction between that person and the attorney was completed within 12 months of the date on which the instrument was registered; or
(b) that person makes a statutory declaration, before or within 3 months after the completion of the purchase, that he had no reason at the time of the transaction to doubt that the attorney had authority to dispose of the property which was the subject of the transaction.

(5) For the purposes of section 5 of the Powers of Attorney Act 1971 (c. 27) (protection where power is revoked) in its application to an enduring power the revocation of which by the donor is by virtue of paragraph 15 invalid unless and until confirmed by the court under paragraph 16—

(a) knowledge of the confirmation of the revocation is knowledge of the revocation of the power, but
(b) knowledge of the unconfirmed revocation is not.

Further protection of attorney and third persons

1–502   **19.** (1) If—

(a) an instrument framed in a form prescribed as mentioned in paragraph 2(2) creates a power which is not a valid enduring power, and
(b) the power is revoked by the mental incapacity of the donor,
    sub-paragraphs (2) and (3) apply,whether or not the instrument has been registered.

(2) An attorney who acts in pursuance of the power does not, by reason of the revocation, incur any liability (either to the donor or to any other person) unless at the time of acting he knows—

(a) that the instrument did not create a valid enduring power, and

(b) that the donor has become mentally incapable.

(3) Any transaction between the attorney and another person is, in favour of that person, as valid as if the power had then been in existence, unless at the time of the transaction that person knows—

(a) that the instrument did not create a valid enduring power, and

(b) that the donor has become mentally incapable.

(4) Paragraph 18(4) applies for the purpose of determining whether a transaction was valid by virtue of sub-paragraph (3) as it applies for the purpose or determining whether a transaction was valid by virtue of paragraph 18(3).

PART 7

JOINT AND JOINT AND SEVERAL ATTORNEYS

Application to joint and joint and several attorneys

20.—(1) An instrument which appoints more than one person to be an attorney cannot create an **1–503** enduring power unless the attorneys are appointed to act—

(a) jointly, or

(b) jointly and severally.

(2) This Schedule, in its application to joint attorneys, applies to them collectively as it applies to a single attorney but subject to the modifications specified in paragraph 21.

(3) This Schedule, in its application to joint and several attorneys, applies with the modifications specified in sub-paragraphs (4) to (7) and in paragraph 22.

(4) A failure, as respects any one attorney, to comply with the requirements for the creation of enduring powers—

(a) prevents the instrument from creating such a power in his case, but

(b) does not affect its efficacy for that purpose as respects the other or others or its efficacy in his case for the purpose of creating a power of attorney which is not an enduring power.

(5) If one or more but not both or all the attorneys makes or joins in making an application for registration of the instrument—

(a) an attorney who is not an applicant as well as one who is may act pending the registration of the instrument as provided in paragraph 1(2),

(b) notice of the application must also be given under Part 3 of this Schedule to the other attorney or attorneys, and

(c) objection may validly be taken to the registration on a ground relating to an attorney or to the power of an attorney who is not an applicant as well as to one or the power of one who is an applicant.

(6) The Public Guardian is not precluded by paragraph 13(5) or (8) from registering an instrument and the court must not direct him not to do so under paragraph 13(10) if an enduring power subsists as respects some attorney who is not affected by the ground or grounds of the objection in question; and where the Public Guardian registers an instrument in that case, he must make against the registration an entry in the prescribed form.

(7) Sub-paragraph (6) does not preclude the court from revoking a power in so far as it confers a power on any other attorney in respect of whom the ground in paragraph 13(9)(d) or (e) is established; and where any ground in paragraph 13(9) affecting any other attorney is established the court must direct the Public Guardian to make against the registration an entry in the prescribed form.

(8) In sub-paragraph (4), "the requirements for the creation of enduring powers" means the provisions of—

(a) paragraph 2 other than sub-paragraphs (8) and (9), and

(b) the regulations mentioned in paragraph 2.

Joint attorneys

21.—(1) In paragraph 2(5), the reference to the time when the attorney executes the instrument is to **1–504** be read as a reference to the time when the second or last attorney executes the instrument.

(2) In paragraph 2(6) to (8), the reference to the attorney is to be read as a reference to any attorney under the power.

(3) Paragraph 13 has effect as if the ground of objection to the registration of the instrument specified in sub-paragraph (9)(e) applied to any attorney under the power.

173

(4) In paragraph 16(2), references to the attorney are to be read as including references to any attorney under the power.

(5) In paragraph 16(4), references to the attorney are to be read as including references to any attorney under the power.

(6) In paragraph 17, references to the attorney are to be read as including references to any attorney under the power.

Joint and several attorneys

1–505   **22.**—(1) In paragraph 2(7), the reference to the bankruptcy of the attorney is to be read as a reference to the bankruptcy of the last remaining attorney under the power; and the bankruptcy of any other attorney under the power causes that person to cease to be an attorney under the power.

(2) In paragraph 2(8), the reference to the suspension of the power is to be read as a reference to its suspension in so far as it relates to the attorney in respect of whom the interim bankruptcy restrictions order has effect.

(3) The restriction upon disclaimer imposed by paragraph 4(6) applies only to those attorneys who have reason to believe that the donor is or is becoming mentally incapable.

PART 8

INTERPRETATION

1–506   **23.**—(1) In this Schedule—

"enduring power" is to be construed in accordance with paragraph 2,

"mentally incapable" or "mental incapacity", except where it refers to revocation at common law, means in relation to any person, that he is incapable by reason of mental disorder (within the meaning of the Mental Health Act) of managing and administering his property and affairs and "mentally capable"and "mental capacity"are to be construed accordingly,

"notice" means notice in writing, and

"prescribed", except for the purposes of paragraph 2, means prescribed by regulations made for the purposes of this Schedule by the Lord Chancellor.

(2) Any question arising under or for the purposes of this Schedule as to what the donor of the power might at any time be expected to do is to be determined by assuming that he had full mental capacity at the time but otherwise by reference to the circumstances existing at that time.

DEFINITIONS

1–507   "bankrupt": s.64(3)
"trust corporation": s.64(1)
"Public Guardian": s.64(1)
"the court": s.64(1)
"deputy": s.64(1)
"property": s.64(1)
"purchaser": s.64(1)
"Mental Health Act": s.64(1)

GENERAL NOTE

1–508   See the notes to s.66(3).

SCHEDULE 5   **Section 66(4)**

TRANSITIONAL PROVISIONS AND SAVINGS

PART 1

REPEAL OF PART 7 OF THE MENTAL HEALTH ACT 1983

Existing receivers

1–509   **1.**—(1) This paragraph applies where, immediately before the commencement day, there is a receiver (R) for a person (P) appointed under section 99 of the Mental Health Act.

(2) On and after that day—

(a) this Act applies as if R were a deputy appointed for P by the court, but with the functions that R had as receiver immediately before that day, and

(b) a reference in any other enactment to a deputy appointed by the court includes a person appointed as a deputy as a result of paragraph (a).

(3) On any application to it by R, the court may end R's appointment as P's deputy.

(4) Where, as a result of section 20(1), R may not make a decision on behalf of P in relation to a relevant matter, R must apply to the court.

(5) If, on the application, the court is satisfied that P is capable of managing his property and affairs in relation to the relevant matter—

(a) it must make an order ending R's appointment as P's deputy in relation to that matter, but

(b) it may, in relation to any other matter, exercise in relation to P any of the powers which it has under sections 15 to 19.

(6) If it is not satisfied, the court may exercise in relation to P any of the powers which it has under sections 15 to 19.

(7) R's appointment as P's deputy ceases to have effect if P dies.

(8) "Relevant matter" means a matter in relation to which, immediately before the commencement day, R was authorised to act as P's receiver.

(9) In sub-paragraph (1), the reference to a receiver appointed under section 99 of the Mental Health Act includes a reference to a person who by virtue of Schedule 5 to that Act was deemed to be a receiver appointed under that section.

Orders, appointments etc

2.—(1) Any order or appointment made, direction or authority given or other thing done which has, **1–510** or by virtue of Schedule 5 to the Mental Health Act was deemed to have, effect under Part 7 of the Act immediately before the commencement day is to continue to have effect despite the repeal of Part 7.

(2) In so far as any such order, appointment, direction, authority or thing could have been made, given or done under sections 15 to 20 if those sections had then been in force—

(a) it is to be treated as made, given or done under those sections, and

(b) the powers of variation and discharge conferred by section 16(7) apply accordingly.

(3) Sub-paragraph (1)—

(a) does not apply to nominations under section 93(1) or (4) of the Mental Health Act, and

(b) as respects receivers, has effect subject to paragraph 1.

(4) This Act does not affect the operation of section 109 of the Mental Health Act (effect and proof of orders etc.) in relation to orders made and directions given under Part 7 of that Act.

(5) This paragraph is without prejudice to section 16 of the Interpretation Act 1978 (c. 30) (general savings on repeal).

Pending proceedings

3.—(1) Any application for the exercise of a power under Part 7 of the Mental Health Act which is **1–511** pending immediately before the commencement day is to be treated, in so far as a corresponding power is exercisable under sections 16 to 20, as an application for the exercise of that power.

(2) For the purposes of sub-paragraph (1) an application for the appointment of a receiver is to be treated as an application for the appointment of a deputy.

Appeals

4.—(1) Part 7 of the Mental Health Act and the rules made under it are to continue to apply to any **1–512** appeal brought by virtue of section 105 of that Act which has not been determined before the commencement day.

(2) If in the case of an appeal brought by virtue of section 105(1) (appeal to nominated judge) the judge nominated under section 93 of the Mental Health Act has begun to hear the appeal, he is to continue to do so but otherwise it is to be heard by a puisne judge of the High Court nominated under section 46.

Fees

5. All fees and other payments which, having become due, have not been paid to the former Court of **1–513** Protection before the commencement day, are to be paid to the new Court of Protection.

Court records

1–514   **6.**—(1) The records of the former Court of Protection are to be treated, on and after the commencement day, as records of the new Court of Protection and are to be dealt with accordingly under the Public Records Act 1958 (c. 51).

(2) On and after the commencement day, the Public Guardian is, for the purpose of exercising any of his functions, to be given such access as he may require to such of the records mentioned in sub-paragraph (1) as relate to the appointment of receivers under section 99 of the Mental Health Act.

Existing charges

1–515   **7.** This Act does not affect the operation in relation to a charge created before the commencement day of—

(a)   so much of section 101(6) of the Mental Health Act as precludes a charge created under section 101(5) from conferring a right of sale or foreclosure during the lifetime of the patient, or

(b)   section 106(6) of the Mental Health Act (charge created by virtue of section 106(5) not to cause interest to fail etc.).

Preservation of interests on disposal of property

1–516   **8.** Paragraph 8(1) of Schedule 2 applies in relation to any disposal of property (within the meaning of that provision) by a person living on 1 st November 1960, being a disposal effected under the Lunacy Act 1890 (c.5) as it applies in relation to the disposal of property effected under sections 16 to 20.

Accounts

1–517   **9.** Court of Protection Rules may provide that, in a case where paragraph 1 applies, R is to have a duty to render accounts—

(a)   while he is receiver;

(b)   after he is discharged.

Interpretation

1–518   **10.** In this Part of this Schedule—

(a)   "the commencement day" means the day on which section 66(1)(a) (repeal of Part 7 of the Mental Health Act) comes into force,

(b)   "the former Court of Protection" means the office abolished by section 45, and

(c)   "the new Court of Protection" means the court established by that section.

PART 2

REPEAL OF THE ENDURING POWERS OF ATTORNEY ACT 1985

Orders, determinations, etc

1–519   **11.**—(1) Any order or determination made, or other thing done, under the 1985 Act which has effect immediately before the commencement day continues to have effect despite the repeal of that Act.

(2) In so far as any such order, determination or thing could have been made or done under Schedule 4 if it had then been in force—

(a)   it is to be treated as made or done under that Schedule, and

(b)   the powers of variation and discharge exercisable by the court apply accordingly.

(3) Any instrument registered under the 1985 Act is to be treated as having been registered by the Public Guardian under Schedule 4.

(4) This paragraph is without prejudice to section 16 of the Interpretation Act 1978 (c. 30) (general savings on repeal).

Pending proceedings

1–520   **12.**—(1) An application for the exercise of a power under the 1985 Act which is pending immediately before the commencement day is to be treated, in so far as a corresponding power is exercisable under Schedule 4, as an application for the exercise of that power.

(2) For the purposes of sub-paragraph (1)—

(a)   a pending application under section 4(2) of the 1985 Act for the registration of an instrument is to be treated as an application to the Public Guardian under paragraph 4 of Schedule 4 and any notice given in connection with that application under Schedule 1 to the 1985 Act is to be treated as given under Part 3 of Schedule 4,

(b) a notice of objection to the registration of an instrument is to be treated as a notice of objection under paragraph 13 of Schedule 4, and

(c) pending proceedings under section 5 of the 1985 Act are to be treated as proceedings on an application for the exercise by the court of a power which would become exercisable in relation to an instrument under paragraph 16(2) of Schedule 4 on its registration.

Appeals
13.—(1) The 1985 Act and, so far as relevant, the provisions of Part 7 of the Mental Health Act and **1–521** the rules made under it as applied by section 10 of the 1985 Act are to continue to have effect in relation to any appeal brought by virtue of section 10(1)(c) of the 1985 Act which has not been determined before the commencement day.

(2) If, in the case of an appeal brought by virtue of section 105(1) of the Mental Health Act as applied by section 10(1)(c) of the 1985 Act (appeal to nominated judge), the judge nominated under section 93 of the Mental Health Act has begun to hear the appeal, he is to continue to do so but otherwise the appeal is to be heard by a puisne judge of the High Court nominated under section 46.

Exercise of powers of donor as trustee
14.—(1) Section 2(8) of the 1985 Act (which prevents a power of attorney under section 25 of the **1–522** Trustee Act 1925 (c.19) as enacted from being an enduring power) is to continue to apply to any enduring power—

(a) created before 1 st March 2000, and

(b) having effect immediately before the commencement day.

(2) Section 3(3) of the 1985 Act (which entitles the donee of an enduring power to exercise the donor's powers as trustee) is to continue to apply to any enduring power to which, as a result of the provision mentioned in sub-paragraph (3), it applies immediately before the commencement day.

(3) The provision is section 4(3)(a) of the Trustee Delegation Act 1999 (c. 15) (which provides for section 3(3) of the 1985 Act to cease to apply to an enduring power when its registration is cancelled, if it was registered in response to an application made before 1 st March 2001).

(4) Even though section 4 of the 1999 Act is repealed by this Act, that section is to continue to apply in relation to an enduring power—

(a) to which section 3(3) of the 1985 Act applies as a result of sub-paragraph (2), or

(b) to which, immediately before the repeal of section 4 of the 1999 Act, section 1 of that Act applies as a result of section 4 of it.

(5) The reference in section 1(9) of the 1999 Act to section 4(6) of that Act is to be read with sub-paragraphs (2) to (4).

Interpretation
15. In this Part of this Schedule, "the commencement day" means the day on which section **1–523** 66(1)(b) (repeal of the 1985 Act) comes into force.

DEFINITIONS **1–524**
"Mental Health Act": s.64(1)
"deputy": s.64(1)
"the court": s.64(1)
"enactment": s.64(1)
"property": s.64(1)
"Public Guardian": s.64(1)
"Court of Protection Rules": s.64(1)
"the 1985 Act": s.64(1)

GENERAL NOTE
See the notes to s.66(4). **1–525**

SCHEDULE 6 **Section 67(1)**

MINOR AND CONSEQUENTIAL AMENDMENTS

1–526   [*Not reproduced*]

SCHEDULE 7 **Section 67(2)**

REPEALS

1–527   [*Not reproduced*]

PART 2

DELEGATED LEGISLATION

THE MENTAL CAPACITY ACT 2005 (INDEPENDENT MENTAL CAPACITY ADVOCATES) (GENERAL) REGULATIONS 2006

(SI 2006/1832)

Dated July 7, 2006 and made by the Secretary of State for Health under the Mental Capacity Act 2005 (c.9), ss.35(2), (3), 36, 37(6), (7), 38(8), 64(1) and 65(1).

GENERAL NOTE

These Regulations define "NHS body" and "serious medical treatment" for the pur- **2–001** poses of certain provisions the Mental Capacity Act 2005 which deal with independent mental capacity advocates ("IMCAs"). The Regulations also contain provision as to who can be appointed to act as an IMCA and as to an IMCA's functions when he has been instructed to represent a person in a particular case. The provisions about the IMCA's appointment and functions apply where the IMCA is instructed under ss.37 to 39 of the Act or under regulations made by virtue of s.41 of the Act (see reg.2(2)).

Regulation 3 defines "NHS body". This term is used in ss.37 and 38 of the Act. Those sections impose an obligation on NHS bodies to instruct an IMCA in certain circumstances involving acts or decisions relating to serious medical treatment or to accommodation.

Regulation 4 defines "serious medical treatment". Under s.37 of the Act, an NHS body must instruct an IMCA where it is proposing to provide, or secure the provision of, such treatment.

Regulation 5 provides that a person can only act as an IMCA if he has been approved by a local authority or is a member of a class which has been so approved. For an IMCA to be appointed, he must satisfy certain requirements as to experience, training, good character and independence.

Regulation 6 sets out the steps an IMCA must take once he has been instructed to act in a particular case. He must obtain and evaluate information about the person he has been instructed to represent ("P") and about P's wishes, feelings, beliefs or values. He must then report to the person who instructed him.

Under *regulation 7,* an IMCA who is instructed to represent P in relation to any matter may challenge a decision made in that matter in relation to P, including any decision as to whether P is a person who lacks capacity. For the purpose of making a challenge, the IMCA is treated in the same way as any other person caring for P or interested in his welfare.

The equivalent to regs 3 to 7 with respect to Wales are regs 3 to 7 of the Mental Capacity Act 2005 (Independent Mental Capacity Advocates) (Wales) Regulations 2007 (SI 2007/ 852 (W.77)).

Citation, commencement and extent

1.—(1) These Regulations may be cited as the Mental Capacity Act 2005 **2–002** (Independent Mental Capacity Advocates) (General) Regulations 2006.

(2) These Regulations shall come into force—

(a) for the purpose of enabling the Secretary of State to make arrangements under section 35 of the Act, and for the purpose of enabling local authorities to approve IMCAs, on 1st November 2006, and

(b) for all other purposes, on 1st April 2007.

(3) These Regulations apply in relation to England only.

Interpretation

2–003   **2.** —(1) In these Regulations—

"the Act" means the Mental Capacity Act 2005; and

"IMCA" means an independent mental capacity advocate.

(2) In these Regulations, references to instructions given to a person to act as an IMCA are to instructions given under sections 37 to 39 of the Act or under regulations made by virtue of section 41 of the Act.

Meaning of NHS Body

2–004   **3.**—(1) For the purposes of sections 37 and 38 of the Act, "NHS body" means a body in England which is—

(a) a Strategic Health Authority;

(b) an NHS foundation trust;

(c) a Primary Care Trust;

(d) an NHS Trust; or

(e) a Care Trust.

(2) In this regulation—

"Care Trust" means a body designated as a Care Trust under section 45 of the Health and Social Care Act 2001;

"NHS foundation trust" has the meaning given in section 1 of the Health and Social Care (Community Health and Standards) Act 2003;

"NHS trust" means a body established under section 5 of the National Health Service and Community Care Act 1990;

"Primary Care Trust" means a body established under section 16A of the National Health Service Act 1977; and

"Strategic Health Authority" means a Strategic Health Authority established under section 8 of the National Health Service Act 1977.

Meaning of serious medical treatment

2–005   **4.**—(1) This regulation defines serious medical treatment for the purposes of section 37 of the Act.

(2) Serious medical treatment is treatment which involves providing, withdrawing or withholding treatment in circumstances where—

(a) in a case where a single treatment is being proposed, there is a fine balance between its benefits to the patient and the burdens and risks it is likely to entail for him,

(b) in a case where there is a choice of treatments, a decision as to which one to use is finely balanced, or

(c) what is proposed would be likely to involve serious consequences for the patient.

Appointment of independent mental capacity advocates

5.—(1) No person may be appointed to act as an IMCA for the purposes of sec- **2–006**
tions 37 to 39 of the Act, or regulations made by virtue of section 41 of the Act,
unless—
  (a) he is for the time being approved by a local authority on the grounds that he
      satisfies the appointment requirements, or
  (b) he belongs to a class of persons which is for the time being approved by a
      local authority on the grounds that all persons in that class satisfy the
      appointment requirements.
(2) The appointment requirements, in relation to a person appointed to act as
an IMCA, are that—
  (a) he has appropriate experience or training or an appropriate combination of
      experience and training;
  (b) he is a person of integrity and good character; and
  (c) he is able to act independently of any person who instructs him.
(3) Before a determination is made in relation to any person for the purposes of
paragraph (2)(b), there must be obtained in respect of that person—
  (a) an enhanced criminal record certificate issued pursuant to section 113B of
      the Police Act 1997; or
  (b) if the purpose for which the certificate is required is not one prescribed
      under subsection (2) of that section, a criminal record certificate issued pur-
      suant to section 113A of that Act.

Functions of an independent mental capacity advocate

6.—(1) This regulation applies where an IMCA has been instructed by an auth- **2–007**
orised person to represent a person ("P").
(2) "Authorised person" means a person who is required or enabled to instruct
an IMCA under sections 37 to 39 of the Act or under regulations made by virtue of
section 41of the Act.
(3) The IMCA must determine in all the circumstances how best to represent
and support P.
(4) In particular, the IMCA must—
  (a) verify that the instructions were issued by an authorised person;
  (b) to the extent that it is practicable and appropriate to do so—
      (i) interview P, and
      (ii) examine the records relevant to P to which the IMCA has access under
           section 35(6) of the Act;
  (c) to the extent that it is practicable and appropriate to do so, consult—
      (i) persons engaged in providing care or treatment for P in a professional
          capacity or for remuneration, and
      (ii) other persons who may be in a position to comment on P's wishes, feel-
           ings, beliefs or values; and
  (d) take all practicable steps to obtain such other information about P, or the act
      or decision that is proposed in relation to P, as the IMCA considers
      necessary.
(5) The IMCA must evaluate all the information he has obtained for the purpose of—
  (a) ascertaining the extent of the support provided to P to enable him to partici-
      pate in making any decision about the matter in relation to which the IMCA
      has been instructed;

(b) ascertaining what P's wishes and feelings would be likely to be, and the beliefs and values that would be likely to influence P, if he had capacity in relation to the proposed act or decision;

(c) ascertaining what alternative courses of action are available in relation to P;

(d) where medical treatment is proposed for P, ascertaining whether he would be likely to benefit from a further medical opinion.

(6) The IMCA must prepare a report for the authorised person who instructed him.

(7) The IMCA may include in the report such submissions as he considers appropriate in relation to P and the act or decision which is proposed in relation to him.

Challenges to decisions affecting persons who lack capacity

2–008   **7.** —(1) This regulation applies where—

(a) an IMCA has been instructed to represent a person ("P") in relation to any matter, and

(b) a decision affecting P (including a decision as to his capacity) is made in that matter.

(2) The IMCA has the same rights to challenge the decision as he would have if he were a person (other than an IMCA) engaged in caring for P or interested in his welfare.

THE MENTAL CAPACITY ACT 2005 (INDEPENDENT MENTAL CAPACITY ADVOCATES) (EXPANSION OF ROLE) REGULATIONS 2006

(SI 2006/2883)

Dated October 30, 2006 and made by the Secretary of State for Health under the Mental Capacity Act 2005 (c.9), ss.41(1), (2), 64(1) and 65(1).

GENERAL NOTE

These Regulations adjust the obligation to make arrangements as to the availability of **2–009** independent mental capacity advocates ("IMCAs") which is imposed by s.35 of the Mental Capacity Act 2005. Under the Regulations, the Secretary of State may also make arrangements to enable IMCAs to be available to represent a person ("P") who lacks capacity to agree to the outcome of an accommodation review or to protective measures taken in adult protection cases.

Regulation 2 provides that arrangements under s.35 of the Act may extend to cover IMCAs who are instructed in the circumstances specified in reg.3 or 4.

Regulation 3 specifies circumstances where an NHS body has made, or a local authority have made, arrangements as to P's accommodation and it is then proposed to review those arrangements. In addition, P must not have capacity to participate in the review and there must be no one else who can be consulted as to matters affecting his best interests.

Regulation 4 specifies circumstances where it is alleged that P is or has been abused or neglected by another person or that he is abusing or has abused another person. In addition, protective measures affecting P must have been taken, or be proposed, by an NHS body or local authority in accordance with any adult protection procedures which have been set up pursuant to certain statutory guidance. The guidance current when these Regulations were made is entitled "No secrets: guidance on developing and implementing multi-agency policies and procedures to protect vulnerable adults from abuse".

Regulation 5 provides that an NHS body or local authority may instruct an IMCA to represent P if the NHS body considers, or the local authority consider, that that would be of particular benefit to P. The NHS body or local authority must take account of information provided by the IMCA and of any submissions made by him.

Paragraph 10.61 of the *Code of Practice* states:

"Responsible bodies are expected to take a strategic approach in deciding whether they will use IMCAs in [the situations set out in regs 3 and 4]. They should establish a policy locally for determining these decisions, setting out the criteria for appointing an IMCA including the issues to be taken into account when deciding if an IMCA will be of particular benefit to the person concerned. However, decision-makers will need to consider each case separately to see if the criteria are met. Local authorities or NHS bodies may wish to publish their approach for ease of access, setting out the ways they intend to use these additional powers and review it periodically."

The equivalent to regs 3 and 4 with respect to Wales are regs 8 and 9 of the Mental Capacity Act 2005 (Independent Mental Capacity Advocates) (Wales) Regulations 2007 (SI 2007/852 (W.77)).

Citation, commencement, extent and interpretation

1.—(1) These Regulations may be cited as the Mental Capacity Act 2005 **2–010** (Independent Mental Capacity Advocates) (Expansion of Role) Regulations 2006.

(2) These Regulations shall come into force—

(a) for the purpose of enabling the Secretary of State to make arrangements by virtue of regulation 2, on 1st November 2006, and

(b) for all other purposes, on 1st April 2007.

(3) These Regulations apply in relation to England only.

(4) In these Regulations—

"the Act" means the Mental Capacity Act 2005;

"IMCA" means an independent mental capacity advocate; and

"NHS body" means a body in England which is—

(a) a Strategic Health Authority;

(b) an NHS foundation trust;

(c) a Primary Care Trust;

(d) an NHS Trust; or

(e) a Care Trust.

(5) In the definition of "NHS body" in paragraph (4)—

"Care Trust" means a body designated as a Care Trust under section 45 of the Health and Social Care Act 2001;

"NHS foundation trust" has the meaning given in section 1 of the Health and Social Care (Community Health and Standards) Act 2003;

"NHS trust" means a body established under section 5 of the National Health Service and Community Care Act 1990;

"Primary Care Trust" means a body established under section 16A of the National Health Service Act 1977; and

"Strategic Health Authority" means a Strategic Health Authority established under section 8 of the National Health Service Act 1977.

Adjustment of the obligation to make arrangements imposed by section 35 of the Act

2–011   **2.** Arrangements made by the Secretary of State under section 35 of the Act may include such provision as she considers reasonable for the purpose of enabling IMCAs to be available to represent and support persons in the circumstances specified in regulation 3 or 4.

Review of arrangements as to accommodation

2–012   **3.**—(1) The circumstances specified in this regulation are where—

(a) qualifying arrangements have been made by an NHS body or local authority as to the accommodation of a person ("P") who lacks capacity to agree to the arrangements;

(b) a review of the arrangements is proposed or in progress (whether under a care plan or otherwise);

(c) the NHS body is satisfied, or the local authority are satisfied, that there is no person, other than a person engaged in providing care or treatment for P in a professional capacity or for remuneration, whom it would be appropriate to consult in determining what would be in P's best interests;

(d) none of the following exist—

(i) a person nominated by P (in whatever manner) as a person to be consulted in matters affecting his interests,

(ii) a donee of a lasting power of attorney created by P,

(iii) a deputy appointed by the Court of Protection for P, or

(iv) a donee of an enduring power of attorney (within the meaning of Schedule 4 to the Act) created by P; and

(e) sections 37, 38 and 39 of the Act do not apply.

(2) In this regulation—

"accommodation" means—

(a) accommodation in a care home or hospital, or

(b) residential accommodation provided in accordance with—

(i) section 21 or 29 of the National Assistance Act 1948, or

(ii) section 117 of the Mental Health Act 1983,

as the result of a decision taken by a local authority under section 47 of the National Health Service and Community Care Act 1990;

"care home" and "hospital" have the same meaning as in section 38 of the Act; and

"qualifying arrangements" means arrangements—

(a) under which accommodation has been provided for P for a continuous period of 12 weeks or more, and

(b) which are not made as a result of an obligation imposed on P under the Mental Health Act 1983.

Adult protection cases

4.—(1) The circumstances specified in this regulation are where—　　**2–013**

(a) an NHS body proposes to take or has taken, or a local authority propose to take or have taken, protective measures in relation to a person ("P") who lacks capacity to agree to one or more of the measures;

(b) the proposal is made or the measures have been taken—

(i) following the receipt of an allegation or evidence that P is being, or has been, abused or neglected by another person or that P is abusing, or has abused, another person, and

(ii) in accordance with arrangements relating to the protection of vulnerable adults from abuse which are made pursuant to guidance issued under section 7 of the Local Authority Social Services Act 1970; and

(c) none of the following provisions apply—

(i) section 37, 38 or 39 of the Act, or

(ii) regulation 3 of these Regulations.

(2) The reference to protective measures in relation to P includes measures to minimise the risk that any abuse or neglect of P, or abuse by P, will continue.

GENERAL NOTE

　　Under this Regulation, an IMCA may be appointed even where P has family or friends　**2–014**
whom it might be appropriate to consult.

Instructing an IMCA

5.—(1) In the circumstances specified in regulation 3 or 4, an NHS body or　**2–015**
local authority may instruct an IMCA to represent P if the NHS body is satisfied,

or the local authority are satisfied, that it would be of particular benefit to P to be so represented.

(2) An NHS body which instructs, or a local authority which instruct, an IMCA under paragraph (1) must—

   (a) in making any decision resulting from a review of arrangements as to P's accommodation, or

   (b) in making any decision, or further decision, about protective measures in relation to P,

take into account any information given, or submissions made, by the IMCA.

THE MENTAL CAPACITY ACT 2005 (LOSS OF CAPACITY DURING RESEARCH PROJECT) (ENGLAND) REGULATIONS 2007

(SI 2007/679)

Dated March 3, 2007 and made by the Secretary of State for Health under the Mental Capacity Act 2005 (c.9), ss.30(6)(a), 34(1), (2) and (3)(b), 64(1) and 65(1)(c).

GENERAL NOTE

These Regulations are made under s.34 of the Mental Capacity Act 2005. They provide **2–016** for certain research, relating to people without capacity to consent to it, to be carried out lawfully where otherwise the requirements of s.30 of the Act would have to be complied with.

Regulation 1 provides for the Regulations to come into force on 1 July 2007 for the purpose of enabling applications for approval of research protocols under the Regulations to be made and determined and on 1 October 2007 for all other purposes.

Regulation 2 provides that the Regulations apply where a research project began before 1 October 2007 and a person ("P") consented, prior to 31 March 2008, to take part in the project but has subsequently lost capacity to continue to consent.

Regulation 3 provides that research under such a project may be carried out using information or material collected prior to P's loss of capacity. The information or material must be either data within the meaning of the Data Protection Act 1998 (c. 29) or material which consists of or includes human cells or DNA. In addition the requirements of Schedules 1 and 2 must be complied with.

Schedule 1 provides that an appropriate body must have approved a protocol for the project which provides for research to be carried out in relation to a person who has consented to take part and then lost capacity. The appropriate body must also be satisfied that there are reasonable arrangements for ensuring that Schedule 2 will be complied with.

Schedule 2, which repeats the relevant safeguards from s.32 and 33 of the Act, sets out requirements as to consultation about P's involvement in the project, as to respecting his wishes and objections and as to assuming that his interests outweigh those of science and society.

Provision for Wales, which in all material respects replicates these regulations, is contained in the Mental Capacity Act 2005 (Loss of Capacity during Research Project) (Wales) Regulations 2007 (SI 2007/837 (W.72)).

Citation, commencement, territorial application and interpretation

1.—(1) These Regulations may be cited as the Mental Capacity Act 2005 (Loss **2–017** of Capacity during Research Project) (England) Regulations 2007 and shall come into force on—

(a) 1 July 2007 for the purpose of enabling applications for approval for the purposes of Schedule 1 to be made to, and determined by, an appropriate body,

(b) 1 October 2007 for all other purposes.

(2) These Regulations apply in relation to the carrying out of research in England.

(3) In these Regulations—

"the Act" means the Mental Capacity Act 2005;

"appropriate body" has the meaning given by section 30(4) of the Act and the Mental Capacity Act 2005 (Appropriate Body) (England) Regulations 2006.

Application

2–018 2. These Regulations apply where—
- (a) a person ("P")—
    - (i) has consented before 31 March 2008 to take part in a research project ("the project") begun before 1st October 2007, but
    - (ii) before the conclusion of the project, loses capacity to consent to continue to take part in it, and
    - (iii) research for the purposes of the project in relation to P would, apart from these Regulations, be unlawful by virtue of section 30 of the Act.

Research which may be carried out despite a participant's loss of capacity

2–019 3. Despite P's loss of capacity, research for the purposes of the project may be carried out using information or material relating to him if—
- (a) that information or material was obtained before P's loss of capacity,
- (b) that information or material is either—
    - (i) data within the meaning given in section 1(1) of the Data Protection Act 1998, or
    - (ii) material which consists of or includes human cells or human DNA,
- (c) the project satisfies the requirements set out in Schedule 1, and
- (d) the person conducting the project ("R") takes in relation to P such steps as are set out in Schedule 2.

SCHEDULE 1   **Regulation 3(c)**

REQUIREMENTS WHICH THE PROJECT MUST SATISFY

2–020 1. A protocol approved by an appropriate body and having effect in relation to the project makes provision for research to be carried out in relation to a person who has consented to take part in the project but loses capacity to consent to continue to take part in it.

2–021 2. The appropriate body is satisfied that there are reasonable arrangements in place for ensuring that the requirements of Schedule 2 will be met.

SCHEDULE 2   **Regulation 3(d)**

STEPS WHICH THE PERSON CONDUCTING THE PROJECT MUST TAKE

2–022 1. R must take reasonable steps to identify a person who—
- (a) otherwise than in a professional capacity or for remuneration, is engaged in caring for P or is interested in P's welfare, and
- (b) is prepared to be consulted by R under this Schedule.

2–023 2. If R is unable to identify such a person he must, in accordance with guidance issued by the Secretary of State, nominate a person who—
- (a) is prepared to be consulted by R under this Schedule, but
- (b) has no connection with the project.

2–024 3. R must provide the person identified under paragraph 1, or nominated under paragraph 2, with information about the project and ask him—
- (a) for advice as to whether research of the kind proposed should be carried out in relation to P, and
- (b) what, in his opinion, P's wishes and feelings about such research being carried out would be likely to be if P had capacity in relation to the matter.

2–025 4. If, at any time, the person consulted advises R that in his opinion P's wishes and feelings would be likely to lead him to wish to withdraw from the project if he had capacity in relation to the matter, R must ensure that P is withdrawn from it.

2–026 5. The fact that a person is the donee of a lasting power of attorney given by P, or is P's deputy, does not prevent him from being the person consulted under paragraphs 1 to 4.

2–027 6. R must ensure that nothing is done in relation to P in the course of the research which would be contrary to—

(a) an advance decision of his which has effect, or

(b) any other form of statement made by him and not subsequently withdrawn,

of which R is aware.

7. The interests of P must be assumed to outweigh those of science and society. **2–028**

8. If P indicates (in any way) that he wishes the research in relation to him to be discontinued, it must **2–029** be discontinued without delay.

9. The research in relation to P must be discontinued without delay if at any time R has reasonable **2–030** grounds for believing that the requirement set out in paragraph 1 of Schedule 1 is no longer met or that there are no longer reasonable arrangements in place for ensuring that the requirements of this Schedule are met in relation to P.

10. R must conduct the research in accordance with the provision made in the protocol referred to in **2–031** paragraph 1 of Schedule 1 for research to be carried out in relation to a person who has consented to take part in the project but loses capacity to consent to continue to take part in it.

ANNEX A

CONTACT DETAILS

The following list provides contact details for relevant organisations.   **A–001**

Action on Elder Abuse

web: *www.elderabuse.org.uk*
telephone helpline: 0808 808 8141
switchboard: 020 8765 7000

Age Concern

web: *www.ace.org.uk*
telephone helpline: 0800 009966
switchboard: 020 8765 7200

Alzheimers Society

web: *www.alzheimers.org.uk*
telephone: 020 7306 0606

British Banking Association

web: *www.bba.org.uk*
telephone: 020 7216 8800

British Institute of Learning Disabilities

web: *www.bild.org.uk*
telephone: 01562 723025

British Psychological Society

web: *www.bps.org.uk*
telephone: 0116 254 9568

Care and Social Services Inspectorate Wales

web: *www.csiw.wales.gov.uk*
telephone: 01443 848450

Carers UK

web: *www.carersuk.org*
telephone carers line: 0808 808 7777
switchboard: 020 7490 8818

Commission for Social Care Inspection

web: *www.csci.org.uk*
telephone: 0845 015 0120 / 0191 233 3323
textphone: 0845 015 2255 / 0191 233 3588

Community Legal Services Direct

web: *www.clsdirect.org.uk*
telephone helpline: 0845 345 4345

Criminal Records Bureau

web: *www.crb.org.uk*
tel: 0870 909 0811

Department of Constitutional Affairs

web: *www.dca.gov.uk/legal-policy/mental-capacity/index.htm*

Department of Health

web: *www.dh.gov.uk/imca*

Disability Rights Commission

web: *www.drc-gb.org*
telephone helpline: 08457 622 633
textphone: 08457 622 644

Down's Syndrome Association

web: *www.downs-syndrome.org.uk*
telephone helpline: 0845 230 0372
switchboard: 0845 230 0372

Foundation for People with Leaning Difficulties

web: *www.learningdisabilities.org.uk*
telephone: 020 7803 1100

Headway – the Brain Injury Association

web: *www.headway.org.uk*
telephone helpline: 0808 800 2244
switchboard: 0115 924 0800

Healthcare Commission

web: *www.healthcarecommission.org.uk*
telephone helpline: 0845 601 3012
switchboard: 020 7448 9200

Healthcare Inspectorate for Wales

web: *www.hiw.org.uk*
telephone: 029 2092 8850

Help the Aged

web: *www.helptheaged.org.uk*
telephone: 020 7278 1114

Information Commissioner's Office

web: *www.ico.gov.uk*
telephone helpline: 0845 630 6060
switchboard: 01625 545700

Local Government Ombudsman

web: *www.lgo.org.uk*
telephone advice line: 0845 602 1983

Mind

web: *www.mind.org.uk*
telephone infoline: 0845 766 0163
switchboard: 020 8519 2122

Mencap

web: *www.mencap.org.uk*
telephone: 020 7454 0454

Mental Health Act Commission

web: *www.mhac.org.uk*
telephone: 0115 943 7100

Morgan Cole Mental Capacity Act website

web: *www.mental-capacity.com*
switchboard: 02920 385385

National Autistic Society

web: *www.nas.org.uk*
telephone helpline: 0845 070 4004
switchboard: 020 7833 2299

Office of the Public Guardian

web: *www.publicguardian.gov.uk* (from October 2007)
switchboard: 0845 330 2900

Official Solicitor

web: *www.officialsolicitor.gov.uk*
telephone: 020 7911 7127

Parliamentary and Health Service Ombudsman

web: *www.ombudsman.org.uk*
complaints helpline: 0845 015 4033

Public Service Ombudsman for Wales

web: *www.ombudsman-wales.org.uk*
telephone: 01656 641150

Rethink

web: *www.rethink.org*
telephone: 0845 456 0455

Royal College of Psychiatrists

web: *www.rcpsych.ac.uk*
telephone: 020 7235 2351

Solicitors for the Elderly

web: *www.solicitorsfortheelderly.com*
telephone: 01992 471568

Young Minds

web: *www.youngminds.org.uk*
telephone: 020 7336 8445

Index

LEGAL TAXONOMY

FROM SWEET & MAXWELL

This index has been prepared using Sweet and Maxwell's Legal Taxonomy. Main index entries conform to keywords provided by the Legal Taxonomy except where references to specific documents or non-standard terms (denoted by quotation marks) have been included. These keywords provide a means of identifying similar concepts in other Sweet & Maxwell publications and online services to which keywords from the Legal Taxonomy have been applied. Readers may find some minor differences between terms used in the text and those which appear in the index. Suggestions to *sweetandmaxwell.taxonomy@thomson.com*.

(All references are to paragraph number)

196